Improving Teaching and Learning

SRHE and Open University Press Imprint

Current titles include:

Catherine Bargh *et al.*: *University Leadership*
Ronald Barnett: *Beyond all Reason*
Ronald Barnett: *The Limits of Competence*
Ronald Barnett: *Higher Education*
Ronald Barnett: *Realizing the University in an Age of Supercomplexity*
Ronald Barnett & Kelly Coate: *Engaging the Curriculum in Higher Education*
Tony Becher and Paul R. Trowler: *Academic Tribes and Territories* (2nd edn)
Neville Bennett *et al.*: *Skills Development in Higher Education and Employment*
John Biggs: *Teaching for Quality Learning at University* (2nd edn)
Richard Blackwell & Paul Blackmore (eds): *Towards Strategic Staff Development in Higher Education*
David Boud *et al.* (eds): *Using Experience for Learning*
David Boud and Nicky Solomon (eds): *Work-based Learning*
Tom Bourner *et al.* (eds): *New Directions in Professional Higher Education*
John Brennan *et al.* (eds): *What Kind of University?*
Anne Brockbank and Ian McGill: *Facilitating Reflective Learning in Higher Education*
Stephen D. Brookfield and Stephen Preskill: *Discussion as a way of teaching*
Ann Brooks and Alison Mackinnon (eds): *Gender and the Restructured University*
Sally Brown and Angela Glasner (eds): *Assessment Matters in Higher Education*
Burton R.Clark: *Sustaining Change in Universities*
James Cornford & Neil Pollock: *Putting the University Online*
John Cowan: *On Becoming an Innovative University Teacher*
Sara Delamont, Paul Atkinson and Odette Parry: *Supervising the Doctorate* (2nd edn)
Sara Delamont & Paul Atkinson: *Successful Research Careers*
Gerard Delanty: *Challenging Knowledge*
Chris Duke: *Managing the Learning University*
Heather Eggins (ed): *Globalization and Reform in Higher Education*
Heather Eggins & Ranald Macdonald (eds): *The Scholarship of Academic Development*
Gillian Evans: *Academics and the Real World*
Andrew Hannan and Harold Silver: *Innovating in Higher Education*
Lee Harvey and Associates: *The Student Satisfaction Manual*
David Istance, Hans Schuetze and Tom Schuller (eds): *International Perspectives on Lifelong Learning*
Norman Jackson and Helen Lund (eds): *Benchmarking for Higher Education*
Merle Jacob and Tomas Hellström (eds): *The Future of Knowledge Production in the Academy*
Peter Knight: *Being a Teacher in Higher Education*
Peter Knight and Paul Trowler: *Departmental Leadership in Higher Education*
Peter Knight and Mantz Yorke: *Assessment, Learning and Employability*
Ray Land: *Educational Development*
Mary Lea and Barry Stierer (eds): *Student Writing in Higher Education*
Dina Lewis and Barbara Allan: *Virtual Learning Communities*
Ian McNay (ed.): *Higher Education and its Communities*
Elaine Martin: *Changing Academic Work*
Louise Morley: *Quality and Power in Higher Education*
Lynne Pearce: *How to Examine a Thesis*
Moira Peelo and Terry Wareham (eds): *Failing Students in Higher Education*
Craig Prichard: *Making Managers in Universities and Colleges*
Michael Prosser and Keith Trigwell: *Understanding Learning and Teaching*
John Richardson: *Researching Student Learning*
Stephen Rowland: *The Enquiring University Teacher*
Maggi Savin-Baden: *Problem-based Learning in Higher Education*
Maggi Savin-Baden: *Facilitating Problem-based Learning*
Maggi Savin-Baden and Kay Wilkie: *Challenging Research in Problem-based Learning*
David Scott, Andrew Brown, Ingrid Lunt &Lucy Thorne: *Examining Professional Doctorates*

Peter Scott (ed.): *The Globalization of Higher Education*
Peter Scott: *The Meanings of Mass Higher Education*
Michael L Shattock: *Managing Successful Universities*
Maria Slowey and David Watson: *Higher Education and the Lifecourse*
Anthony Smith and Frank Webster (eds): *The Postmodern University?*
Colin Symes and John McIntyre (eds): *Working Knowledge*
Peter G. Taylor: *Making Sense of Academic Life*
Richard Taylor, Jean Barr and Tom Steele: *For a Radical Higher Education*
Malcolm Tight: *Researching Higher Education*
Penny Tinkler and Carolyn Jackson: *The Doctoral Examination Process*
Susan Toohey: *Designing Courses for Higher Education*
Paul R. Trowler (ed.): *Higher Education Policy and Institutional Change*
Melanie Walker (ed.): *Reconstructing Professionalism in University Teaching*
Melanie Walker and Jon Nixon (eds): *Reclaiming Universities from a Runaway World*
David Warner and David Palfreyman (eds): *Higher Education Management of UK Higher Education*
Gareth Williams (ed): *The Enterprising University*
Diana Woodward and Karen Ross: *Managing Equal Opportunities in Higher Education*

Improving Teaching and Learning

A Whole Institution Approach

Vaneeta-marie D'Andrea and David Gosling

Society for Research into Higher Education
& Open University Press

Open University Press
McGraw-Hill Education
McGraw-Hill House
Shoppenhangers Road
Maidenhead
Berkshire
England
SL6 2QL

email: enquiries@openup.co.uk
world wide web: www.openup.co.uk

and Two Penn Plaza, New York, NY 10121–2289, USA

First published 2005

A catalogue record of this book is available from the British Library

ISBN-13 978 0335 21068 8 (pb) 978 0335 21069 5 (hb)
ISBN-10 0 335 21068 6 (pb) 0 335 21069 4 (hb)

Library of Congress Cataloging-in-Publication Data
CIP data has been applied for

Typeset by RefineCatch Limited, Bungay, Suffolk
Printed in the UK by Bell & Bain Ltd, Glasgow

Contents

Foreword

In many countries there is renewed debate about the purposes of higher education, the respective contributions of various academic roles, the need for reflection on effective practices, the assurance of quality and realizable commitments to enhancement. Employability of graduates and the contributions which higher education can make to national (and international) economies are often powerful drivers behind governmental perspectives and those of the funders of institutions and the higher education sector.

From a different standpoint, academics and others fear a dangerous narrowing of purposes and a trend towards greater convergence of mission, notwithstanding the public rhetoric of a commitment to, even a desire to promote, institutional diversity. Massification, widening access and increased demands for accountability, along with globalization and the accelerating impact of communication technologies are all further complicating factors. In this context, traditional notions of what it means be a teacher in higher education are becoming increasingly disputed.

In this timely volume the authors enter this contested territory. By observing the classic academic tenets of thoughtful analysis and reflection, thorough research and referencing, and transparent and weighted evaluation, they have contributed to the dialogue about institutional change and the place of teaching in higher education. The volume deals with important topics. It seeks to inform discussions and practice. The authors aspire to inform and influence policies to create a development culture within higher education. So when you read the volume you should ask yourself, what aspects of my current policy and practice does this confirm and what, if anything, will I change? What will improve and enrich the learning experiences of students and how would I know?

George Gordon
University of Strathclyde

Preface

The origins of this book lie in our experience of working in higher education for the past thirty years. We have both been academics working in disciplinary fields: sociology and philosophy. We have both had a keen interest in the teaching of our subjects and in supporting our students to be successful. We both believe that it is important to open higher education to students from groups that have traditionally been under-represented. It was because we were engaging with questions related to the process of teaching and learning that we came to work in educational development in the latter years of our academic careers.

However, working in the field of educational development we have often found ourselves caught between our loyalty to academic traditions and the changes occurring in higher education generally. In this book we have tried to address the pressures that academics, as teachers, face and to discuss what recent research has to say about them. We suggest ways in which academics can respond effectively to changing demands without losing sight of a commitment to traditional academic values. Our major challenge was to understand how to support desirable change while preserving the values that we believe in.

We support the idea of having a student focus that sees each student as a person with an individual social identity and personal needs. However, we think it is important not to lose sight of the teacher who has a complex professional identity, with commitments to a subject, and sometimes conflicting roles to perform. We want to bring back questions of academic values in the discussion of teaching and to understand the teaching role as more than a set of skills and competences.

We have tried to identify the changes that are desirable for professionalizing teaching in higher education while preserving values of criticality and scholarship. We leave it to the reader to decide whether we have succeeded.

Acknowledgements

I would wish to acknowledge the support of my students and colleagues at City University, the University of Roehampton and at the Carnegie Academy for the Scholarship of Teaching and Learning (CASTL) who have sparked a number of the ideas that are reported in this book. In particular, I would wish to thank the research assistants who have provided assistance to us: Paola De Orsi and Kevin Humby.

Vaneeta-marie D'Andrea
22 November 2004

I want to acknowledge the contribution of my colleagues in Educational Development Services at the University of East London from 1993 to 2002 with whom I had many valuable debates about teaching and supporting students in higher education. In particular I remember with affection the conversations I had with Dave O'Reilly who sadly died in 2002.

David Gosling
22 November 2004

Abbreviations

AAHE	American Association for Higher Education
AQIP	Academic Quality Improvement Program
ASA	American Sociological Association
C&IT	communication and information technology
CASTL	Carnegie Academy for the Scholarship of Teaching and Learning
CEQ	Course Experience Questionnaire
CMC	computer-mediated communication
CNAA	Council for National Academic Awards
CPD	continuing professional development
DfES	Department for Education and Skills
EDC	educational development centre
FDTL	Fund for the Development of Teaching and Learning
FIPSE	Fund for the Improvement of Postsecondary Education
GLAD	Group for Learning in Art and Design
HE	higher education
HEA	Higher Education Academy
HEFCE	Higher Education Funding Council for England
HEIs	higher education institutions
HEQC	Higher Education Quality Council
ICT	information and communication technology
IT	information technology
KI	knowledge intensive
LTSN	Learning and Teaching Support Network
MLE	managed learning environment
NQF	national qualifications framework
NSF	National Science Foundation
NSSE	National Survey of Student Engagement
NTF	National Teaching Fellowship
PBL	problem-based learning
PDP	personal development planning

Ped D	Pedagogical Development
Ped R	Pedagogical Research
QA	quality assurance
QAAHE	Quality Assurance Agency for Higher Education
QD	quality development
QE	quality enhancement
RI	restricted identity
RAE	Research Assessment Exercise
SEEC	Southern England Consortium for Credit Accumulation and Transfer
SHEFC	Scottish Higher Education Funding Council
SoTL	scholarship of teaching and learning
STEM	science, technology, engineering and mathematics
TQEF	Teaching Quality Enhancement Fund
TQM	total quality management
UUK/SCOP	Universities United Kingdom/Standing Conference of Principals
VLE	virtual learning environment

Introduction

It seems that every higher education institution wants to boast that it offers 'high quality learning and teaching'. Mission statements consistently claim that universities and colleges seek to provide excellent teaching and a high quality learning environment. But it is less than obvious that institutions are either clear about what these goals mean or actually pursuing these goals with strategic vision. In most cases neither of these key goals is well defined: what is excellent teaching and what constitutes a high quality learning environment? And the manner in which institutions are attempting to achieve these goals is many and varied. Often the approach simply reflects the historical traditions of a particular institution and its associated values and practices.

Given the diversity of origins and values of higher education institutions, can we assume that any and all approaches are equally effective? To what extent do institutions know whether what they do is an effective strategy to enhance student learning? Institutions with selective student intakes, with excellent results and a high reputation might still be underachieving. But would they know? And if they did know, would they know how to make improvements in areas identified as less than 'high quality'? If they did know what would make a difference, would they have the institutional will to follow the process through? This last question is a key one because, as we shall discuss, there are conflicting pressures on higher education institutions (HEIs), which require prioritization and differential levels of attention.

One of these pressures is the increase in student numbers. In the developed world, where participation in higher education approaches, or exceeds, half of young adults, traditional forms of teaching come under mounting pressure to change. The changes that are required amount to a transformation of higher education, with implications for teaching, course design, use of learning technologies, scholarship and quality management. Teaching and learning within higher education cannot be isolated from all the other activities which impact on faculty/staff and students. Any attempt to improve teaching and learning must take account of this complexity at both an institutional and a personal level; a complexity that is as much about competing values and epistemologies as it is about organizational structures.

Teaching is only one of an academic's roles, each of which competes for time and priority. Yet these roles do not exist in isolation. They overlap and influence each other. The teaching role of academics is coloured by their role as a researcher, scholar, administrator, manager, and adviser to students. There are pedagogical communities to which academics owe loyalty and from which they draw their identity, their language and their knowledge. But these communities of understanding can also create barriers and boundaries through conflicting value systems and contradictory allegiances.

We propose that a key condition necessary to meet the challenges of improving teaching and learning in higher education is an institution-wide strategic approach. This means that it is important to take account of the teacher's behaviour, their views of teaching, their understanding of student learning and so on, and also the wider cultural and institutional context within which these behaviours and beliefs are developed, maintained or even undermined. Improving teaching requires attention to the complete range of activities that make up higher education: it benefits from taking a holistic approach.

Equally, student learning cannot be understood in isolation. Students are never simply 'learners', and 'learning' is not simply a psychological process. Students also have to manage role conflict and a multiplicity of value systems and identities. Gender, ethnicity, nationality, class, personal and value commitments, these have been given less attention in much of the recent literature on teaching and learning which has tended to focus on purely psychological processes, such as deep and surface approaches to learning and taxonomies of understanding.

The psychological paradigm that has dominated much of the teaching and learning literature ignores the importance of learning as a set of social practices. It has also had the effect of ignoring important questions about the goals of education. If 'learning' is regarded as an end in itself, and 'effective learning' is the extent of the goal to which teaching is aimed, we bypass the question of the purpose of that learning. 'Effective learning' is such a 'thin' description of the goals of teaching that, as a concept, it actually impoverishes the debate that we ought to be having about what constitutes 'improving teaching and learning'.

We argue that higher education has a social purpose that is not merely about transmitting knowledge and skills. In our view it should also engage students in a transformational process by encouraging critical reflection on their learning and actions. This is as much a social process as it is a psychological one, and is clearly a relational process between teacher and students and the ideas shared. It is a process that is also intimately influenced by the wider cultural environment and of the institution. Nevertheless, the focus on learning has been important in challenging traditional forms of teaching. The paradigm shift characterized as 'from teaching to learning' has become widely adopted and many institutions now at least pay lip service to 'student-centred' learning in their learning and teaching strategies, and for some there is a serious attempt to turn the rhetoric into reality.

A critical approach to the concept of 'improvement'

Attempts to turn the rhetoric into reality are seen as improvements to the teaching and learning process in higher education. Since this book is entitled 'Improving Teaching and Learning' we want to say something about the notion of 'improvement'. Whereas change can be for the better or worse, improving something implies changing it for the better. Improvement suggests that the status quo is being regarded as inadequate in some way. The process of improving, when it is the result of intentional action, requires that there is an agent who is acting in response to the perceived weaknesses and with the belief that the action taken will be instrumental in addressing the problems or inadequacies identified. It implies a dynamic process rather than a point of arrival.

Improving is a teleological and a normative concept, that is, it is directed activity aimed at achieving a valued goal. As such, it is necessarily open to dispute. There can be disagreement about the description of the status quo or baseline, the analysis of the inadequacies of the status quo, the means chosen to address the perceived problem, and the goal. There can also be disagreement about the costs, financial or otherwise, involved in undertaking the improvement, and about the consequences or anything else that could impact on the process of improvement.

In this book we discuss many changes in higher education which may be regarded as improvements by some but disputed by others, either because of what is lost in the process or because they are unconvinced that the new state of affairs will actually be better. Even those who promote change, and believe there are good reasons for doing so, recognize that there are costs involved in change.

Sometimes there appears to be a naive faith in the value of 'innovation' and a confidence that 'best practice' can be identified and 'disseminated' to others. Increasingly popular in the recent policy rhetoric in education is the idea of 'excellence'. Unlike the process of dynamic change implied by 'improving', the idea of 'excellence' implies that a state of exceptionally high performance has already been achieved. Higher education institutions are being urged to identify and proclaim their excellence in order that the validity of their claim may be judged – by a selected few. Those accorded the status of 'excellent' have the role of serving as exemplars for the remainder of the sector.

Part of the anxiety about these trends towards identifying 'best practice' and 'excellence' is that they are symptomatic of a wider trend towards reduced professional autonomy and closer surveillance of professional activity. As Popper (1966) has argued, a belief in certainty can easily become totalitarian, if those with power do not allow alternative beliefs and ideals to thrive. When ideas about what is good or best practice are over-determined, this can easily lead to a desire for control by those who are convinced they know best and have the means of imposing those views on others. The result is over-regulation and a multiplication of forms of control.

> Professional self-discipline or self-regulation has been recast as a form of social surveillance; self-examination and an ethos of learning from experience has been transmuted into one of public blaming, naming and shaming.
>
> (Cooper 2000: 128)

The new forms of accountability have imposed forms of central control that are antithetical to the academic culture. What is needed is a renewal of trust within academic communities (see Chapter 8).

> We argue that the restoration of a culture of trust and professional accountability within all educational institutions is a necessary pre-requisite for the maintenance of a robust and prosperous democratic society.
>
> (Olssen *et al.* 2004: 197)

Nevertheless, we believe it is important that the notion of improving is kept alive because it motivates activity designed to solve problems. But it is important never to forget that 'improving' is a contested concept that needs to be critically debated. The fallibility of judgements about what constitutes improvement always needs to be kept in mind. Consequently, we would caution that naive forms of 'evidence-based practice', that assume evidence will 'demonstrate' conclusively the best course of action, and how the improvement can be measured and achieved, also need to be critically assessed.

We recognize the anxiety there is in higher education about well-meaning strategies designed to 'improve' but which have consequences that many are unhappy with. Sometimes this is because a good idea that works well in one context is over-generalized and made to apply where it is not appropriate. Sometimes it is because an innovation has been insufficiently researched before it is recommended to all. As Elmore has said: 'improvement is a function of learning to do the right thing in the setting where you work' (quoted in Fullan 2001: 270).

The localized and situated nature of improvement must be remembered, but this should not mean that general principles and values are entirely abandoned in pursuit of a wholly particularist agenda. We believe there are values that are at the centre of higher education which must be articulated and defended. Without ideals, situated thinking can easily become a form of exceptionalism ('this does not apply to us') that pre-empts any improvement. Ideal forms, like Habermas's 'ideal speech', serve a function as a benchmark against which we can judge our actual behaviour (Habermas

1984). Nevertheless, exactly what these ideals mean, and what implications they have for action, do need to be interpreted locally.

A 'whole institution' approach

The significance of 'the institution' as a locus for improving teaching and learning is by no means obvious. Why should anyone setting out to achieve improvements in teaching begin with the institution, and, if they were to do so, what would this mean?

Among educational developers there has often been a preference for working with individuals who are seen as 'change agents'. These are people who are willing to lead on innovations and who can interest other faculty/staff in working with them. In this way an innovation spreads to other members of a department/school/faculty and then more widely across the institution, or, through the subject community, into other institutions. There are numerous reports on the success of this strategy. The National Teaching Fellowship programme in the UK, Carnegie Scholarships in the USA, 3M scholars in Canada and other similar schemes exemplify this approach.

This might be called the 'heroic' theory of change, although the messiness and difficulties of promoting change faced by these individuals shows a much more mundane process of fighting lone battles in complex organizational settings. Skelton (2004) has suggested the model is based on 'transfer' theories of learning. Awards schemes on both sides of the Atlantic seem to be based on the assumption that by rewarding individual excellent teachers others will be encouraged to emulate them. 'First-rate teachers can, and do, work in isolation, but surely part of the purpose of marking them out as superlative is to enable others to learn from them so as to raise the overall standards of teaching' (S. Brown 2003: 5).

In both the (UK) National Teaching Fellowship scheme and the (US) Carnegie Academy scheme, award winners undertake development projects that provide them with the opportunity to extend their influence and there is also an attempt to assist them to have a collective influence as a group and across the groups.

Studies have shown that change agents within institutions often remain relatively isolated and initiatives designed to raise the status of teaching remain vulnerable if central funding is removed (Hannan and Silver 2000). Although there are undoubtedly enthusiasts for improving teaching and learning throughout higher education, the more cautionary view suggests that 'small groups of self-selected reformers apparently seldom influence their peers' (Elmore 1995: 20) and the implicit 'cascade' model of change is rarely effective (Elton 1995b). This suggests that, unless the strategies to improve teaching and learning are aimed at the majority of faculty/staff and embedded within institutional structures, individual innovators will continue to remain peripheral to the main culture of the university. Of course, the individual should be supported and encouraged, but as a change strategy a 'whole institution' approach has a greater capacity to effect change.

There is considerable research that suggests that teachers in higher education feel their principal identity is determined by their subject or discipline, more than by the institution (Henkel 2000; Becher and Trowler 2001). Academic staff move between institutions and some remain relatively aloof from whichever institution they may inhabit.

> The logic seems indisputable: the first loyalty of academic staff is to their discipline, or sub-discipline and subject, rather than to their department, which tends to be their second source of loyalty, or their institution, which tends to be their third source of loyalty. Working through subject networks and creating discipline-specific staff development, courseware and on-line learning environments would seem an obvious change strategy.
>
> (Blackwell and Preece 2001: 4)

We support this suggestion and endorse the idea that discipline-specific development is necessary and useful. This is not opposed to an organization-based approach. Indeed the two strategies should be seen as complementary. A whole institution approach does not necessarily imply a centralist managerial model in which all improvement is described in 'generic' terms. A whole institution approach allows for different types and levels of devolution. It recognizes disciplinary differences, because there is an important sense in which teaching can only be understood as teaching something, namely a subject, discipline or profession. But there is value also in interdisciplinary critical enquiry. Indeed, this can generate some of the most useful forms of learning. Placing disciplinarity, and therefore disciplinary differences, at the core of a scholarship does not abolish the need for, or supplant interest in, generic teacher knowledge (Andresen 2000).

We recognize that institutions vary enormously in their structures and management styles. In some there is a close sense of a single community in which change is agreed and implemented collectively. This can only happen in relatively small institutions with a specialist focus. Alverno College in the USA is a well-known example. In a large university with many departments, hundreds if not thousands of staff and tens of thousands of students, spread across several campuses, as well as those learning at a distance, it would be less than helpful to imply that a whole institution approach means singularity of purpose or that it implies a one-size-fits-all model of teaching.

The ideal strategy finds the right balance between the interconnectedness needed to create learning organizations (see Chapter 2) and implement effective strategies for all students, while valuing and preserving what is distinctive about disciplines. Finding the right balance means navigating between some of the principal dilemmas, or tensions, that can often paralyse the improvement process. Some of the principal tensions are between:

- traditional notions of academic identity and new roles demanded within a mass higher education system;
- discipline identities and cross-disciplinary approaches to teaching;
- maintaining standards and innovating in teaching;
- increasing research productivity and improving teaching quality;
- principles of pedagogy and the requirements of learning technologies.

Our view is that these are oversimplified dichotomies that need not be diametrically opposed. Sometimes the tensions can be increased, rather than resolved, by inappropriate use of managerial methods that are counterproductive within an academic community. Sometimes the agenda for improving teaching seems to be wholly initiated and defined by those who have a specialist interest in teaching pedagogies. This too can create, rather than resolve, tensions between the central policy makers of an institution and those at the periphery within subject schools and departments.

Successful and strategic management of improving teaching and learning must be inclusive of all those who are affected by the improvements, responsive to disciplinary differences and flexible in the manner in which the change is implemented. Such an ideal cannot always be attained, particularly when regulations require a consistency of approach in order to achieve fairness for students. Innovation that is imposed without taking account of the multiplicity of ways in which that change will be understood and interpreted is doomed to being undermined. 'Transformation depends on how well managerial and faculty values become intertwined and then expressed in daily operating procedures' (Clarke 1998: 137). This entails that the change agenda must work both vertically, to include both bottom-up and top-down strategies, and also horizontally across organizational structures. We suggest that involving academic staff in the process of researching their teaching practice increases ownership of improvements, encourages a scholarly approach to teaching and helps inform decisions at all levels of the institution. This is an approach that is consistent with academic identities and does not run counter to it as so much managerially driven change appears to do.

We will be clarifying through this book the ways in which we believe that an approach to institutional change which is firmly rooted in what we know about learning has a better chance of succeeding than models of change based on the culture of corporate business. Learning occurs through participation in social practices, in which meaning is constructed and negotiated and identities formed and re-formed. As we shall see, this approach to learning is as important to understanding faculty/staff attitudes to changes in the higher education environment as it is for appreciating the struggle that many students engage in as they find their way into the subject or disciplinary knowledge. Faced with new contexts, we are all 'learners'.

We begin by discussing the important question of values in higher education – too often ignored or missing in discussions of this kind. In the second chapter we look at the key concept of learning and begin to fashion a thesis which argues that the learning of students and of teaching staff need to be understood if the process of developing higher education is to be successful. In Part 2 we consider the major areas in a cross-institutional approach to improving teaching and learning: the staff, students, the curriculum, learning technologies, research, teaching and scholarship and quality enhancement. In the final chapter of the book we summarize the various approaches we have suggested for developing, implementing and evaluating learning and teaching strategies and for managing and supporting improvements to learning and teaching.

Part 1

The Aims of Higher Education

1

The Changing Higher Education Environment

> Education is not a service for a customer but an ongoing process of transformation of the participant.
>
> Harvey 2002: 253

Introduction

As more students enter universities and colleges than ever before, traditional forms of teaching are under increasing pressure to change. These pressures derive from a variety of sources: a more diverse student profile, globalization, flexibility in modes of delivery, marketization of higher education, funding, and accountability. Each of these has implications for teaching and learning. We briefly explore in this chapter some of the trends in teaching that indicate how the possibilities for innovation have been taken up and supported in universities and colleges. In the UK, the response to these changes has been somewhat contradictory. On the one hand, the effect has been to drive higher education towards greater segmentation and differentiation, but on the other there have been pressures towards greater standardization and uniformity through the intervention of government and its agencies.

These changes have affected the ways in which higher education is managed. There has been a shift from traditional collegial models towards more managerial or corporate styles of management. As a result of this shift, faculty/staff have faced major changes to the environment in which teaching and learning takes place. Almost all, but particularly middle managers (a concept that would not have been used with respect to academics thirty years ago), seem to have faced a growing burden of restructuring, devolved budgeting, target setting, documenting practice, policy writing, and faculty/staff review.

Finally there have been major shifts in the most fundamental issue of all: the purpose of higher education. Universities have become agents of political and social change, in particular by being required to change the social class and ethnic composition of the graduate population through changes to admission policies. This demand for opening access is partly driven by beliefs about social justice, but it is also symptomatic of a wider shift that has seen higher education being viewed as part of economic policy, serving the needs of the economy by producing the skilled workforce required for a 'knowledge society'.

Later in this chapter we argue that demands for improvement and innovation have paid insufficient attention to the question 'what is higher education for?' Unless there is an understanding of the aims, we cannot say what counts as 'improving' student learning. Simply learning more effectively is not enough if that learning is misdirected or inappropriate. In this chapter, we discuss what the goals of higher education might be as an essential precondition for any debate about how to improve teaching and learning in higher education.

Teaching and learning in flux

Diversity in a mass system

As participation rates rise, the student profile in universities and colleges becomes more diverse on a variety of fronts: educational achievement on entry, age, social class, ethnicity, religious and cultural traditions. Although no institution escapes these changes entirely, the impact of this diversity varies considerably between institutions. Roughly speaking, the 'recruiting institutions' with more open admissions policies are considerably more diverse than institutions that have higher selection criteria (Connor *et al.* 2004). This is one important feature that differentiates institutions in the developed world. Whereas in the USA there has been a mass higher education system for some decades, the changing student profile presents new challenges for many institutions in countries where there has been a recent and rapid expansion of so-called non-traditional students, for example in the UK and South Africa. Some institutions under pressure from government to change their admissions policy have seen their student profile shift dramatically. The extent to which they have made commensurate changes to their teaching and learning support remains open to question. We examine these issues in greater detail in Chapter 4.

Student numbers are rising across the globe, and student mobility between countries is also increasing. This has resulted in growing numbers of students from diverse national and ethnic cultures being 'traded' between nations. The internationalization of higher education is a global phenomenon, but one which disproportionately advantages universities in the developed world as the receivers of students from poorer countries (Chen and Barnett 2000; Marginson and Rhoades 2002). The combination of globalization of higher education and advances in communication technologies is creating more examples of 'borderless education' (Middlehurst 2000), that result in the blurring of boundaries between national systems.

Competition for students and resources

Competition for students between universities is intensifying, both within and across national boundaries. This competition for students creates institutional and departmental changes in patterns of enrolment. When the overall demographic trend is upwards, this basic feature of competition may be temporarily disguised. In any case, universities, colleges and disciplines need to pay attention to attracting students, or face the prospect of closure or contraction. This has led to increasing attention being paid to marketing programmes to attract students, and treating students as quasi-customers (Morley 2003b). Programmes of study, indeed knowledge itself, have become products in this commodified environment. The shifting market trends in subjects, the ups and downs of their popularity with students, have significant implications for the careers of academic staff. These market forces largely drive shifts in programmes offered, for example from home to international students, or from undergraduate to postgraduate students.

Universities are increasingly entrepreneurial in their character and objectives (Clarke 1998) and have been forced to seek a higher proportion of their income from corporate bodies as neo-liberal economic polices in governments have led to reduced state funding. This change impacts particularly on those academic areas that work closely with business and industries, such as pharmaceuticals, medicine, food and agriculture, and engineering. In some areas it is the relationship with public bodies that is the more significant, for example, with the National Health Service in the UK. The nature and extent of these corporate links play a significant role in defining the character and the financial status of institutions. The trend is towards creating partnerships between higher education institutions and both public and private corporations to provide tailor-made programmes of study (Jarvis 2001).

Higher education institutions also compete for funding from government-sponsored schemes, such as the Research Assessment Exercise in the UK, and from charitable foundations. The method of allocating research funding impacts significantly on teaching and learning. There is strong evidence in the UK that the Research Assessment Exercise has driven a damaging wedge between teaching and research (McNay 1999). In Chapter 7, we suggest ways of countering this bifurcation.

Changing conceptions of knowledge

Both research and teaching are equally affected by changing conceptions of knowledge, which have challenged traditional conceptions of 'disciplines'. Some have argued that these changes are putting the very existence of universities at risk (Barnett 2000), whereas others suggest that there are new modes of knowledge transforming knowledge production and transmission (Gibbons *et al.* 1994). Foucault (1970) has claimed that scientific and disciplinary knowledge are constructed from historically specific situations and postmodernism has called into question whether familiar ways of dividing knowledge are legitimate (Griffin 1997). Others have questioned the extent to which the 'forms of knowledge' used in western universities are historically contingent formations shaped by elites in western culture (Scott 1997). Globalization, through the 'network society', challenges traditional cultural forms in favour of decentralized networks (Castells 2001) and new technologies may also be creating new ways of thinking (J.S. Brown 2000) which are not bounded by existing ways of dividing subjects. This complexity, or 'supercomplexity', as Barnett has described the situation, for universities in the postmodern world and the uncertainties that are endemic in the 'risk society' (Beck 1992) mean that the straightforward transmission of knowledge in traditional didactic ways is of questionable value and legitimacy. The implications of these shifts for course design are explored in Chapter 5.

As the numbers of students entering higher education rise, the demand for efficiency and cost-effectiveness drive much of institutional policy. This affects the nature and organization of the curriculum as well as the physical environment within which teaching occurs. Much of the so-called McDonaldization of higher education (Ritzer 1993; Hayes and Wynyard 2002) is driven by this concern for greater efficiency. Semesterization, although sometimes sold as increasing access and flexibility, has principally been driven by attempts to achieve greater efficiency. The combined effect of these changes and the decline in student and faculty/staff ratios has led to a depersonalization of the relationship between teacher and student.

Accountability

In parallel to the driving down of the resources, there is a demand that the money spent on higher education be accounted for in more public ways than was traditionally required. As the effects of the increase in student numbers have become more apparent in student achievement and retention, the call for ever more demanding and intrusive processes of quality assurance has become stronger. Such processes are designed to reassure both politicians and students that their public and private investment in higher education is giving them value for money (Harvey 1995). In practice these processes add to the pressures on faculty/staff by creating more bureaucratized systems, in which every aspect of the teaching–learning relationship is required to be recorded, evidenced and scrutinized. As reported in the UK:

> There has certainly been a strong trend towards increasing consumer choice through the publication of information about service standards in different institutions. This has heralded a growth in the use of

> performance indicators, the construction of 'league tables' and a growth and strengthening of management cadres within public sector organisations of all kinds. So too within universities and colleges, new management positions, administrative units, procedures and codes of practice have been introduced. These have brought a measure of standardisation and centralisation into institutions that had traditionally been marked by decentralisation and the professional freedoms of their staff.
>
> (Brennan *et al.* 2003: 7)

These characteristics of modern higher education have clearly had a significant impact on academic life across the developed world. Many faculty/staff feel alienated by the increased levels of bureaucracy and administration forced on them. The pace and extent of change have led to weariness and resistance to what is perceived to be externally imposed shifts in the higher education environment. There is a sense of powerlessness in the face of state-driven policy change and market-driven transformation of what had been a familiar academic culture.

The fear undoubtedly exists that these changes in the culture of universities are having a number of negative effects on teaching (Rowland 2000; Walker 2001b; Morley 2003a). However, as we will see in later chapters, while some have resisted and subverted change, others have responded to these challenges by modifying their teaching and have seized the opportunity to experiment and innovate. New developments in teaching and learning have resulted in many practices becoming common which would once have been rare in traditional forms of teaching in higher education. Some examples of innovations that are now often found in programmes of study include: group work, project work, oral presentations, peer- and self-assessment, student-led activities and independent learning of many kinds, work-based activities, volunteering, and using new communication technologies in teaching (Hannan and Silver 2000). More important, perhaps, have been ways in which the approach to designing teaching has profoundly altered over recent times. Ideas about active learning and student-centred learning, outcome-based course design, authentic assessment, 'constructive alignment' (Biggs 1999) have become influential among large sections of the academic community, as we discuss in detail in Chapter 5.

The climate for innovation remains fragile (Hannan and Silver 2000; Hannan 2002), despite clear policy statements and funding opportunities that have been made available in many countries. Examples are the Teaching Quality Enhancement Fund (TQEF) in England and the Fund for the Improvement of Postsecondary Education in the USA. It is difficult to evaluate the impact of these national initiatives, not only because the response to them is so variable between and within institutions, but also because there are contradictory messages that emerge from national bodies. In the UK, for example, during the same period that there has been a declared attempt to raise the status and quality of teaching there has also been a further intensification of efforts of higher education institutions to secure research funding. But these national initiatives do illustrate an important fact, namely that the policy environment now includes explicit reference to the quality of teaching in higher education in a way that did not exist even ten years ago.

We have outlined a wide range of changes that are impacting on teaching and learning in higher education, and yet, it may be that the changes have not been sufficient to meet the challenges of the new, open-access, mass higher education. There is no evidence that the pressure to change is reducing. Scott (1995) has argued that, in the UK context, the system continues to operate with many elitist assumptions even in the face of massification. More modifications to traditional approaches to teaching will be required, and especially, as we shall suggest, through the development of universities into learning organizations.

Thus far we have identified a number of factors (reduced funding, competition from research, increased levels of bureaucracy) that seem to be undermining teaching, and yet there is more public and political interest in the quality of the teaching. The strategies employed by government agencies and most universities have failed to resolve this paradox satisfactorily. This is a paradox because one might have expected that if there is greater interest in teaching then this would have raised its significance in the minds of those managing and teaching in higher education. But, this does not follow. In practice, we have a tension between the rhetoric of valuing teaching, enhancing the status of teaching and rewarding excellent teachers, and the reality which continues to suggest that teaching is very much a lower priority, subservient to research and income-generating activities (R. Brown 2000a). In the next two sections we consider some of the policy responses and changes in management styles that contribute to the current situation with respect to teaching and learning.

Policy responses to a changing environment

Lists of changes occurring to the university in the late twentieth and early twenty-first century have become commonplace (Schuller 1995; Scott 1995; Becher and Trowler 2001), but there is an important point here for the focus of this book. It would be misleading to propose ways of achieving improvements to teaching and learning in higher education without taking into account the wider economic, social and political environment within which the notion of improvement is articulated and implemented. Equally important is how the improvement is received within the diverse groups of people and communities of practice (Wenger 1998) that is sometimes referred to simplistically as 'the academic community'. Higher education in most national systems is highly diverse with respect to its wealth, status, mission, student profile and many other dimensions, and such diversity creates multiple academic communities and multiple student experiences. Yet much of the teaching and learning literature and some policy documents are decontextualized. We hear a lot about 'best practice', 'the student learning experience', 'quality enhancement' as if these were definable single entities. The idea that it is possible to define 'best practice' is not only misleading but also counterproductive. It implies that there is a single best way in which practice should be performed and that faculty/staff should be modifying their existing practice so that it conforms to 'best practice'. This fails to take account of two important facts. Firstly, for most social situations there are multiple ways of understanding and achieving an objective. Secondly, teaching is situated in specific ways, not only in relation to factors such as institutional context, subject specialism, level of study, students' profile, but also in relation to the personal characteristics of the teacher as an individual agent. Teaching and assessing students is a 'socially situated interpretive act' that resists generalization (Shay 2004).

Unfortunately, much of the generic literature on teaching and learning has given the impression, possibly unintentionally, that it ignores these points. This has led to a strong reaction against generic educational development (see for example, Rowland 2003). It also partly explains the hostile response to some national initiatives, although recent schemes in the UK, including the creation of the Learning and Teaching Support Network and the Centres of Excellence in Teaching and Learning, have taken into account subject identities from the outset, and the Carnegie Academy's support for the scholarship of teaching and learning in the USA has had a strong disciplinary focus. We return to examine these developments in detail in Chapters 3 and 7.

Organizational cultures of higher education

There have been several attempts to categorize organizational cultures of higher education. It has been argued that in the past the academic collegial culture was dominant, but that this has been replaced today by a managerialist culture (Becher and Kogan 1992; Bergquist 1992; McNay 1995; Evans 2002). Any such contrast is bound to be a simplification, and possibly a reflection of not a little nostalgic thinking about some rather undefined and indeterminate golden age. There are, however, clear changes that support this general thesis.

In the collegial model the university was defined as a community of scholars who shared governance through processes of collective peer review and rotating peer leadership. Institutional values reflected a liberal concept of higher education in which the goal for students and staff was predominantly defined by the search for increased knowledge within disciplinary areas. Teaching staff held tenured posts as a guarantee of their academic freedom. Success was judged in qualitative terms and promotion was based on demonstrated merit within the discipline. Research and scholarship were central activities that were driven by the interests of individuals and were largely unmanaged.

By way of contrast, the university in the managerial model is much more strongly led by an executive minority using line management to ensure that the will of the executive is implemented. The result is a much more hierarchical structure in which performance is measured in terms of productivity and efficiency in meeting corporate goals. There is stronger accountability for both financial and quality matters using devolved responsibility to middle managers who have to meet predetermined output targets. Outputs for teaching and research are measured principally using quantitative financial criteria for income generation: numbers of students recruited, student retention, research grants awarded, and so on. The model is based on the assumption that institutions are seeking to improve their competitive advantage over other institutions operating within the same markets. Students are perceived as customers purchasing the knowledge products on offer. Employers, government and corporations are known now as stakeholders in the university enterprise. Faculty/staff are more likely to be non-tenured and part-time, moving between the commercial and educational worlds, with increasing specialization in either research or teaching, but not necessarily both.

This shift in the focus of higher education from a collegial to a managerial model and the consequences for the ways of working has created significant tensions in higher education that need to be addressed. The tensions arise because the dominant academic culture is in many ways antithetical to the idea of universities as businesses. In the past, the discovery and transmission of knowledge were viewed as an important enough outcome for society to justify the funding of universities, but as higher education faces competition from other sources of knowledge creation, this is no longer taken for granted. As a number of commentators have pointed out (Becher and Kogan 1992; McNay 1995; Jarvis 2001), universities are required to act in market-like ways because they face competition from knowledge providers in the corporate world and because governments, influenced by neo-liberal economic theories, from Thatcher and Reagan onwards, have driven down state funding and forced institutions to seek income from other sources. This has led to a move from a strongly planned managerial culture to a more market-driven, competitive culture.

This change creates tensions because of a further organizational culture found in higher education: the bureaucratic (McNay 1995; Jarvis 2001). While universities are certainly bureaucratic in many respects, imposing complex rules for course approval, quality assurance and research assessment, they are, at the same time, expected to become more entrepreneurial (Clarke 1998). When, managerial processes are used to set ever more detailed standards and targets, and bureaucratic procedures become more restrictive and burdensome, the opportunity for staff to become entrepreneurial risk takers is clearly reduced. The tension between these models which coexist within many institutions has proved to be demoralizing and demotivating for many staff (Knight and Trowler 2001).

Bergquist (1992) describes a new organizational culture that emerged in academe in the 1970s in the USA. This he calls the 'developmental culture', and it emerged as a response to the limitations of each of the collegial and managerial cultures. The collegial culture lacks organizational coherence, is slow to adapt to external changes in the environment and is often elitist and paternalistic, with few opportunities for women and minorities to participate in decision making. The managerial model reduces academic autonomy and can create 'repressive' and 'uninspired' places to work (Bergquist 1992).

The developmental culture emerges as an attempt to heal the rift between the collegial and managerial cultures. It seeks to discover points of compatibility between personal and organizational well-being and assumes that the concerns of individuals and organizations must be brought into harmony. The developmental culture is characterized by an emphasis on 'furthering the personal and professional growth of all members of the collegiate community', it values openness between all members of the academic community and places confidence in systematic institutional research as a rational basis for organizational planning.

We recognize many points of convergence between Bergquist's developmental culture and the general thrust of this book. However there is one issue concerning the 'untested assumption about the desire of all men and women to attain their personal maturation, while helping others in the institution to become more mature' (Bergquist 1992: 5) that we would wish to consider further. Embedded change has often failed to occur in institutions because the principal proponents of the developmental culture in institutions, often the staff in educational development centres, have focused on individual development. This failure to achieve long-term impact is partly a reflection of the marginal status of educational development centres (Gosling 1996, 2001b), and it also reflects the principal change mechanisms employed by them. Workshops, short courses, short-term funded projects, consultancies with individual enthusiasts, newsletters and websites can all generate short-term excitement, without guaranteeing any significant change in the longer term. What the early forms of the developmental culture lacked was a coherent strategy for affecting change across the institution. How can this be done without perpetuating managerialism?

To help us find an answer, we turn to the idea of 'knowledge-intensive' organizations proposed by Frenkel *et al.* (1999 cited in Jarvis 2001: 98). It is this organizational form to which universities might increasingly aspire, as we shall be suggesting in different ways in this book. Knowledge-intensive organizations are 'based on normative relationships and reciprocity', and work relations are 'based on intrinsic motivation aimed at encouraging creativity and innovation'. The university as a knowledge-intensive institution operates as a learning organization in which the emphasis is on cross-functional sharing of knowledge, continuous processes of evaluation and feedback, and maximizing employee empowerment through decentralized decision-making (Senge 1990a; Watkins and Marsick 1993).

Throughout the book we use learning theory to argue that faculty/staff are more likely to adapt to change within the model of a learning organization than under the current heavily managed environments, because only in this way can trust be rebuilt between managers and academics. Universities and colleges must find more imaginative ways of utilizing and developing the skills and knowledge of the staff that work in them if they are to develop and change to meet the challenges outlined at the beginning of this chapter. This requires a commitment to professional development and promoting critical dialogue. We return to this theme in Chapter 2.

Professional knowledge

If universities are to be knowledge-intensive learning organizations with respect to teaching as well as with respect to their research activity, then it is essential that the kind of knowledge needed for professional development is understood. Yet it would appear that little research has been undertaken to identify the professional knowledge utilized by higher education teachers. However, at school level, some conceptual frameworks have been developed which can be helpful for us in higher education. Turner-Bisset (1999) suggests the following ways of categorizing teachers' professional knowledge:

Subject knowledge

- Substantive subject knowledge – facts, concepts, theories, frameworks.
- Syntactic subject knowledge – generation and verification of knowledge.
- Beliefs about the subject – teacher's belief system about the nature and value of the subject.

Pedagogy

- Curriculum knowledge – curriculum materials, software.
- General pedagogical knowledge – craft knowledge, expository skills, classroom management, questioning.
- Knowledge/models of teaching – approach to teaching, beliefs about teaching.
- Knowledge of learners:
  Cognitive – theories of learning, development
  Empirical – experiential knowledge of students.
- Knowledge of self.
- Knowledge of educational contexts.
- Knowledge of educational ends, purposes and values.

The problem with a list such as this is that it formalizes knowledge in a way that suggests that teachers could be tested on their knowledge of each category. It suggests that professional knowledge is an accumulated set of propositions known or believed to be true and a repertoire of identifiable skills. But much professional knowledge is not at all like that. Eraut (2000) has emphasized in his writings that much professional learning is 'informal' and much of the knowledge is 'tacit'. Informal learning occurs through a variety of processes, some of which are 'implict', defined as 'the acquisition of knowledge independently of conscious attempts to learn' (Reber 1993 cited in Eraut 2000: 115), some are 'reactive', near spontaneous and unplanned, and only partly 'deliberative', that is, when time is set aside to review past actions and reflect systematically on them. Eraut further suggests that most of professional knowledge is acquired through, or emerges from, social processes of action. When there is available relevant scientific knowledge, it has to be conceptualized and integrated into the teachers' understanding of the specific context in which it is used. Knowledge transfer is 'the learning process involved in resituating some aspect of one's knowledge into a new context' (Erault 2000: 133). Tacit knowledge, he suggests, is acquired in variety of different ways:

- knowledge acquired by implicit learning of which the knower is unaware;
- knowledge constructed from the aggregation of episodes in long-term memory;
- knowledge inferred by observers to be capable of representation as implicit theories of action, personal constructs, schemas, etc.;
- knowledge which enables rapid, intuitive understanding or response;
- knowledge entailed in transferring knowledge from one situation to another;
- knowledge embedded in taken-for-granted activities, perceptions and norms.

Of course there is a role for formal and deliberative learning. Space needs to be given for this, particularly for those entering the profession of teaching in higher education. Some of the proposals in this book also suggest that there is scope for professional development relating to improving teaching and learning to occur through the activities of professionals working with each other, talking to each other and investigating their own work.

When academics express concern 'about the sort of knowledge that is coming to count as worthwhile for all professionals' (McWilliam 2002) and the failure to problematize the nature of the knowledge often transmitted through what passes for 'staff development workshops', it is because the highly situated nature of professional knowledge is ignored or disparaged. Many academics simply do not recognize the relevance of pedagogical 'theory'.

'The whole idea I think of a theory of teaching, or theorising about the activity rather than just doing it, or even of seeing the teaching as distinct from the pursuit of philosophising doesn't come easily to people in the (X discipline) community' (personal communication 2004).

Nevertheless, when the nature of the teaching task is radically altered by significant changes in the higher education context and the student profile, then habitual ways of using existing professional knowledge derived from informal experiential processes are put under extreme pressure. Problems arise which cannot be solved on the basis of experience alone. In these circumstances, which are increasingly common in higher education, new structures for learning and new ways of promoting and informing conversations are needed. The challenge is not to invent new ways of persuading academics to attend staff development workshops, but rather to create an institutional ethos that encourages such conversations to occur in a systematic and constructive way.

Thinking critically about the goals of teaching

We have outlined the changes that are occurring in higher education and reflected on the kinds of professional knowledge that need to be built on in order to respond to the challenges facing academics today. The changing relationship between higher education, the state and society not only impacts on organizational structures but also challenges traditional assumptions about the purpose of higher education. Indeed, Barnett (2000: 99) has claimed that 'the university no longer knows what it is to *be* a university'. Reflecting this crisis of radical uncertainty about the identity of the university are competing notions of the goals of higher education. This uncertainty is demonstrated by the diversity of institutional goals and cultures that we find across the developed world.

This book advances a development model of teaching and learning, which means that it is important to be clear about what universities and colleges are developing towards. We contend that it is essential to clarify the goals of higher education. In much of the literature on learning and teaching and on educational development, the concept of development is treated uncritically, as if we all knew what we were developing towards. But this is far from the case. Development is similar to the concept of improvement, as we pointed out in the Introduction, in being a teleological concept that implies that there is a growth or change towards a desired or natural end. As Webb (1996) has argued, the goals of educational development are highly contested and cannot be taken for granted. Yet as Thompson (2004: 43) has commented, 'educational developers speak as though it is self evident what we do and what we are trying to achieve as we work'.

In some writing, the notion of learning has been regarded as a good in itself and the goal of development is 'improving student learning'. The emphasis has been on helping student learning to become more effective or more efficient. One of the best-known books in learning and teaching in recent years speaks of 'teaching for quality learning' and the principal tool for achieving 'quality learning' is 'constructive alignment' (Biggs 1999). The subtitle of the book is 'What the student does', which is a useful reminder that 'what the student does is actually more important in determining what is learned than what the teacher does' (Shuell 1986 cited in Biggs 1999). This is an important antidote to the traditional notion of teaching as delivery, but the thrust of the Biggs' book is that if courses are designed to achieve alignment between what are referred to as 'desired outcomes', teaching methods and assessment tasks, then we have improved the 'quality' of student learning. We return to this question of alignment when we consider issues in course design in Chapter 5. The point we want to make here is that this approach side-steps the question 'what are desired outcomes?' and simply focuses on learning as a competence and the outcome of learning as performance. It does not consider epistemological issues or any value commitments. The approach illustrates what Lyotard (1984) has described as a characteristic of postmodernity, namely what he calls 'performativity', where efficient performance is valued without reference to any value system or overarching goals (see also Usher *et al.* 1997; Barnett 2000).

Biggs, like others who have been influential in the literature on learning and teaching, is working within a predominately 'psychological model' of teaching. An example is Biggs' discussion of the learning environment where negative factors such as 'anxiety' and teachers' cynicism are discouraged because they 'make a mess of student priorities' by focusing attention on matters irrelevant to the 'proper task – engagement' (Biggs 1999: 63). This leaves open the possibility that if research on learning showed that anxiety increased students' engagement with the proper task then it could be encouraged as part of the 'learning climate'. There is no place in this account for ethical considerations of the teacher–student relationship or of value commitments that might suggest that anxiety-inducing behaviour is not just reducing the efficiency of learning, but also damaging to trust between student and teacher and can affect students' self-confidence and self-perception. The literature on adult learning (see, for example, Brookfield 1985; Welton 1995) more often considers the social and ethical commitments which underpin the teaching/learning enterprise.

Learning effectively is not just a psychological process, it is also about the relationship between the learner and subject knowledge. This relationship is partly a matter of how the students regard what is being learned in relation to their own social identity and values. It is also about the students' understanding of the status of the evidence for the knowledge learned, what counts as appropriate evidence and how secure the evidence needs to be to be regarded as knowledge. This understanding is critical for the teaching of a discipline that is centrally about the value attached to forms of evidence and types of discourse. As Rowland (2000: 113) has pointed out: 'our commitment to our subject infuses us with the values embodied in it'.

Furthermore there is a danger that the focus on the single term 'learning' results in an impoverishment of the educational process. This is for two reasons. The first is that it could lead to an underestimation of the extent to which the student must come to a position of intellectual autonomy (Barnett 1990). This is not just a matter of learning, it is also a matter of making judgements, making value commitments, taking positions. This is what we want students to do *with* their learning as they move from an apprenticeship role at the periphery to one as a member of a community of practice (Lave and Wenger 1991). The second, but linked, point is that students do much more than learn: they discuss, debate, perform, act, create, argue, experiment, treat patients, research, make business plans, and much more. Of course, through these performative acts they may also be learning, but all these acts cannot be *reduced to* learning alone.

Understanding goals

The notion of goals is a complex one. In order to cut through some of this complexity we make a distinction between three types of goals. First there are the goals that students have as personal objectives for themselves. We call these 'personal goals'. These are the reasons students have for entering and persisting with higher education. Typically, students' personal goals include such things as 'getting a better job', 'increase my knowledge', 'learn more about a subject', 'build my confidence'. For university students, personal goals may be more about being part of a community than strictly educational goals. These include goals such as, 'to meet new people', 'have fun', 'pursue a sport' or 'engage in' politics or other personal interest. These social goals have an important influence on student recruitment and retention and so cannot be ignored. However, students' goals are not fixed. There is evidence that students' goals change as a result of their experience of higher education (Astin 1993).

The second category of goals comprises those that are outcomes of programmes of study. We call these 'outcome goals'. These include such things as 'the ability to think critically', 'to work with others in a team' and 'to show initiative and personal responsibility'.

The third type of goals we term 'system goals'. These are the goals that the higher education system as a whole is expected to achieve and they are usually set by governments or academic associations such as Universities UK and the British Psychological Society. System goals include 'meeting the needs of the economy', 'providing a trained workforce', 'socially responsible citizenship', 'lifelong learning' and 'widening participation'. Such goals reflect different ideological commitments, or high-level social and political values, for equality of opportunity, social justice, democratization, sustainability, capitalism and so on. These are too vaguely conceptualized and highly contested to be specific goals or outcomes.

It is possible to arrange these three levels of goals in a hierarchy of generality (see Table 1.1). However, reality is much more complex than such a neat hierarchy suggests. Goals can be indeterminate, unarticulated and

Table 1.1 Hierarchy of higher education goals

Level of goal	*Legitimating groups*	*Example*
Highest-level socio-political values	Society/political leadership	Equality of opportunity
System goals	Agencies of the state/ academic representatives	Widening of social class or ethnic participation
Outcome goals	Academic staff/managers/ employers	Employability
Personal goals	Students/clients	Achieve a better career

unrecognized. Rationalizing vague aspirations into tidy lists always creates a false sense of clarity that is rarely matched in either institutional or individual behaviour. Furthermore, there are intermediate goals that may be seen as ends in themselves or as means to higher-level aims. For example, student autonomy may be regarded as a worthwhile end in itself, but can also be seen as a means to helping the individual student be more employable or a more successful lifelong learner.

Many of the goals that are seen as ends, as improvements in teaching and learning, are only means to a higher-level goal. A typical set of goals for enhancing teaching and learning might include:

- active learning
- deep learning
- diversifying assessment
- learner-managed learning
- peer review of teaching
- personal development planning
- problem-based learning
- scholarship of teaching and learning
- student-centred learning
- using learning technologies
- work-related learning.

These are often treated as if they were ends in themselves, but we would argue that they are only a means to some other end. An implication of this point is that in order to evaluate the effectiveness of any of these processes or activities it is necessary to find ways of measuring, or estimating, their contribution to the achievement of the higher-level goal. We return to the question of evaluating the impact of changes on learning and teaching in Chapter 9. Here, we are making the point that we must not lose sight of what it is we are trying to achieve. Perhaps it is obvious that if we seek to promote problem-based learning it is because we think it will help students to be better critical thinkers. Or if we advocate student-centred learning it is because it will enable students to be more autonomous and more effective lifelong learners. Unfortunately the means too often becomes the end in itself and we lose sight of the ultimate system goals and, at programme level, outcome goals that the changes implicitly or explicitly are designed to foster.

Angelo (1995) has proposed a useful model to clarify what goals a particular teaching strategy is designed to achieve. The Teaching Goals Inventory includes the following:

- higher-order thinking skills
- basic academic success skills
- discipline-specific knowledge and skills
- liberal arts and academic values
- work and career preparation
- personal development.

Readers will want to create their own list of goals, but the important point here is that we must clearly associate the strategy with the goals it is designed to achieve.

What is labelled as 'development' in relation to a given goal, may be regarded as a retrogressive step by others who have not bought into the (often implicit) goal that the development seeks to achieve. What is taken to be a merely technical improvement by a 'developer' is seen as ideologically motivated by subject specialists who do not share, or who have not been invited into a discussion of these goals (McWilliam 2002). A clear example of this in many UK institutions has been the move to a credit accumulation model where this has been imposed from above with little attempt to debate its merits among staff. It is presented as a regulatory change, when in practice it has significant implications for teaching, course design and assessment. The result is resistance, tokenism and subversion of the policy as Trowler's (1998) account has demonstrated. We discuss the important issue of the response of teaching staff to change in Chapter 3.

Ethical goals of teaching

The goals of teaching are inextricably linked to ethical choices about the good life and human good. In these days of instrumental thinking, when many staff and students see education as simply a route to a better paid job, and in which governments emphasize above all else the contribution of higher education to the economic well-being of the nation, it is worth reminding ourselves of this fundamental point. When we defend a goal as an appropriate end for education we endorse it as being in some sense for the good of the person being educated. This leaves open the question what is 'the good'.

There is a long tradition of arguing that intellectual and critical powers are good in themselves. Aristotle thought the ultimate goal of human life was *eudaimonia*, variously translated as 'happiness' or 'human flourishing' but this is not 'happiness' in the simple sense of a feeling of pleasure or enjoyment, rather it is the highest form of human life. For Aristotle this was leading the life of the intellect. John Stuart Mill declared that it was better to live the life of a Socrates dissatisfied than that of a pig satisfied. This may be unfair to pigs, but intellectualists wishing to justify an education that is principally about developing the higher capacities of the mind have seized on the key point. Its best-known advocate is Newman in the *Idea of the University*, first published in 1853. According to Newman (1853: 112), the purpose of a university education is 'to open the mind, to correct it, to refine it, to enable it to know, and to digest, master, rule, and use its knowledge, to give it power over its own faculties, application, flexibility, method, critical exactness'.

Liberal education, viewed in itself, is simply the cultivation of the

> intellect, as such, and its object is nothing more or less than intellectual excellence.
>
> (Newman 1853: 121)

One appeal of liberal education today is that it appears to be morally neutral between alternative life-choices that, it is claimed in this relativist and postmodern world, should be the choice of individuals rather than that of a state-sponsored educational system. Liberal education facilitates individual choice by making it better informed, but it does not determine what the choice should be. But the intellectualist tradition rests on an ethical position about the value of rationality in human life. Barnett (1990) argues for three levels of rationality, which he calls groundedness (giving adequate reasons for beliefs), enlightenment (transformation through understanding) and emancipation (creating new possibilities for thought and action). He concludes: 'The radical conception of a person-centred liberal education amounts to nothing less than a total transformation and emancipation of the individual student' (Barnett 1990: 191).

When it comes to considering any ethical dimension to this 'transformation', however, it amounts to no more than the moral virtues of the intellectual life, characteristics such as sincerity, honesty, truthfulness, the avoidance of self-contradiction, intellectual courage, and openness to other viewpoints (Barnett 1990). While not wishing to question the importance of the value of these intellectual virtues, there does appear to be something missing from this account. Our anxiety is that relying only on intellectual virtues leaves open the possibility of what Geras, writing a post-Holocaust political philosophy, has called 'the contract of mutual indifference: under which people in acute danger or trouble may be simply left there, so far as their situation is considered to be the business of anyone else' (Geras 1998: 169). This tendency to mutual indifference has had dire consequences, not only in the Holocaust but also in other more recent threats to human life, not least the persistence of avoidable poverty, malnutrition and early mortality in the developing world. What is needed, Geras argues, is not some ideal of human nature, which is a highly contested notion, but rather the 'notion of certain shared human characteristics and vulnerabilities' (1998: 133).

We find a similar idea in Rorty, namely the notion of 'human solidarity' as a goal of 'moral progress'.

> The view I am offering says that there is such a thing as moral progress, and that this progress is indeed in the direction of greater human solidarity. But that solidarity is not thought of as recognition of a core self, the human essence, in all human beings. Rather, it is thought of as the ability to see more traditional differences (of tribe, religion, race, customs, and the like) as unimportant when compared with similarities with respect to pain and humiliation.
>
> (Rorty 1989: 192)

But does higher education contribute to this, or any other version of moral progress? Should universities and colleges have a role as significant players in promoting ethical responsibility, human solidarity, democratic values, social responsibility and lifelong learning? It is true that the Dearing Committee (Dearing 1997: 8) recognized that higher education should be 'part of the conscience of a democratic society' and talked about 'respect for the rights of the individual and the responsibilities of the individual to society as a whole', and there is a growing awareness of the importance of teaching ethics (Macfarlane 2003; CIHE 2004; Illingworth 2004) as an integral part of professional preparation. Nevertheless, ethical goals have received far less attention in the higher education policy context than, for example, widening participation and employability. We wish to argue that ethical responsibility and democratic values are equally important, and potentially create just as significant an agenda for change in universities.

> The ethical turn must, then, also be a political turn framed by the society we would hope to build, a concern for oppressed and marginalised groups, and a reflexive recognition of the ways on which universities perpetuate relationships of power and domination, even while they challenge them.
>
> (Walker 1998: 293)

At the present time, it seems that few higher education institutions in the UK give prominence to these social and ethical values. In a review of UK institutional learning and teaching strategies, Badley and Wickes noted:

> One new university . . . describes itself as developing student awareness of civic society, equality, human need and social justice. Is it just surprising (or ironic), or sadly dispiriting, that this is the only reference to democratic values in any university's strategic vision that we could find?
>
> (Badley and Wickes 2002: 6)

Perhaps this is surprising given that universities have had a long tradition of radical politics. In a democracy higher education should stand for the values of social engagement, participation, tolerance, and the 'open society' (Popper 1966). The intellectual values of critical thinking, challenging what is taken for granted, searching for truth, these ultimately have value because they contribute to a better society and more fulfilled individuals. Without them, as Mill (1962) argued, we are left with mere dogma and superstition. The significance of these values become clear in the context of the changes that occur when societies move from being ideologically closed to becoming 'open societies'. The changes occurring now in higher education in Russian and other eastern European countries demonstrate what has to happen in the curriculum and in teaching if democratization is to take root (Tomusk 1999).

> The norms, values, attitudes, ethics and knowledge that tertiary institutions can impart to students constitute the social capital necessary to

> construct healthy civil societies and socially cohesive cultures as well as to achieve good governance and democratic political systems.
>
> (World Bank 2001: 16)

Clearly the authors of this World Bank strategy believed that tertiary or higher education has an important role in transmitting and maintaining sets of values and attitudes. These values of higher education are not necessarily directly 'taught'. Rather they are exemplified in its practices, in its admissions policies, in its choice of research, in the relationship between teachers and students. The injustices of the apartheid regime in South Africa, for example, were reflected in the country's education system. Addressing these historical injustices is only now becoming a driving feature of the South African university sector.

> The principle of equity requires fair opportunities both to enter higher education programmes and to succeed in them. Applying the principle of equity implies, on the one hand, a critical identification of existing inequalities which are the product of policies, structures and practices based on racial, gender, disability and other forms of discrimination or disadvantage, and on the other a programme of transformation with a view to redress. Such transformation involves not only abolishing all existing forms of unjust differentiation, but also measures of empowerment, including financial support to bring about equal opportunity for individuals and institutions.
>
> (Department of Education 1997: para 1.18)

In the developed world we cannot afford to presume these goals have been achieved. Discrimination, inequalities and injustices continue to exist within our universities and some scholars have argued that the values of truth seeking and scholarship are under threat from the increasingly close relationship between universities and their corporate paymasters (Evans 1999).

In the USA there is a strong tradition of 'service' to the community as the third goal of universities, along with research and teaching. This commitment to serving the local or regional community is less clear in the UK, but the impact of universities on their neighbourhood is still strong through adult education, community learning, and their role in supporting voluntary movements.

It could be argued that university researchers lead the way in thinking about ecology and green politics, for example animal ethics and anti-globalization. But equally universities are linked to large corporations and military research. In this respect higher education merely reflects the values of the wider society that funds the research. The conclusion might be that universities are no more likely to be moral institutions than any other, despite the overt commitment to certain ethical values such as truth-telling, respect for freedom of thought, tolerance of alternative views, equal opportunities and so forth. The growing interest in professional ethics may be more a pragmatic reflection of the growth of professional regulation in nursing, social work and kindred disciplines than a desire to expand the moral education of students.

Our position is that ethical values cannot be ignored as part of any discussion about what constitutes 'improving teaching and learning'. We suggest that there are three main ethical dimensions that need to be developed. These relate to (1) the activities of teaching, (2) the learning of students and (3) the nature of the knowledge taught.

The ethical basis of teaching

In his book *The Courage to Teach*, Palmer states: 'Good teaching cannot be reduced to technique; good teaching comes from identity and integrity of the teacher' (1998: 13). The identity of a teacher is constructed from a complex interplay of factors (discussed further in Chapter 3) that include not only the values of the discipline or profession of which the teacher is a member, but also the personal values, history and commitments that the teacher brings to the task of teaching. Integral to this notion of identity are ethical beliefs. When Rowland (2000) talks about the most fundamental aim of teaching being to imbue students with a love of the subject, he is expressing an ethical commitment at the heart of teaching.

But we have other commitments to our students which are equally ethical: that alternative views should be respected, that students should be rewarded for effort, that students should be successful, to be honest with students about our own beliefs, the development of students' capacity to be critical, the duty to provide students with feedback on their learning within a time period that is useful to them in their studies. There is a long list of commitments, duties and responsibilities that are central to the activity of teaching. Much of what is called professionalism is the conscientious acting out of these ethical principles (Ottewill 2001; Macfarlane 2003). But as Macfarlane has pointed out, teachers are often faced with dilemmas in their professional lives that require them to prioritize their principles. His solution is to propose a set of 'virtues for university teaching': respectfulness, sensitivity, pride, courage, fairness, openness, restraint and collegiality.

In reality we all fall short of our own ideals, sometimes because of pressures or role conflicts or personal failings. Whether we succeed or not in matching our actions to our ideals, teaching is at heart an ethical activity. Among all the talk of developing the technical competences of teachers in higher education, we must not forget this fundamental point.

The ethical development of students

The ethical development of students happens in a variety of ways. Firstly, we have referred already to the intellectual virtues integral to academic work. Commitment to these virtues is one reason why plagiarism is treated seriously by institutions of higher education. Secondly, students' ethical understanding should be developed through their exploration of ethical issues arising within their studies, whether this be about the application of genetics, the ecological impact of tourism, the place of morality in art, social inequality in history and today. Students are implicitly and explicitly being made aware of the ethical dimensions to their subject and provided with more sophisticated tools to respond to them. Thirdly, students preparing for professional careers will be introduced to, and will be expected to demonstrate their commitment to, professional standards of behaviour. Fourthly, colleges and universities could promote, through the curriculum, moral commitments to the promotion of human good, social justice, tolerance and democratic values.

The ethical basis of the knowledge taught

The third dimension relates to the ethical basis of disciplines and professions. Each subject incorporates a variety of ethical commitments and poses characteristic ethical dilemmas. No subject can be value free, either in relation to the way in which knowledge is collected and understood or in the application of that knowledge in society. Teachers of subjects need to explore these value questions with their students to ensure that they are explicitly acknowledged and analysed (Skelton 2002). Furthermore, many subjects in higher education have ethical goals in the more explicit sense that the behaviour required of professionals has an ethical base. Students will therefore need to develop an awareness of personal responsibility and professional codes of conduct and will need to incorporate a critical ethical dimension to their studies.

It has been suggested that approaches to the teaching of ethics can be of three kinds (Illingworth 2004). The first is simply a pragmatic response to the regulatory frameworks laid down by professional bodies; the second embeds standards of behaviour in the professional training of students, and third is the more theoretical study of morals and ethics. If students are taught the ethical code of a profession, or standards of professional behaviour, without subjecting that code or those standards to critical scrutiny, then their learning lacks a central characteristic of higher education. Students need to know not only how to behave according to professional ethics, but also why. Without this they will lack the ability to make choices when principles conflict, as they often do. Ethical behaviour cannot be controlled simply through ever more detailed prescriptive professional codes of practice without concern for the ethical values which underpin the professional life. As Brien (1998: 394) states:

> These measures focus on what people do rather than the sort of person an agent is and so they fail to engender ethical norms. Such measures fail to take sufficient account of the fact that an important part of being

a professional is being a certain sort of person who values certain things in certain ways.

We have seen that teaching incorporates ethical choices and commitments in a variety of ways. When the current discourse emphasizes skills and knowledge acquisition, then this ethical aspect of teaching can become neglected or ignored. In our view, transforming students is as much an ethical process as it is about cognitive development.

Teaching as transformation

The tradition of a liberal education remains strong despite the battering it has received from the marketization and commodification of knowledge and from the growth of vocationalism in higher education. The 'liberal' view sees the supreme value of education as lying in the development, or the 'transformation', of the individual. For example, Harvey (2002: 253) has argued that: 'Education is not a service for a customer but an ongoing process of transformation of the participant.'

But what is the meaning of transformation? There have been a variety of approaches to understanding this process. One is the tradition of experiential learning (Boud and Walker 1993; Boud and Miller 1996); others are linked to traditions in adult education (Brookfield 1985; Welton 1995), the independent studies movement (Robbins 1988) and learner-managed learning (Graves 1993; O'Reilly *et al.* 1999) which emphasizes the overriding importance of the personal growth of the individual. A commonplace in the rhetoric of higher education today is phrases like 'student-centred learning' (CNAA 1992), 'student focused strategies' (Prosser and Trigwell 1999), 'the autonomous learner' (Gibbs 1992; Baume 1994), which might imply that self-management and personal autonomy are being addressed. However, too often these phrases stand for little more than a reduction in faculty/staff contact hours, rather than a process of enabling students to acquire the capacity to be more self-confident and independent.

The growth of personal development planning (Jackson and Ward 2001; Gosling 2003) is a response to the recognition that students must be encouraged 'to reflect upon their own learning, performance and/or achievement and to plan, for their personal, educational and career development' (Ward 2001: 2). If we are serious about encouraging students to be self-reflexive and to achieve 'the discursive openness and continuing critical evaluation for a genuinely open society' (Barnett, 1997: 169), then we must organize our teaching in a way that does more than acknowledge the epistemological uncertainties that we discussed earlier in this chapter.

Furthermore, students who are marginalized within society and their universities by virtue of their race, gender, age, religion, sexual orientation or disability, can feel that the vast apparatus of the dominant traditions and conventions of their subject gives them no space to develop a position of their own without being penalized. The experience of higher education for students from minorities can feel oppressive and disempowering, as this student explains: 'Black people don't matter as they are not included in the curriculum. This makes life more difficult because part of what is left out is "me". This is sad, but it is expected and that is the real sadness' (Nehusi and Gosling 2001: 295).

Feminist writers have similarly resisted the silencing of women in the history of the disciplines and have struggled to ensure that alternative voices are heard within the academy. Other groups, the disabled, working-class students, have reported similar feelings that their identity has been denied by being ignored.

This denial of the multiple social identities of students presents a difficult issue for the notion of education as a transformative experience. Education is clearly about learning, and learning implies a change to the mental models through which individuals understand their world. When students learn to use new concepts, new ideas, new outlooks, their sense of themselves inevitably changes. Meyer and Land (2003: 2) have talked about the 'indissoluble inter-relatedness of the learner's identity with thinking and language'. As students come to understand key concepts, or threshold concepts, as Meyer and Land refer to them, this leads to 'a transfiguration of identity'. The realization of the potential impact on their current identity by adopting the schemas of their discipline, or some subset of the discipline, can lead some students to resist adopting those concepts because they fear that their core identity is being colonized by an alien system of thought. Those who are less threatened by a way of thinking will be less troubled by making the transition to a new conceptual framework and may embrace it with enthusiasm. Between the resisters and the enthusiastic adopters there will be those who will engage with the ideas in a critical way to challenge them and recast them. Out of this can emerge some of the most engaged, creative and interesting student work. Some of these students will go on to postgraduate study and become the next generation of thinkers who will challenge the hegemony of previously accepted norms and theories.

One way the teacher can encourage students to achieve this change is to 'democratise knowledge' (Skelton 2002). Skelton argues that this requires four things. Firstly, in addition to a deep knowledge of the subject they are studying, students need to have 'an awareness of the historical and philosophical development of the discipline, which allows them to undertake the justificatory and explanatory tasks within its conventions' (Skelton 2002: 196). Secondly, students need to have access to the areas where knowledge is contested within their discipline and understand the different traditions that exist within a field of knowledge. Thirdly, students should be encouraged to step outside the discipline in order to critique it, particularly from the perspective of those who are marginalized by the dominant traditions of the subject. Finally, students can be encouraged to take up a personal position on the discipline by reference to 'meta-criteria' that can be drawn from personal values or ethical positions.

Distinctive values of teaching in higher education

Despite the changing context that we have outlined at the start of this chapter, we nevertheless believe that there are distinctive values in higher education that must be preserved. These include a commitment to developing critical thinking and higher-level cognitive skills, maintaining the relationship between research and teaching, aiming for collegiality and the value commitments that define each discipline and profession. We have argued that the overriding goal is the transformation of students' understanding of themselves and their world. Successful programmes of study engage students in actively developing their conception of themselves and others by providing access to new insights and new ways of acting in the world. What ensues, for teachers and students, is a somewhat unpredictable journey with uncertain destinations, because we cannot predict how students make use of the knowledge we encourage them to acquire. Our role as teachers is to try to make that journey exciting and challenging.

The implicit promise we make to students is that their lives can be improved by engaging in study, not just, or not necessarily, materially, but by being better able to think clearly, to gather and analyse evidence, to work with others, to be a more autonomous, self-directed person and appreciate the value of knowledge. The promise we make to society is that higher education contributes to a better society by creating people who have been taken through a programme of learning which is rigorously and fairly assessed and which creates motivated and creative people who will go on to be successful learners throughout their lives. We can, as teachers in higher education, achieve these goals by being self-critical and better informed about teaching, being willing to experiment and investigate the impact of our teaching, by ensuring that at all times we are responding to the development and learning needs of our students.

These values need to be defended in the context of mass higher education and the other changes we discussed in the earlier part of this chapter. We do not expect all our readers to share the same values, but we are arguing that there is a need to be open and explicit about which social and value commitments are driving the desire to bring about change. Innovation is not a good in itself. Change is not necessarily for the better. It is therefore imperative that the values that underpin an institutional approach to improving teaching and learning are clearly articulated.

In this book we explore how the goals of higher education should inform the management of change. Improving teaching requires attention to teachers, students, the design of courses, the use of information technology, research and teaching, and quality systems. The result of successful learning inevitably means that their learning changes individuals, both teachers and students.

2

The Learning University

> Learning is a basic human drive which most healthy people . . . choose to pursue.
>
> Martin 1999: 69

Introduction

The aim of this chapter is to share our understanding of how institutions can improve teaching and learning through a whole institution approach. We entitle this chapter 'the learning university' because, corresponding to the goals we outlined in Chapter 1, we believe that learning is central to everything that universities do, whether it be the learning of researchers from new discoveries, the learning of teachers from the interaction with discipline content, the learning of students from pedagogical experiences, the learning of managers through trial and error or the learning from any other university activities. In line with Stata's claim that 'the rate at which individuals and organisations learn may become the only sustainable competitive advantage, especially in knowledge-intensive industries' (cited in Meade 1995: 113), it is our position that universities that understand learning in all its capacities will be most able to cope with the pace of change discussed in Chapter 1. We are less inclined to describe universities as industries; nevertheless we do accept the basic premise behind Stata's point as the rationale for the development of learning universities.

We begin the chapter by summarizing the work of scholars and theorists who have attempted to understand the university as an organization and who, through their research, have identified the unique dimensions of change as it occurs in this context. We also briefly outline the relevant literatures on learning organizations, learning communities and learning theory. From these literatures, our own research and professional experience we have developed a range of approaches that can assist with creating a learning university. It is our view that these approaches have the potential to be successful levers for improving teaching and learning, as well as mechanisms for dealing with change, in universities today.

We conclude the chapter with a number of suggestions for academics, support staff, managers/administrators and students on how these approaches can support learning development across the whole institution in order to manage change in teaching and learning.

What makes universities different from other complex organizations?

In the early 1990s an article by Smith (1992) set out the key differences between universities and other complex structures. Smith's view is based on his ten-year experience as a dean of business at a Canadian university. He uses business organizations as the main comparator. His work remains a useful reminder of the challenges that university managers/administrators and academics must understand when faced with internal and external change initiatives that can impact on the student learning experience.

As discussed in Chapter 1, the scope and number of changes are more complex than ever before. We would like to suggest that the approaches we propose in this chapter provide a useful basis for a university to respond to the many changes that it might face and prepare the institution to cope with these changes in ways that can improve teaching and learning.

Firstly, let us look at what Smith (1992) identified as the key organizational differences that impact on how universities cope with change. He notes six:

- the goals of the university;
- efficiency measures;
- devolved power arrangements;
- competitive forces vary from programme to programme;
- publicly funded institutions must be accountable to the public;
- employment conditions are often misunderstood and questioned.

How is each of these different from other complex organizations? Most organizations have clearly articulated goals. In the world of academe, 'home of the articulate', it might be expected that goals would be easy to produce. In Chapter 1 we discussed some of the reasons why this would be difficult; we noted how goals in higher education are highly contestable. Smith also suggests that another of the reasons why there are not clearly articulated goals in higher education institutions is the potential that clear and measurable goals have for creating internal conflict. Although, as we discussed in Chapter 1, the main aim of all universities is similar, the specific goals within an institution are less so because of the range of disciplinary and professional areas included under its umbrella of work. Aligned to this, and equally affecting the goal-defining process, is the difficulty of accurately measuring the outcomes of university work, whether it is research or teaching. Outside of academe, growth and profitability are viewed as measures of success, whereas inside academe neither one nor both may be applicable to all subject departments of a university. Society needs a full complement of subjects to be investigated and taught, and not all will meet these kinds of typical organizational efficiency expectations.

Furthermore, seeking to be efficient in higher education oftentimes leads to measuring the wrong thing. If growth and profitability, that is productivity, cannot be defined, how can they be measured? The item most often measured is the number of publications produced by each academic member of staff or by departments or schools. This can lead to the unnecessary production of publications as products that do not necessarily add to the useful pursuit of knowledge and ideas or to students' learning.

Another constraint on efficiency measures is the fact that seeking answers in science often leads to 'failures' because answers are not always found or the answers found prove a thesis wrong. The negative case and 'failures' nonetheless can move ideas onwards and, as a result, universities do provide an important contribution to society that by the usual measures of success, focusing on efficiencies and specified outcomes, would not be calculated as such. 'In sum, efficiency is a difficult concept to apply to the major task of universities' (Smith 1992: 4)

Devolved governance in universities is also an organizational anomaly since most other types of organizations are hierarchical in structure and function. The fact that, in universities, high-ranking employees – the professors – have potentially as much power as their bosses, creates a dual authority structure uncommon in other complex organizations. Authority in this case comes from the specialist knowledge held by the academics who know the most about what should be researched and taught. This requires a dual decision-making process over curriculum issues and goal setting which then often results in a fragmented policy-making process. An added factor to this scenario is the tradition of universities to engage in consultative consensus-building processes when engaged in decision making. This is often seen by outsiders as problematical since it delays response time which, in a fast-paced modern environment, can make universities less able to cope with change. Smith (1992) defines this as a distinguishing feature of universities as compared with private businesses – although, he adds, it does not necessarily make them different from other large, complex organizations.

Universities have traditionally understood consultation to happen through committees. There are many more committees in universities that are permanent and meet on a regular basis and are larger (in order to properly represent various university groups) than in other organizations. Smith (1992) notes that, despite what might seem like a recipe for disaster in decision making, university committees have been found to reach final decisions at about the same speed as other organizations. In fact, it is thought that standing committees may actually speed up this process and, most importantly, the process is perceived as arriving at decisions through a culturally acceptable process that helps to ensure broad-based participation in the outcomes. Although not all academics would necessarily participate in the process, they would see themselves as having a right to do so. We come back to university committee work in the last section of this chapter, where we identify how committees can be a useful mechanism for creating a learning university through engaging in their work as learning communities.

Related to the problem of measuring output is the problem that universities are seen as insufficiently accountable. The consumer choice/profitability scenario in business does not directly apply in higher education. As Smith (1992: 4) notes: 'While it is possible for students to select alternative programs, this possibility is likely to have little impact on undergraduate programs . . . particularly those oversubscribed.' Although he is referring to Canadian universities in particular, recent experience in the UK would suggest that student choice of undergraduate programmes is leading to the closure of some subject areas where there is no compensating income source. Nevertheless, it does not follow that a business model applies, since universities can choose to sustain programmes for reasons other than student numbers when it is believed to be important for the achievement of the institutional mission.

Smith continues this analysis by looking at postgraduate programmes and indicates that in that context the pressures to achieve high research outputs and the rewards that go with them create a different kind of situation that is more highly competitive at that level. He further suggests that this then places too much focus on research as an area of accountability where even here the results can take years to realize. Thus, 'the informed qualitative judgement of peers may be the best we can do' (Smith 1992: 3) to be accountable in higher education. This is what is commonly called peer review and is used extensively as a mechanism for both accountability and quality control in higher education. We discuss the features of the peer review process later in the chapter, and elsewhere in the book, when we consider various approaches to creating a learning university.

Academic leaders, for the most part, come up through the ranks of academe having been successful teachers and/or researchers. Thus, they are rarely prepared for the role they will need to play as academic managers/administrators. Many are reluctant candidates for their posts since most higher education managers are often viewed suspiciously in the academic community. This is mainly because the management role does not include the usual work of academics. It is not teaching or research but rather is concerned with ensuring proper management of both staff and budgets. Because the work of the academic manager is significantly different from the academic role, it is often difficult to garner the support of colleagues for the strategic planning required of managers. The time in post is usually limited so this, too, makes long-term planning difficult.

Management style must also be sensitive to the academic culture (Bergquist 1992). 'In a large university effective leadership must be largely unobtrusive, causing academics, whether knowingly or unknowingly, to end up where the leader wishes them to go' (Smith 1992: 7). As noted earlier, a shared consensual decision-making model of academic governance is most compatible with a non-directive management approach. Most telling about this management model in universities is Rosovsky's view that 'the quality of a school is negatively correlated with the unrestrained power of administrators [managers]' (cited in Smith 1992: 7). Again, this marks university organizations as uniquely different from those in business and industry.

Conditions of employment in universities are also very different from those in other organizations. Academic freedom and the corollary 'right to fail' mentioned earlier allow most full time workers in academe to pursue their careers with a greater degree of job security than in many other contexts. The increasing use of part-time academics is, however, leading to a casualization of the higher education workforce that potentially threatens the traditional autonomy of academics. 'Society benefits from the protection of truth telling that is the responsibility of universities. That there is some social cost associated with providing this benefit is to be expected' (Smith 1992: 8). In the business world this would, in effect, be the equivalent of a 'loss leader' and necessary to ensure the types of outcomes we described in Chapter 1.

The tradition of sabbaticals, taking uninterrupted time out from normal teaching duties to produce academic work, has become an increasingly important condition of employment for traditional universities to maintain a competitive edge in research productivity. It is, however, less common in those institutions where research is a lower priority. As early as 1968, Bok noted that 'while it took Harvard 275 years to collect its first 1 million books, it took only five years to add the most recent 1 million' (Smith 1992: 8). If universities are to remain competitive in the context of this rate of production, staff must have sufficient time set aside to achieve this goal.

However, these 'timeouts' are not well understood by those outside academe, though there are some businesses that have recently adopted similar schemes for their employees. Sabbaticals and other 'perks' of the job, such as facilities to conduct research, travel funds to conferences to meet others working in similar areas of interest, and other office support systems, are conditions that many academics enjoy, that are relatively rare in other complex organizations, and are often more important than salary considerations. As we point out in other parts of this book, notably Chapter 7, anything that gives academics more time to do the main functions of their job, that is to engage in research and teaching, is of critical importance to their ability to produce even what might be perceived as 'unmeasurable' outcomes.

When creating a whole institution approach to managing change through teaching and learning, it is important to remember each of these key areas where universities differ from other organizations. It is also important to take account of disciplinary loyalties of academic staff. Loyalty to the department, and the degree programmes it offers, often outweigh any loyalties an academic might have to the institution as a whole. We discuss disciplinary identity and its impacts later in the book, in Chapters 3 and 7.

If either of these unique characteristics is not taken into account or is not aligned properly with the structures, customs and culture of academic organizations, the chances are that the approaches taken to improve teaching and learning will not be welcomed by the inhabitants of the university and consequently less likely to succeed in tackling the changes needing to be addressed. We suggest some ways to take account of the unique characteristics of universities in the sections that follow. First, we will take a look at learning as a organizational dynamic and then discuss how the unique organizational dimensions of universities align with those of learning organizations more generally.

Learning and change

Even a cursory review of the ideas contained in the literature on learning would recognize learning as a driver for change in its own right (Lave 1993; Brew and Boud 1995a, b; Martin 1999). What is surprising is the conclusion that, although in Lave's terms learning is 'ubiquitous in ongoing activity', it is rarely recognized in the context of educational developments or as part of a change process in higher education. The link between learning and change is, however, more evident in 'the student learning literature [which] emphasizes that learning is change, that is, change in ways of seeing and understanding' (Martin 1999: 76). The point here is that change *requires* learning. We will look at ways that universities, as organizations, can learn from themselves, and can become a teaching resource for themselves as well.

In this section we identify how a university, as an organization, can become more connected to its main outcome – learning – and use learning to understand and deal with change. We draw on the work of Martin (1999) for this task because she has provided a systematic review of the learning literature and, in particular, has produced a summary of the relationship between the literature on learning with the literature on learning organizations (see Table 2.1). She also describes what we would call an applied learning model to institutional change. We draw on her model when establishing the foundation for our proposals supporting universities on becoming learning organizations.

The comparison of student and organizational learning needs, as illustrated in Table 2.1, suggests that an application of pedagogical knowledge to organizational change is another important consideration when developing universities into learning organizations. Each of the learning dimensions can be matched against an organizational change dimension. And when learning theory is directly used in this analysis, the application of a learning model can be developed even further: for example, 'Staff can be bullied into compliance and do the minimum, similar to those students who adopt surface approaches. But . . . useful, heuristic outcomes do not result from surface approaches' (Martin 1999: 73; see also Boud 1995; Lawler and King 2000). Is this not a case of 'teacher teach thyself'? This understanding of the role of

Table 2.1 Martin's summary of student learning and organizational learning literatures

Student learning literature	*Organizational learning literature*
'Learners need to see the salience of what they are being asked to learn and how they are being asked to change.'	'The needs and strengths of staff, as well as the force of external demands, require attention.'
'Learners must engage with the learning task.' 'Learners need guidance as well as independence.'	'Shared commitment, not imposition and mandate, brings about successful change.' 'Independence and self-reliance are essential for collaboration.'
'Assessment must link to desired learning. Desired learning must be what is rewarded and recognized.' 'Assessment processes must support not get in the way of desired learning.'	'Develop organizational structures which support and reward the desired learning processes and outcomes.'
'Regular and supportive feedback is necessary for learning. Learning involves change.'	'Change can be painful but also liberating.' 'Support, including the opportunity for new learning and for personal development, is essential.'

Source: Adapted from Martin (1999: 73).

learning theory and pedagogic knowledge is an important one in the context of supporting universities to become learning organizations because it takes account of some of the organizational uniqueness noted earlier.

What is a learning organization?

Definitions of a learning organization have been appearing for nearly a decade and half now. As is well known, Senge (1990a) has led the development of this idea. We provide his definition as the starting point for understanding this conceptualization.

> [A learning organization is a place] where people continually expand their capacity to create the results they truly desire, where new and expansive patterns of thinking are nurtured, where collective aspiration is set free, and where people are continually learning how to learn together.
>
> (Senge cited in Meade 1995: 114)

Other definitions include an emphasis on acquiring new knowledge (Garvin 1993; Meade 1995), transferring and disseminating new knowledge across an organization (Garvin 1993; Meade 1995), and modifying current ways of working and thinking (Meade 1995). Meade (1995) has also emphasized the collective process involved and noted that others see learning organizations as 'consummately adaptive' organizations (Dumaine 1989; Kiechel 1990; Lessem 1991). Blackwell (2003) has noted James's (1997) position that 'structured serendipity' is sometimes advocated as the hallmark of the learning organization. Barnett (2000: 127) has suggested that 'we need to couple it with the idea of *unlearning*: the university has to be an unlearning organization'. This latter point is an important challenge to the learning paradigm that also needs to be considered in the development of universities as learning organizations.

Senge (1990a, 1996) has provided a list of five 'disciplines' that he suggests are needed for a learning organization to work. We discuss each of these below and, because Senge's work was mainly aimed at the world of business and management, we have added the views of others who have considered these disciplines in the context of higher education. We identify how each discipline can be encouraged in universities.

Personal mastery

Personal mastery is not unlike independent and autonomous learning. It is in essence personal mastery over work and the workplace in order to make it a better environment for the individual and their colleagues. When the work environment undergoes rapid and radical change, for example when the student profile shifts dramatically, academics' sense of personal mastery can be put under extreme pressure. In these circumstances, personal mastery is challenged.

Deming (1988) has noted three ways that organizations discourage employees from doing their best, in effect how they are discouraged from achieving personal mastery:

- excessive paperwork;
- attitudes that denigrate enthusiasm and commitment;
- negative sanctioning of employees who offer ideas and critiques out of line with official policy.

The organizational environment of universities, as we have discussed earlier, in many ways encourages personal mastery and has few sanctions for critiques of official university policies, in fact we would say that the principle of academic freedom gives academics a licence to be critical. If universities can find a way to manage the recent increase in paperwork that is associated with amplified external regulatory function, then universities could succeed in achieving this discipline.

Mental models

Mental models are what academics deal with on a daily basis and are closest to what is known in the academic world as paradigms of thought. Congruence of mental models is important for the effective functioning of a learning organization. Conflict occurs when there is variation in the mental models. These conflicts occur in universities mainly because of the expectation that consultation in decision-making is the academic norm and an important element of the traditional university working environment. Almost any area brought forward for consultation could be met with a wide range of views based on a variety of disciplinary paradigms. However, universities have survived for centuries coping with the debates surrounding conflicting mental models so it would seem that this would not necessarily decrease their chances of successfully becoming learning organizations.

Shared vision

According to Martin (1999), the main points of a shared vision in a learning organization include:

- beginning with personal vision;
- developing a climate of creative tension;
- stimulating commitment and enthusiasm (much more effective than compliance);
- providing time, tolerance and understanding.

These conditions again appear to fit the working patterns within the typical university. We have noted earlier that academics are encouraged and supported to develop a personal vision through the work they do as researchers and teachers. Personal vision is an integral part of the academic role. Again, the consultation process surrounding decisions creates a climate of creative tension. The tradition of academic debate also supports these creative tensions. Except for the recent demands surrounding academic accountability, which in turn is beginning to create a compliance culture around quality assurance issues, most academic work stimulates enthusiasm and commitment because it emanates from individual academics themselves. The sabbatical options we mentioned earlier can best illustrate the fourth point concerned with time, tolerance and understanding. It would appear that universities operate under conditions that are conducive to achieving the 'discipline of a shared vision'.

Team learning

Teamwork is about groups of academic staff working towards an agreed outcome. Martin (1999) has noted an interesting contradiction around this discipline. On the one hand, university research teams epitomize the essence of teamwork, where, working together, research teams achieve more than any one individual could do on their own. On the other hand, university committees, as currently organized, tend to be less about teamwork and more about the expression of individual views on matters related to the governance of the university. It is here that a 'thousand flowers bloom', and consequently the outcomes can include increased conflict instead of the sought-after consensus.

However, we would suggest that university committees have the opportunity to contribute to a learning university by employing similar methods as research teams. They have the potential to drive and change universities into learning organizations. They can create 'teachable moments' for all participants in them. If appropriate teaching approaches are employed in the running of committees, learning can be the key outcome. Committees are an opportunity for applying the scholarship of teaching and learning and they also provide an opportunity for meaningful staff development. They can take care of university business in a creative and purposeful way while providing staff with the opportunity to learn from each other about the issues of the committee and the broader work of the university itself. Later in this chapter we discuss ways that learning committees can be created to exploit this range of possible outcomes and contribute to the development of a learning university.

Systems thinking

The discipline of systems thinking is about a holistic approach to understanding change, it is about meta-analysis of the organization and the changes it faces. One response to the outcomes of systems thinking is an 'unlearning process', suggested earlier by Barnett. 'The boundaries that mark out the inner life of the university have to be eroded. The forging . . . of a culture of collective self-scrutiny has to be worked at continually' (Barnett 2000: 137). Martin (1999) specifically proposes that for universities aiming to become learning organizations they must unlearn those ways of working that militate against the successful achievement of Senge's five disciplines.

Barnett has described universities as a mosaic made up of different parts of different shapes and sizes with all parts connected to each other via several other pieces of the mosaic. He has also identified three conditions for universities to meet the challenges of changing times. Each condition could be used to support one or other of the five disciplines and the development of universities as learning organizations. These include:

- *The knowledge condition.* The more actors understand about their situation, the more they will be able to make judgements and take actions that are likely to anticipate emerging circumstances.
- *The interaction condition.* A challenge facing universities is to bring as many of the pieces in touch with each other as possible.

- *The condition of communication.* A key issue, therefore, in constructing the university is the extent to which its members communicate with each other (given these conditions of mutuality and co-understanding). (Barnett 2000: 135 6)

What we suggest in the remainder of this chapter is a rethink of how the pieces of the university mosaic, as currently configured, can produce a more meaningful outcome for students, faculty/staff and managers/administrators and can allow the university to become a learning organization true to its central mission and purpose. Our focus here is on both the structure and the functioning of the university in new and more effective ways. We would wish to make clear that these suggestions are neither part of a reconstruction of the university for managerialist purposes nor a deconstruction for ideological purposes.

How can universities become learning organizations?

In order for universities to become learning organizations they would have to determine what changes might need to occur for this to happen. One way they can do this is to assess themselves against the most common features of learning organizations and then decide how many of the features they would need to address in order to become a learning organization. It is our view that the first thing universities need to do in the process of becoming a learning organization is to create a new kind of conversation (Hutchings 2000).

> Cultural theorists have suggested that conversations are distinct from the other modes of interaction (such as debates and discussions) because the topic of conversation cannot be pre-determined. In this sense a conversation allows something new to emerge because the participants do not try to pre-determine its outcome.
>
> (J.S. Brown 2000: 11–12)

Conversations of this type could allow universities to meet the requirements of several of both Senge's five disciplines and Barnett's three conditions for change. Conversations could allow for common issues of concern to surface, and from these, more structured interactions could be organized that matched against the checklist of outstanding features identified by each university. Conversations, and the follow-on activities, would be consistent with most universities' commitment to empowering staff to make and manage change. Empowerment is a central construct of learning organizations and this would be an important dimension to maintain throughout the process of creating a learning university (Perlman *et al.* 1988).

Understanding the role of leaders in a learning organization is also important to consider.

> In a learning organization, leaders' roles differ dramatically from that of

> the charismatic decision maker. Leaders are designers, teachers and stewards . . . leaders in learning organizations are responsible for *building organizations* where people are continually expanding their capabilities to shape their future – that is, leaders are responsible for learning.
>
> (Senge 1990b: 9)

In the context of higher education institutions, this type of leadership role would seem to be especially appropriate. Higher education leaders 'can help to promote collaborative self-learning that transcends the natural boundaries in which the academics have their identities' (Barnett 2000: 138). Unlike other complex organizations, the academic traditions we discussed earlier are not only supportive of this model of leadership but also create a capacity in the higher education system generally for developing this type of leadership.

Meade (1995: 114) has developed a useful list of expectations for university leaders to follow when establishing a 'learning culture'. In his view this requires a leader who:

- encourages staff members to learn and to share their knowledge with others;
- supports formal and informal staff development and ensures that members have the time and resources to engage in such activities;
- challenges staff by giving them responsibility and the opportunity to try out new things and to take risks;
- tolerates mistakes and values these as opportunities for learning, innovation and discovery;
- links the learning of individual staff members with the learning of the faculty;
- is adaptive, open to innovation and embraces change to meet the uncertainties and challenges of the future.

Again, this list echoes the ideas of Senge and others who are proponents of learning organizations.

In addition to creating conversations and maintaining empowering leadership, establishing learning communities within universities is another part of the process of changing a university into a learning organization. We consider what they add to the conversations that create and support empowerment of faculty/staff, students and managers and how they help sustain the culture change once initiated. They are especially appropriate in the context of higher education since as 'Bailey (1977) notes, universities . . . operate as a "community culture" ' (Becher 1994: 151).

What are learning communities?

Definitions of learning communities commonly include a list of characteristics similar to those applied to learning organizations, for example purposeful, open, just, disciplined, caring and celebrative (Boyer 1990). Boyer applied his definition to colleges and universities as a whole; others limit application of the term to smaller, face-to-face groups with more clearly identified members (Baker 1999). Central to learning communities is the notion that 'all members of the group are learners, and the group is organised to learn as a whole system' (Cox 2004: 6).

Learning communities are, in effect, the forum for university-wide conversations. Learning communities, like the type of conversations we have been discussing, encourage *all* participants to share their knowledge, in a non-judgemental, non-hierarchical environment that is supportive of individual/group change, development and enhancement. Baker (1999) notes that 'classes, committees, advisory groups, interdisciplinary teaching teams, departments, and residential colleges have the potential to be – but may not be – learning communities' (cited in Cox 2004: 6). It is our view that universities are more likely to become learning organizations if all of the groups Baker mentioned can be supported to become learning communities. These communities, in turn, would support the development of the university as a learning organization.

Cox and Richlin (2004: 1) have found that faculty/staff learning communities can also influence 'the degree to which an institution can become a learning organization'. Their work reviews faculty/staff learning communities as a university-wide programmatic activity. 'Creating a faculty learning community program is one approach that engages community in the cause of student and faculty learning and of transforming our institutions of higher education into learning organizations' (Cox cited in Cox 2004: 5).

Learning communities as a lever for change in learning organizations

There are two major ways to approach the development of learning communities. The first is through the existing structures of the organization, mainly its committees; the second is through the creation of new structures that address specific areas of institutional learning. The latter might include learning networks, communities of practice and learning sets. In this section we look at each of these structures and suggest some practical ways they can contribute to the development of the learning communities and the university as a learning organization.

Learning committees

Universities typically have more committees than most other organizations of similar size. As we reported earlier, this was one of Smith's key differences between universities and other complex organizations. Since this is the case, it would seem that there is an opportunity for universities to create a learning community within its standing committees. The committees are clear structures already in place that have the potential to make a major contribution to the development of a learning university.

Any committee can redefine itself as a learning community by changing the way it works. University committees, for example, usually spend most of their time dealing with the business of the committee. For example, a teaching awards committee would spend its time deciding on criteria for selection of awards and reviewing award applications. Rarely are there discussions of the ideas, research or principles underpinning the work of the committee. In the case of a teaching awards committee this discussion could be on the meaning of excellence in teaching or how it could be defined at the specific university.

One way to help committees to become learning committees is to change the agenda of the meetings to include a period set aside to debate selected issues, research findings, or a set of principles underlying the decision-making processes. In the case of the teaching awards committee, published articles on teaching excellence might be a useful device to allow for a more informed discussion of the process, the criteria used and the selection of award recipients. This could be done in a number of ways and at any point in the time already set aside for the meeting. One approach would be to adopt a seminar style for the meeting and apply the principles on teaching through discussion to the process. For example, a member of the committee could act in the role of seminar facilitator and the group could establish ground rules for how the discussion would be run. Changing the focus of the committee work from business only to a combination of business and learned discussion would redefine both the work and the relations of the committee and its members and could contribute to the development of the university as a learning organization.

Learning networks

The focus of learning networks (Brookfield 1985) is different from learning committees in that they do not have a responsibility to carry out any decision-making functions for the university. They are more informal than committees but, like most committees, they concentrate their activities on one specific area of concern. The work of networks usually achieves several of Senge's five disciplines, including personal mastery, a shared vision and team learning.

H. Brown (2001) notes that she found that academic staff were more likely to engage in continuing professional development (CPD) if it were part of a professional network.

> Joining a network was psychologically more acceptable to designers than formally signing up to CPD which may be associated with an unwelcoming admission that they did not know everything and had something more to learn.
>
> (H. Brown 2001: 6)

However, as has been pointed out by Liberman (1999), networks are usually much more fragile than other more permanent structures within the university, such as standing committees. Their activity usually requires

> finding a balance between 'inside knowledge' of practitioners and 'outside knowledge' of reformers and researchers: building collaborative governance structures neither too centralized nor too decentralized; being informal and flexible rather than rigidly holding onto forms and activities that no longer work; and deciding how inclusive or exclusive membership should be.
>
> (Liberman 1999: 47)

A community of practice is another name given to networks. Wenger (2004), who coined the phase, lists networks as one form of community of practice. These groups are characterized by their members' shared interest related to the work they do and the fact that members meet specifically to learn from each other, as in the example of the CPD network mentioned above. Communities of practice contribute to the development of the university as a learning organization through providing members of the university with the learning opportunity directly linked to the jobs they perform within it.

Learning sets

Learning sets (McGill and Beaty 1995) are more focused on problem-solving activities than are networks or communities of practice. They are sometimes referred to as action learning sets because of the focus on concrete learning outcomes from the group's activities. The idea behind learning sets in the context of higher education institutions is that they can provide academic staff the opportunity to openly discuss concerns related to their work in order to test out with their colleagues possible solutions to the problems they face in carrying out their job.

Typically, learning sets are small, around 5–8 people at most, each of whom brings a problem to the group. The members commit to meeting at a regular time and operate on a shared time principle for the discussion, that is, each person in the group has an equal share of the group's time to explore their issue and receive feedback from the other members of the group. Following the meetings the suggestions are put into action; this would be followed up by a report back at the next meeting. In effect, learning sets are an example of Kolb's learning cycle put into practice: experiencing, reflecting, conceptualizing and planning (Kolb 1984).

One example given to illustrate the idea of a learning set is the Nobel Prize winners at the Cavendish Laboratory in Cambridge, what some would call a 'think-tank' environment.

> Every Wednesday they met together to discuss their experiments. They didn't meet to convince each other how clever they were but 'to see if we

> can understand our own difficulties'. In other words, these eminent people came together to speak not of their triumphs but to discuss the problems they were encountering in their work, in order to learn from one another.
>
> (Bourner *et al.* 2000: 3)

Meta-learning communities

Another mechanism that can contribute to the development of a university into a learning organization is something we have discussed in earlier work on this issue (D'Andrea and Gosling 2000a). We have observed what we have called 'meta-learning communities' can exist. The usual purpose of these structures is to bring people together from the larger learning community to engage in higher-order policy discussion and decision making. Meta-learning communities take on many forms, they might be ad hoc groups established to review university strategies, they might be a university-wide curriculum initiative, and they can even be embodied in educational development centres. Another feature is that they have an inclusive membership from the full range of constituencies within the university: academic staff, support staff, managers/administrators and students. The underlying philosophy of meta-learning communities is based on the premise that by bringing faculty/staff and students together in a common learning space, or through specific curricular developments, or as part of a policy creation process, there is a greater opportunity for democratic decision-making skills to be developed than occurs through more traditional university structures thus supporting the university as a learning organization.

One concrete example might help to illustrate how a learning university could be built through creating appropriate learning structures. This example links to the discussion in Chapter 7 on the development of the scholarship of teaching and learning. It also relates to the recent changes occurring in higher education that we discussed in Chapter 1, in particular the concern for the professionalization of teaching. The example helps to illustrate how working to create a university as a learning organization can be a useful mechanism for dealing with change.

The scholarship of teaching and learning (SoTL) is, in Huber's (1999: 1) words, 'a deeply communal enterprise . . . [that] can flourish only with the development of communities of scholars who share, critique and build upon each other's work'. Assuming this is the case, then it would seem that SoTL could be the focus of a learning set, bringing together academics who are engaged in SoTL projects and who wish to address the specific problems they are facing to a group of colleagues working on similar kinds of problems. SoTL could also flourish through a learning network of all academics interested in SoTL more broadly and who wish to expand their general knowledge about SoTL. Additional SoTL activities could be supported through a programmatic approach via a committed learning community that would consequently have wider impact on the learning related to SoTL across the university as a whole.

> Scholarship in teaching is a learning process involving various combinations of instrumental, but primarily, communicative and emancipatory learning processes. If learning falls into one of the latter two categories, professors validate their knowledge about teaching through critical discourse within a community of peers.
>
> (Kreber 2000a: 75)

What would a learning university look like and what would it do?

The five main activities of a learning organization include: (1) systematic problem solving, (2) experimentation with new approaches, (3) learning from experience, (4) learning from the experiences and practices of others, (5) transferring knowledge quickly and efficiently throughout the organization (Garvin 1993; Meade 1995). If these ideas are linked to the concrete suggestions made by Cambridge (2004) with regard to starting campus conversations on teaching and learning (see Figure 2.1), universities have a strong chance of creating a solid foundation for becoming a learning organization.

Finally, a learning organization needs supportive structures for it to function. Huber (1999) has progressed this dimension in her work on university forums for learning. We have summarized her suggestions on the types of forums which can exist within universities (see Table 2.2) and we have

1. Student–faculty/staff collaborations
   - **funded** student–faculty/staff research teams
   - **seminars** for students and for faculty/staff
2. Enquiry groups followed by institutional action
   - **enquiry** groups for faculty/staff
   - **study** groups with expanding circles of participation
3. Peer support for teaching and the scholarship of teaching
   - **mentoring** among faculty members and graduate students
   - **formative** peer review
4. Creation of a community of scholars across the campus
   - **identifying** teacher scholars
   - **instigating** new collaborations across a campus
   - **building** a community of scholars of teaching and learning

Figure 2.1 University-wide strategies for creating conversations
Source: Cambridge (2002).

Table 2.2 University forums for learning, by format

Type	*External forums*	*University-wide*	*Groups by discipline*	*Groups by school*	*Groups by function*
University central services	✓	✓			✓
Committees		✓	✓	✓	✓
Networks	✓	✓	✓	✓	✓
Learning sets		✓			✓
Listservs	✓	✓	✓	✓	✓
Discussion circles	✓	✓	✓	✓	✓
Publications	✓	✓	✓	✓	✓
Journals	✓	✓			
Newsletters	✓	✓		✓	✓
Conferences	✓	✓			
Programmes/seminars	✓	✓	✓	✓	✓
Awards/fellowships	✓	✓	✓	✓	✓
Grants	✓	✓	✓	✓	

Source: Adapted from Huber (1999).

Table 2.3 University forums for learning, by type

Type	*External forums*	*University-wide*	*Groups by discipline*	*Groups by school*	*Groups by function*
External issues		✓	✓	✓	✓
Student development	✓	✓	✓	✓	✓
Teaching and learning	✓	✓	✓	✓	
Research and scholarship	✓	✓	✓		
Quality enhancement	✓	✓	✓	✓	

Source: Adapted from Huber (1999).

mapped them against the specific activities these forums could engage in to achieve new learning (see Table 2.3). Many of these were discussed earlier in this chapter, and there are others that are new to this list. These tables are a useful guide for anyone in universities who wishes to link their work to more specific learning opportunities.

How will the university know if learning is taking place?

'As Brown has noted, 'It is often difficult to recognize when learning is taking place since it is a ubiquitous and continuous process.' And as we indicated in Chapter 1, most professional learning is informal and situated. 'Situated learning theory does not separate action, thought and feeling. By contrast, traditional cognitive theory is 'distanced from experience' and divides the learning mind from the world. Situated activity provides different perspectives on learning and its contexts:

> 1) knowledge always undergoes construction and transformation
> 2) learning is an integral aspect of activity in and with the world at all times
> 3) 'what is learned' is always complexly problematic
> 4) acquisition of knowledge is not a simple matter of taking in knowledge but requires reconceptualisation'.
>
> (H. Brown 2001: 9)

The irony of much of the 'all is change' literature is that it usually offers some new certainty, usually a pet management technique (Talbot 1996). Some may suggest that promoting learning organizations is just such a pet project. We would contend that, even if it is, it is the one that is most closely connected to the work of universities. As we discuss in subsequent chapters, all other change mechanisms can be considered as a consistent component of the university if it is a learning organization.

> To experience the intensity of success, institutions of higher education must be willing to examine themselves critically; they must come to know what type of organization they are, and they must understand their individual strengths and weaknesses.
>
> (Perlman *et al.* 1988: 58)

In other words, universities can increase their capacity to cope with change by becoming a learning organization.

Part 2

Developing Higher Education

3

Academic Identities and Professional Development

Any successful change management process aimed at improving teaching and learning depends ultimately on the willingness of the people involved to change. Universities include such a diversity of interests and values, and are such multifaceted organizations, that achieving a willingness to change across an institution is a complex and difficult matter. It is easy to underestimate the difficulties and the time needed for achieving shifts in the mental models that underpin working practices. Fullan (2003: 186) has suggested that 'leadership commitment to a particular version of change is negatively related to the ability to implement it' precisely because the difficulty of the task has not been well understood.

Consequently, when change fails to happen, those who put up 'resistance' are made scapegoats for the failure. But, of course, resistance is a positive position from the perspective of those who fear that the change will reduce 'standards' or undermine academic values. In order to understand academics who are labelled in this way we need to consider not just the motivations and interests of individuals, but also the cultures of the 'communities of practice' (Wenger 1998) that create these important attitudinal responses that can make or break any innovation or development. Any attempt to appreciate the processes involved in change must have 'a developed understanding of the underlife of higher education' that takes account of 'ways in which action is implicit in structure, how structures are perceived, socially constructed and responded to in variegated ways' (Trowler 1998: 152).

In this chapter we focus on some key issues relating to academic and support staff in higher education which impact on the process of creating change in learning and teaching. We have suggested in Chapter 2 that it is important to recognize, and to take due account of, the factors that are specific to higher education. In the rush to adopt managerialist methods, universities and colleges can too easily lose sight of the distinctiveness of the culture of educational organizations. When individuals become simply 'human resources' and managers talk about 'driving the agenda forward' and 'rolling out the programme', the indications are present that the people affected by the change are being ignored.

We need to take account of what have been described as 'academic tribes', of academics' self-concepts and aspirations, of relationships between academics and support staff and, not least, the role played by students in any change process. None of these considerations remains static, even if the notorious conservatism of the academic community, what has been called the 'impermeable cultures of resistance' (Hannan and Silver 2000: 96), sometimes creates the illusion of an immovable object. A number of studies (Trowler 1998; Hannan and Silver 2000; Henkel 2000) have shown that academics adapt to change, or resist and subvert it, in many, and sometimes creative, ways.

The shifting environment of higher education that we looked at in Chapter 1 is creating many pressure points and tensions that are causing stress, role conflict, increasing workloads and 'innovation fatigue'. A variety of environmental factors can override the impact of national policies designed to improve teaching. In the UK, a number of studies have provided evidence of the negative impact of the Research Assessment Exercise on teaching (Jenkins 1995; McNay 1999; Yorke 2000; Jenkins *et al.* 2003). The consequences of a 'monolithic' quality assurance process (Martin 1999) are also often cited as a reason for a climate that is inhospitable to developing teaching and learning (Hannan 2002; Morley 2003a). Increasing bureaucracy, increasing need for documentation, over-prescriptive requirements for course approval have all been mentioned as a reason for this climate, but increasing focus on budgets, financial stringency and reduced resources also plays a part in blocking change.

The problems of achieving change in learning and teaching have been perceived as a conflict between perceptions of academic identity. The difficulties of achieving change result from academics dragging their feet and blocking change because of rather ignoble motives: 'vested interests', 'inertia', 'clinging to existing satisfactions' and 'role ambiguity' (Luedekke 1997). Morley (2003a: 114) talks in terms of staff using a 'range of micro political strategies to protect and promote their own interests, life histories and career trajectories'. Outram (2004), quoting Hultman (1998), lists ways in which change is resisted, both actively and passively, and gives some of the same reasons as those noted above.

While not denying that all these difficulties do exist, we need a more complete explanation of the barriers to change that is rooted in an understanding of academic cultures and their institutional contexts. Successful change needs to be framed in a way that does not assign blame and imply a failure of past practice (Eckel *et al.* 1999). As in all learning processes, change must start from how people make sense of themselves and their place in social structures they find themselves. Only when we have a more complete understanding of the reasons that academics have for the stance they adopt than the knee-jerk reaction that 'all resistance is bad', can we move on to suggest some strategies for effecting change. As Outram

(2004: 4) says, 'Not all change is positive and not all resistance is negative.'

Starting from the disciplines

Academic identity has received considerable attention in recent years. It is a concept increasingly used to explain and predict the behaviour of teachers and researchers in higher education. Depending on your point of view, it can be a term of abuse or a reverential appeal to some mythical golden age.

The first point we would wish to make on the topic of academics' identity is that people do not have one identity, but several. Neither are these identities always neatly prioritized. Although the idea of an identity suggests some stability over time, it also can shift and take different forms in response to different situations. Identities are social constructions involving reflexive awareness. They have a symbolic significance that enables us to give meaning to what we do. Identity is part of what Bourdieu calls 'habitus':

> . . . an acquired system of preferences, of principles, of vision and division (what is usually called taste) and also a durable system of cognitive structures (which are essentially the product of internalisation of objective structures) and of schemes of action which orient the perception of the situation and the appropriate response.
>
> (Bourdieu 1998: 25)

P.G. Taylor (1999) suggests that there are three levels at which academic identity is constructed, one linked to the site of work, the second through reference to the person's discipline, and the third is a universal construction of what it means to be an academic. Kogan (2000) also points to three types of identity. One comes from being a distinctive individual, with a unique personal history, striving for esteem, security and recognition. A second is embedded 'within communities and institutions which have their own languages, conceptual structures, histories, traditions, myths, values, practices and achieved goods' (Kogan 2000: 210). The third is the idea of a professional identity that is both individual and social and brings together personal value commitments and roles largely determined by communities and institutions.

The following combines Taylor's and Kogan's categorizations of academic identities; however, we would emphasize that these categories occur in different combinations, each with a different resonance for individual academics and having influences that vary across time. We see three types of identities:

1. The identity of a distinctive individual, formed by the cross-cutting categories such as gender, ethnicity, class, age, personal values, ideologies and history. For some academics, these personal identities are pre-eminent and collective identities such as: 'the women's group' or 'black staff' or 'socialists', can matter more than anything else.

2. The identity formed by institutional memberships, including department, faculty, school, campus. Institutional culture (McNay 1995) and institutional subsector (Scott 1995) can be very influential in the academic's identity. These can be seen in expressions such as: 'I've always been an Oxford/Harvard man/woman', or 'I am very committed to the access agenda of this university'. Institutional roles such as head of department, admission tutor and course leader can also provide important frames for how academics think of themselves.
3. The identity of academics includes:

   (a) discipline or sub-disciplinary specialism: chemist, philosopher, geographer. It may be the specialism rather than the 'parent discipline' that is the strongest influence (Becher and Trowler 2001);
   (b) professional identity: lawyer, engineer, educator, nurse, doctor. These applied fields can be strongly influenced by the ethos of professionals outside of the academic community;
   (c) universal academic identity: 'researcher', 'teacher', 'cosmopolitan', 'intellectual'. As Taylor (1999) suggests, this aspect of identity is often an aspiration to an imagined ideal or 'folkloric myth'.

In recent years it has become commonplace to focus on 3(a) in this schema and to argue that implementing change is best advanced from within discipline identities. Indeed, strategies to enhance teaching and learning in both the UK and USA have been predicated on this assumption. Huber, writing about the US context, has stated:

> To be sure there are many issues that cut across fields. But it's important to start with disciplines first, because that's where most faculty are coming from when they think about teaching and learning and it's where many of their best aspirations for students lie.
>
> (Huber 2003: 91)

Healey and Jenkins (2003) suggest that a scholarly approach to developmental change must engage with academics' discipline identity. 'Working within and with disciplinary communities is central to developing academic, or rather educational, development as a scholarly activity' (2003: 47). Proponents of this view tend to contrast the advocacy of discipline-based focus of developmental activity with what is called a 'generic' approach, which, according to Healey and Jenkins (2003: 49), reduces teaching to 'the technical matter of performance'. Similarly Rowland (2003) has argued that a 'generic' approach often leads to one or the other of two false conclusions being drawn. The first that teaching and learning is 'primarily a practical, rather than theoretical, activity', and the second that teaching and learning are 'the special concerns of educationists and educational researchers who develop educational theory' (Rowland 2003: 15).

The significance of disciplinary based identities has been explored in a number of studies (for example, Evans 1988, 1993; Hativa and Marincovich 1995; Trowler 1998; Becher and Trowler 2001; Henkel 2000; Moore 2003).

The research for Becher's (1989) *Academic Tribes and Territories* was originally undertaken in the 1980s and focused on traditional 'research-led' universities, in both the UK and USA. It is worth noting that in the revised second edition, with Trowler in 2001, the portrayal of the academic world continues to focus on the research dimension while missing out the teaching dimension. The book makes the important claim that 'membership of the academic profession in elite departments is defined in terms of excellence in scholarship and originality in research, and not to any significant degree in terms of teaching capability' (Becher and Trowler 2001: 28).

Disciplines have 'recognizable identities and particular cultural attributes', and this gives rise to the 'tribal aspects of academia' such as the heroes of the tribe, artefacts that adorn the offices of tribal members, traditions, custom and practices, and distinctive forms of professional language used to praise work within a discipline. Historians like to be 'masterly', mathematicians 'elegant', sociologists 'persuasive' and physicists 'accurate and rigorous' (Becher and Trowler 2001). These symbolic forms of differentiation represent more fundamental differences in the epistemology of the subject.

Henkel (2000) found that the extent to which academics defined themselves principally by their research or in terms of the integration of research and teaching, varied by discipline. For scientists, the research identity is strong, and the discipline forms a 'tangible social as well as epistemological construct' (Henkel 2000: 189), whereas in the humanities the picture is more mixed. Historians had a strong sense of their cohesion as a community, but English, because it is a more fragmented discipline, much less so.

Major UK and US national initiatives to support teaching have been based on the assumption that the principal location for change is through academics' disciplinary identity. The Fund for the Development of Teaching and Learning (FDTL: in England), the Learning and Teaching Support Network (LTSN: UK-wide), and the Carnegie Scholars program (USA) all start from this basis. The evidence from evaluations of the LTSN suggests that most academics like this approach (Department of Educational Research 2002). This is not surprising given our propensity to prefer people with whom we share common goals and language. 'We are social and emotional beings and we need public discourses and spaces which can orchestrate, enable and symbolise communities which are the necessary framework for creating social cohesion and individual identity' (Rutherford 2004: 14).

Single disciplinary groupings perform this function for many, although by no means all, academics. They are liked precisely because they reaffirm the avowed identity and confirm existing forms of social cohesion. But the consequence is a tendency to reinforce the reproduction of the traditional values and practices of the group. Universities, like all organizations, have within them forces for both reproduction and transformation. In order to bring about change it is necessary to find social groupings that will assist the process of transformation rather than reproduction without sacrificing or threatening individual identities. From the point of view of sponsoring change, working across and between disciplines can be a productive strategy because, as Wenger (1998: 234) has argued, 'in the process of organising its learning, a community must have access to other practices'.

Another significant qualification to be made about the primacy of disciplinary identities is that the very notion of 'disciplines' has come under increasing question in recent years and the legitimacy of traditional ways of dividing knowledge has been called into question (Barnett and Griffin 1997). Kogan has also warned against overemphasizing narrow disciplinary identities for another reason. He says: 'My impression is that those closest to each other in subject interests are more likely to be critical of and competitive with each other than those in other or adjacent areas. Fraternal relationships can include those on the Cain and Abel model' (Kogan 2000: 213). Within a single department the possibility that some staff will have a strong antipathy to the ways of working and the published results of their colleagues is always present.

The debate about the significance of academic identity reflects wider issues in our society about the pursuit of individual self-fulfilment and self-determination. But this pursuit is increasingly against the background of greater alienation and anxiety (Giddens 1991). Academics report that they feel more isolated as higher education organizations become larger and more fragmented, as structures such as schools and faculties become more artificial reflecting management decisions to group subjects together for pragmatic reasons of organizational convenience rather than because they reflect organic relationships between them. Individuals have to make sense of their own set of values, commitments and practices within the social frameworks that they find themselves.

> We desire to experience an individual life as unique and meaningful to ourselves, but we equally feel a need to belong to and define ourselves through broader collectives. It is in our relationships with others – in what is constituted as the social – that we attempt to reconcile this paradox and make sense of a self that feels authentic.
>
> (Rutherford 2004: 14)

Change is facilitated by creating social spaces in which new identities can be formed through conversations between people who do not as a matter of course speak to each other, or between people who do speak to each other but are encouraged to talk about new things. Hannan and Silver (2000) have reported the isolation often felt by innovators, and Shulman (in Huber 2004) makes the point with respect to Carnegie Scholars who have pursued the scholarship of teaching route, that in doing so they defied the expectations of their disciplinary communities. Their career choice to focus on teaching and learning within their disciplines required them to take 'paths not normally taken' and to become 'distinctively excellent in unconventional inquiries' (Shulman in Huber 2004: ix). National Teaching Fellows in the UK have similarly felt a tension between their discipline identity and their role as Teaching Fellows (Frame *et al.* 2003; Skelton 2004). This would suggest that those who are working towards improving teaching and learning have to challenge, and not merely reproduce, existing stereotypes of the discipline-based scholar.

Becoming interested in 'teaching and learning', 'educational development' or 'scholarship of teaching' is an identity in itself, with its own networks, literature and reference groups (Cooper 2004; Kahn 2004). Commonly, the self-concept of these innovators is at odds with the dominant values of the departments within which they are working. A National Teaching Fellow recalled that when she announced her award, the response of her head of department was to say, 'I hope this won't interfere with your job' (personal communication 2002). Creating groupings that cut across existing organizational structures (see Chapters 2, 5 and 7) provides the possibility for new collectives within which conversations can be held that would be impossible in the familiar relationships of the home department.

Successful change strategies need to work with and build on disciplinary identities, but it is also important to utilize cross-institutional, interdisciplinary and multidisciplinary approaches (Walker 2001a). The tendency to locate change in teaching and learning within an oversimplified dichotomy of academic identities as either disciplinary-based or generic is unhelpful. A more constructive approach recognizes that disciplinary-based development builds on research that may be 'generic' or may have been carried out within other disciplinary fields, because, without the capacity to draw on the generic literature, each discipline has to invent for itself its own theoretical and empirical base. Too often this leads to low-level reinvention of the wheel within closed disciplinary communities that are unwilling to look beyond their own boundaries. Equally, generic research and developmental activity need to be mediated through the language and the interests of the community of practice that seeks to exploit and interpret the generic literature in ways which are relevant to its concerns. Furthermore, as Rowland (2003) has argued and as we have noted in Chapter 1, a critical approach to teaching and learning must consider broader questions that relate to wider social values and purposes that go beyond individual academic sub-fields.

Changing demands on academic staff

The changing organizational structure of universities in the 1990s that Henkel summarizes as becoming 'more professionalised and more flexible' has required staff to have 'more diverse and more specialised knowledge and skills' (Henkel 2000: 61). Within a teaching department it is increasingly commonplace to find staff with specialized expertise in, for example, diagnostic testing for students 'at risk'; online delivery of courses, webdesign and using virtual learning environments; implementing student profiling or personal development planning; liaison with employers, partner institutions and work-based learning; course evaluation and student feedback; credit accumulation and transfer and accreditation of prior learning; quality assurance and quality assessment. These are skills that require time, commitment and, often, specialized training. The days of the gifted amateur have gone. 'There has been a significant shift from thinking that clever people can do anything to a recognition of the complexity and diversity of academic work' (Brew and Boud 1996: 18).

Although there is general agreement that teaching is being professionalized, there is little agreement about what this means and whether this is a positive or negative trend. There are a number of reasons why academics have reservations about professionalization of teaching in higher education. In the first place, as we have seen, the majority of academics have a strong discipline-based professional identity that, it is feared, could be diluted or threatened by any attempt to impose a generic professional category of 'teacher'.

Secondly, there is a suspicion that a trend towards professionalization is yet another form of social control and regulation and is by implication a reduction of trust in academics to self-regulate, because the current levels of professional knowledge and skills of teachers in higher education are assumed to be inadequate. Professionalization is therefore seen as a deskilling process in the sense that the premise of the call for professionalization is that academics have an inadequate base for their teaching and that this situation needs to be remedied through a process of professional development, assessment and registration (Olssen *et al.* 2004).

Thirdly, resistance to professionalizing teaching comes from a fear that it will lead to greater uniformity and therefore mediocrity. According to some critics, the combined effects of teachers being taught similar skills and techniques in their initial preparation to teach (Lindsay 2004), and quality assurance processes assessing teaching against equally moribund criteria, will lead to 'dumbing down at the top, dumbing up at the bottom and dumbing into the middle' (Ryan 2004: 13).

We believe that the way to counter these critiques of professionalization is by proposing ways of enhancing teaching quality which (a) are in line with academic traditions of critical enquiry and scholarship, (b) recognize the variations in roles and functions of teachers within diverse institutional types, and (c) recognize the learning processes required of all those involved. In order to pursue this approach it is necessary to acknowledge how the role of the teacher in higher education is changing. Undoubtedly, part of the problem is that teaching has become increasingly complex as a result of the factors we have outlined in Chapter 1. The demands made by increasing student diversity are considerable, as we shall see in the next chapter, and learning technologies require new skills to be learned and applied.

Furthermore, there is a growing range of specialized roles that impact on teaching, and which are redefining the professional identity of teachers in higher education (Nixon *et al.* 2001). A combination of the power of the university management to command funds and growing demands from policy makers, for example to widen access or to work with local communities, has led to a growth of teaching-related centres. The biggest growth in specialized roles has been staff with information technology (IT) related functions.

A UK investigation into the roles of those working with learning technologies identified eleven distinct roles within three broad categories (Beetham and Bailey 2001). In the first category were the 'new specialists': educational developer, educational researcher, technical/researcher/developer, materials developer, project manager and learning technologists. Then there were academics who were involved as 'innovators' and managers of projects developing the use of learning technologists. Finally, there were 'learning support professionals', staff in non-academic roles with specialist information and communication technology (ICT) skills.

The learning technology staff were seen to have a strong focus on the quality of student learning, a positive orientation to change, a belief in collegiality and teamwork, and a commitment to building networks; they disapproved of cost-cutting and time-saving measures (Beetham and Bailey 2001). A paradox of their position is that they were marginal to most of the power structures of institutions, often on temporary contracts, and yet they felt they were important in terms of institutional change.

Where funding is available to support innovation in teaching and learning, for example in the English Fund for the Development of Teaching and Learning, a new type of specialist comes into being: the project manager. The elements of project management include the ability to define project objectives and outcomes, production and implementation of a plan of action, team building, leading and motivation, good communication skills, and close monitoring and control of the project, review and evaluation processes (Baume *et al.* 2002). The implementation of a strategic approach to teaching and learning also requires some academics to undertake specialized work relating to specific targets identified in the strategy, for example in relation to enhancing students' employability or improving student retention (Johnston 2003).

Offices devoted to supporting student learning and teaching functions are another reflection of this trend. Examples of such offices include English language and study skills support for students, services for disabled students, an international office, counselling services, and educational development centres.

Another growth area has been in functions related to quality assurance and it is here that there is the greatest resentment among teaching staff. Shore and Wright (1999: 567–8) talk in terms of 'parasitical new professions' who are 'agents for subjecting staff to a new normative gaze and instilling its rationality into their working life'. Morley (2003a: 113) found that 'colleagues who invest their time in quality assessments are often perceived as lacking a research focus or track record. They were constructed as fraudulent academics or imposters.'

These developments have the potential to create two kinds of tensions. One is between the 'centre' and the 'periphery' (Henkel 2000; Clegg 2003), between the role of the 'service' or 'support' staff and academics with responsibility for teaching. The second is between the expectations of academic staff to undertake research and to fulfil these specialist functions.

Few academic staff are able to sustain both an active research role and the fulfilment of the specialist teaching functions that we have been discussing. Increasingly they make the choice to develop an area of pedagogical expertise as a career route. This clearly has implications for promotion and other forms of recognition and reward.

Professional development for improving teaching in higher education

In Chapter 1, we emphasized the importance of being clear about the goals of professional development. We discussed the distinctive values of higher education that should, in our view, inform any developmental activity. We also outlined the types of knowledge that form the basis of teaching as a complex human activity. In this section we discuss some strategies for engaging staff at all levels in activities designed to improve the knowledge base for teaching and learning. Formal acquisition of pedagogical knowledge is only a small part of these learning processes. It is more important to identify activities, all of which can be seen as forms of 'professional development', that will raise interest in, and debate about, teaching and learning, enhance the status of activities related to teaching and learning, and promote scholarly enquiry. This is because we believe that this approach is likely to be more effective in promoting the kinds of learning that will enhance the professional knowledge of teachers in higher education and that this is so partly for pragmatic reasons about what academic staff can realistically be expected to engage with, and partly on epistemological grounds, outlined in Chapter 1, about the nature of professional knowledge about teaching.

The ultimate aim of professional development activity is to improve the quality of teaching and learning to the benefit of students. The approach we are advocating 'does not presume that particular knowledge or skill increments lead directly to better teaching; their impact is achieved indirectly by enhancing the professional repertoire from which teachers draw' (Hegarty 2000: 464). Enhancing the professional repertoire is essential for improving teaching in higher education. Finding ways of talking about teaching that are socially engaging, intellectually stimulating and actually relate to and build on people's experience will contribute to this process.

Achievement of this goal is constrained by 'a limited "surface" language of "teaching and learning" ' (Walker 2002). The problem, it has been suggested, is that the technocratic approach to teaching as a set of skills fails to recognize either the emotional commitments that are made in the act of teaching, or the contested field of values and political commitments which underpin different pedagogical approaches.

> We rarely talk with each other about teaching at any depth – and why should we when we have nothing more than 'tips, tricks and techniques'

> to discuss? That kind of talk fails to touch the heart of the teacher's experience.
>
> (Palmer 1998: 11)

Rowland comments that,

> It is difficult to think of a more fundamental educational aim for anyone who teaches in a university than to imbue in one's students a love of the subject. It seems to express what is at the heart of the vocation of teaching. Yet the statement sounds oddly romantic and naïve, or even empty, in the present context of concern for the quality of teaching. How can one speak of 'love' or 'inspiration' in evaluations and investigations when teachers are merely 'human resources' to be managed, teaching is framed around such notions as 'competence', and skill is the determining criteria for evaluating both the outcomes and the processes of learning?'
>
> (Rowland 2000: 74)

The blame for encouraging a technocratic, skill-orientated discourse about teaching is often placed at the door of quality assessors and educational and/or staff developers, but there is evidence from peer observation of teaching schemes that teachers in higher education, with good intentions to improve teaching, tend to use a uniformly bland, unimaginative and disengaged form of language when talking about teaching (Gosling 2004).

In his 1993 paper, Shulman relates his disappointment that the reality of joining a department did not match his vision of the solitary scholar entering the social order, becoming a member of the community, interacting with others, in the classroom and elsewhere, as a teacher. For what he found was not a community of teachers, but isolation.

> We close the classroom door and experience pedagogical solitude whereas in our life as scholars, we are members of active communities: communities of conversation, communities of evaluation, communities in which we gather with others in our invisible colleges to exchange our findings, and methods and our excuses.
>
> (Shulman 1993: 6)

He goes on to suggest that in order to make teaching community property there must be something 'shared, discussed, critiqued, exchanged, built upon'. But this requires the development of a climate that allows and encourages teachers to talk frankly about teaching. The danger is that, in the absence of a tradition of talking about teaching, 'there is a focus on the technicalities of teaching, such as the use of the whiteboard, because these are easy to highlight and quantify and, although these are not unimportant, they are surely not the essence of the teaching' (Cosh 1998: 172).

There are a variety of explanations for the difficulty we have in talking about teaching, some of which are structural. One source of the problem is 'fragmented communications patterns that isolate individual faculty members and prevent them from interacting around issues of undergraduate education' (Massy *et al.* 1994: 18).

Hannan and Silver (2000) have argued that the isolation often felt by innovators is related to the changing culture of higher education.

> The increasing lack of collegiality, not just the attitudes of specific colleagues, was identified as an obstacle to innovation. Such a lack intensified the feeling of staff committed to the improvement of teaching and learning that they ran the risk of becoming even more of the loner in a restructured academic universe.
>
> (Hannan and Silver 2000: 112)

To avoid a situation in which innovators in teaching are 'loners' requires a climate in which staff are willing to be open to new learning, to take risks, and to have trust in a process which is likely to be discomforting and challenging. Unfortunately the ethos of the modern university does not easily tolerate such risk taking. In their 1996 study, Ramsden and Martin found that the wider management climate was responsible for creating mistrust of strategies for improving teaching. Managerial schemes that are characterized by compulsion, insufficient negotiation and judgmental outcomes will almost certainly create distorted and insincere dialogue, in which compliance is given precedence over genuine engagement in a debate on teaching. As a result, strategies such as peer review are likely to be met with resistance motivated by fear, defensiveness, and personal protection. The comment one of us heard recently, 'He would have died rather than be observed teaching . . .', indicated the level of personal antipathy some staff can feel about the prospect of their teaching being reviewed. Departmental cultural values that require academics not to appear vulnerable create a fear of an authentic engagement. We need to recognize the personal emotions that attach to teaching. Teaching can be difficult, emotionally testing, draining of energy and disheartening, but it is not easy to admit to these feelings. Keeping the conversation on safe ground, for example by using the whiteboard, avoids the embarrassment of potentially emotionally charged exchanges of views but does not address the real issues.

Nevertheless, it is important to find ways both to increase the dialogue about teaching and to improve the quality of that dialogue. We have already emphasized the importance of organizational structures that enable this dialogue to happen (see the previous chapter). Let us look now at some specific examples of professional development activities.

Peer review

Peer collaboration and review of teaching, as Hutchings (1995) has shown, can be a valuable tool for making teaching public. By the term 'peer review of teaching', she suggests a broad definition of formal and informal processes in which 'faculty can be more effective colleagues to one another in improving their work as teachers'. This includes 'not just classroom observation, [but also] the variety of processes faculty can use to document and explore their teaching' (Hutchings 1995: 3). Collaborative peer review is designed to facilitate talking about teaching, not just about the performance of teaching, but also about course design, curriculum content, ways of assessing students, ways of stimulating student engagement, ways of challenging settled ways of thinking, provoking argument and gaining trust.

Peer collaboration and review of teaching take many forms. The American Association for Higher Education (AAHE) suggested the following list of possible activities: teaching circles (small groups of faculty committed to regular discussion); departmental teaching seminars; teaching portfolios and course portfolios; reciprocal classroom visits; attention to teaching in the hiring process; coaching and mentoring; external peer review.

The use of peer review is common in some contexts, ranging from approval of research proposals and publications in journals to accreditation, course approval and audit; but when it comes to teaching, the use of peer review is much less common. The exception, in the UK, has been the use of peer observation of teaching that became more prominent during the period of Subject Review (1995 to 2003), when the observation of teaching was used by the quality assessors to provide evidence of teaching quality. Unfortunately, this use of peer observation as a quality control mechanism has partially undermined its use as a genuine developmental tool.

Observations of teaching schemes are designed to break through the barrier of silence on matters relating to teaching and student learning. They provide a formalized context in which teachers can learn about other departmental practices and, in response to comments on their own teaching, reflect on and discuss their own approach to teaching. To make the most of peer observation requires a commitment both to a collective agreement about how such a scheme should be implemented and to the professional development of all involved (Beaty and McGill 1995; Blackwell and McLean 1996; Fullerton 1999; Bell 2001). The major shortcoming of peer observation of teaching is that it focuses on the performance of the teacher and does not take account of all those aspects of the learning process that are not directly observed by someone sitting in the back of a lecture hall or seminar room or laboratory. However, if observation can be established with ground rules that protect confidentiality and clearly separate the process from any judgemental purpose such as appraisal or promotion, then a scheme that is genuinely peer-based can offer a good opportunity for developing a dialogue about teaching (Gosling 2005).

We believe that there is considerable potential to develop the use of peer review processes to encourage debate about teaching and learning which go beyond the use of peer observation (D'Andrea 2001). For example, the learning networks and learning sets discussed in Chapter 2 provide opportunities for professional development of this kind. When peer review is established with a developmental, as opposed to a judgemental purpose, the mindset must be different and, as a result, the nature of the discourse changes. Peers work together to understand the matter under debate better; they set out to learn rather than to defend a position.

Peer review aims to operate within what Habermas (1984) has called an emancipatory discourse. Such discourse is free of unequal power relations, concealed strategic orientation, structural restrictions, closed thinking, fixed assumptions, one-way communication and domination by one party to the communicative interaction. Freedom from these constraints on 'communicative rationality' constitutes what Habermas calls the 'ideal speech situation' which

> must ensure not only unlimited discussion, but discussion that is free from distorting influences, whether their source be open domination, conscious strategic behaviour, or the more subtle barriers to communication deriving from self-deception.
>
> (McCarthy 1984: 306)

It is fair to say that academic discourse rarely meets the standards of the 'ideal speech situation', nevertheless it does provide the benchmark against which we measure how far our intentions to have genuinely supportive peer review are succeeding.

The strength of peer review is that it can avoid the pitfalls of a top-down managerial model, since it relies on peers as equals to consider issues and make recommendations. It builds on a strong tradition within the academic culture and encourages collective ownership of outcomes reached and contributes to the development of a learning organization. Peer review is flexible and adaptable to many different contexts and can take many different forms, as we have seen.

Dialogue and critical debate leading to collective learning can thrive within a collegial ethos, although it is necessary to build confidentiality into some peer review processes, such as providing feedback to individual teachers about their teaching. However, these confidential issues can be brought into the public arena for collective debate, while individuals remain protected by anonomizing and aggregating matters arising through the peer review process.

Using these broad principles, peer review processes can be used to promote conversations about teaching, the curriculum, course design and assessment, reward processes, and continuous professional development (CPD) schemes.

Recruiting and appointing teaching staff

If teaching is to be given greater strategic importance in higher education, then one area that needs to be developed is the way in which new academic staff are recruited. The process of advertising and recruiting staff is an essential element in addressing the quality of teaching in higher education. This critical step in an institutional strategy to improve teaching is often missed.

Paying attention to teaching in the appointment process not only reflects the actual workload that staff undertake, but also carries an important message about the priorities within the institution.

Typically, in the UK, applicants are asked to make a presentation and are interviewed. Judgements about the applicant's ability to teach are based on their communication skills demonstrated in the presentation and interview. Not only are these contexts remote from typical teaching situations, the judgement focuses only on general communication skills and does not allow any exploration of complex issues of relationships with students, understanding of student learning, course design, assessment methods, using information technology and all the other aspects of teaching.

The first step in the recruitment process is to be clear about the university's expectations of teaching quality in the advertisement and job description and to specify the areas of teaching development the candidate will be responsible for if appointed. The application form can be used to ask candidates to specify not simply their teaching experience, but their teaching philosophy, examples of innovations or specific teaching and learning approaches they employ in their own work, and any evidence from evaluation of their teaching, such as from a peer review process.

The shortlisting process needs to be explicit about teaching criteria and the weighting given to teaching alongside other criteria such as professional experience or research output. At the interview stage, candidates can be asked to bring further evidence of their teaching experience, for example a teaching portfolio including examples of courses developed and learning materials designed. They can also be asked to discuss how they would respond to teaching and learning situations. Role-plays are also possible, or candidates can be asked to conduct a 'sample seminar'. However, the artificiality of these scenarios militates against their usefulness as a valid means of assessing commitment to teaching. Presentations with titles like 'how my research informs my teaching (or vice versa)', 'how I would develop a course for a multicultural student group', 'how I use assessment for learning', can also be useful. Inexperienced staff will have less evidence to present, but their commitment to, and interest and in, teaching can be assessed nevertheless.

All candidates need to be informed about the department's and the institution's expectations regarding CPD and initial professional development. Promotion criteria and opportunities for seeking funding for teaching developments should also be provided. (For further details on recruiting good teachers, see Gosling 1997.)

Induction/orientation

The process of orientation is about negotiating entry into new 'communities of practice' and, as an emergent social process, it is about engagement, establishing a sense of belonging, mutually defining group identities and negotiating the language of the institution. 'People assume you know what they're on about, when you don't. Like when I was told "please moderate these exam papers"' (personal communication 2004). Orientation happens in many different 'emergent' contexts within the academic staff member's own department and as a result of actions taken, and interactions experienced, by the persons themselves. These are often spontaneous, unpredictable, and sometimes contradictory.

Formal academic staff induction/orientation, by contrast, is at a time of the organization's choosing, with a fixed programme and designed to communicate institutionally approved messages. It is important to give academic staff an opportunity to express their concerns, ask questions and begin to orientate themselves to the institution and the department. Group activities based on a problem-solving approach can be used to introduce them to typical scenarios of what they will encounter, the relevant university policies and the appropriate course of action they could take. This approach mirrors the much longer process of transition and negotiation that will take at least a year to complete.

It takes time for newcomers to find their way into the organization, make connections and to arrive at a relatively stable position in relation to different aspects of the organization's practices. New academic staff are often preoccupied with their teaching responsibilities and with finding ways to become confident in their own approach to teaching (Henkel 2000). Henkel's research suggests that younger staff 'were more likely than their seniors to have incorporated theory and practice from pedagogy in their approach to teaching' (Henkel 2000: 265). Not all staff accept that it is part of their role as an 'academic' to be a professional teacher. The disciplinary department has an important role to support them through this transition to becoming a teacher.

The difficulties of transition can be exacerbated for those on short-term contracts:

> When they arrive, they know they've been picked only because they have some research money in hand or a batch of upcoming research papers that will earn RAE credits. They're on short term contracts and if the department doesn't keep its 5, they'll be out on their ears. That means they want to do the minimum of teaching so that they can do research.
>
> (Taylor 2004: 21)

Henkel (2000: 177) also found that, 'for some people the preoccupation with teaching meant that for the first time the development of their research profile was less important'. New researchers also recognize that teaching assists their publication output by forcing them to 'develop a much closer understanding of . . . [the] subject' (Stokes 1996: 7), and, as one of Henkel's informants says of their teaching: 'my own written work now has changed as a result of having to be much clearer for undergraduates' (Henkel 2000: 177).

Mentoring schemes

New academic staff come under considerable pressure form a variety of directions – requests to teach a course/module, deliver a lecture, develop a new course, find new funding, publish their research, complete their PhD – and all the while they are still teaching for the first time. These pressures are hard to resist and hard to balance one against the other, and they occur while the process of negotiation with new norms and behaviours is ongoing. A valuable way of helping academic staff at this difficult period in their career is to offer some form of mentoring. Mentoring appears to be common practice in British universities (Blackwell and McLean 1996), but the form the mentoring takes can vary enormously. Some mentoring is part of a formal initial professional development programme; some is based on very informal arrangements; some is conceived as peer relationships in which support and friendship are key elements, while in yet other institutions mentoring is more hierarchical, using senior and experienced staff to help initiate the newcomer into the practices of the department.

A successful, award-winning, mentoring scheme has been operating at Miami University (Ohio), USA, since 1979 (Cox 1998). The key features of this scheme are that it is embedded in a broader, year-long Teaching Scholars Program, it is campus-wide and typically includes 10 to 14 junior faculty. Mentor training is provided by the Office for the Advancement of Scholarship and Teaching, but it is flexible and low key. 'Protégés' select their mentor and may have more than one; about half select a mentor from within their department and one from outside. About 25 per cent of mentors are former protégés. Formal mid- and end-of-year evaluations have suggested that both parties to the programme benefit from the process. Activities include consulting on teaching projects, observation of classroom teaching (live or using video), discussing small-group teaching, joint attendance at seminars on teaching, advising on research, publishing and probationary (tenure) requirements. Social activities are also an important part of the programme. Mentor rewards are mostly intrinsic, but there are also complimentary books on teaching, some free lunches and recognition from senior management/administration of the mentors' service to the university.

This example serves as an illustration of a successful scheme, but the complexities involved in mentoring, and the resources and energy needed to run a successful scheme, must not be underestimated. Decisions must be taken on the level of support offered, guidelines provided, training for mentors, the formality/informality of the process, boundaries of the mentor role, whether it is institution-wide or departmentally based, and how it will be evaluated. Evidence from studies inside and outside education (Megginson and Clutterbuck 1995; Blackwell and McLean 1996) suggest that mentees approve of mentoring schemes, but they need to be resourced to allow appropriate training, support, monitoring and evaluation to occur.

Supporting new teaching staff through initial professional development

Many programmes to improve teaching and learning have focused on providing professional development for newly appointed academic staff with teaching responsibilities. Gibbs (2001a) found that, in England, one of the most frequent uses of institutional Teaching Quality Enhancement Funds (TQEF) was provision of professional development for full-time teachers (47 per cent) and for part-time and graduate teaching assistants (20 per cent). One hundred and fifteen UK-based higher education institutions (HEIs), representing 90 per cent of all HEIs with more than 500 academic staff (from all parts of the UK), now have nationally accredited professional development courses (UUK/SCOP 2004).[1] There will be others with similar programmes that are not yet nationally accredited.

In the USA there has been a similar trend towards 'preparing future faculty', although it is by no means universal (D'Andrea 1996; Gaff *et al.* 2000). The dominant model differs from the UK approach in that professional development is aimed at graduate students undertaking their PhD and is therefore completed prior to taking a full-time teaching appointment.

The trend towards preparing new staff for their teaching role marks a relatively recent change in attitudes to the academic's role that has occurred only as university systems have shifted from being elite to mass systems. Perhaps it is significant, as Wareham (2002) has pointed out, that 'the phrase "reading for a degree" has all but disappeared and in its place the notion of being taught, and being taught effectively, has gained ascendancy'.

But if the idea of 'teaching' in higher education is still novel, the idea that teachers in higher education need to be taught how to do it, is even more recent. Although the Robbins Report (Robbins 1963), in the UK, recommended that academic staff needed some instruction on teaching, the earliest programmes were not developed until the 1970s, and then only in only a handful of institutions (Elton 1995b). These programmes were restricted to a few short introductory sessions with a certificate attached and with little or no requirement that academic staff took a scholarly approach to their teaching. The major growth in accredited postgraduate programmes occurred in the latter part of the 1990s (Gosling 2001b) and has continued apace since (Bamber 2002). In 1995, accredited postgraduate courses could still be written about as an 'innovation' (Andresen 1995), but now almost all British universities have such courses (UUK/SCOP 2004).

Elton (1995b) has suggested that, by focusing professional development activity on junior staff, the professional development of academic staff has come to be seen, for the majority of those in authority, as associated purely with inexperienced staff. Given that it could take twenty years before the majority of academic staff will have received this level of professional development for their teaching role, the strategy of concentrating on new appointments is in danger of leaving the dominant culture untouched. The explanation for this phenomenon is simple. New academic staff are the easiest to target (a) because it is relatively simple to amend the contracts of new staff to require them to attend initial professional development courses and (b) because it might be thought that they were more sympathetic to the idea that they should be schooled in pedagogy than their seniors. This proposition is supported by the limited evidence available (Henkel 2000). The Preparing Future Faculty initiative in the USA found that 'graduate students are enthusiastic about opportunities to learn about the complexities of teaching and service and to begin integrating them with their ability to conduct research' (Gaff *et al.* 2000: xi).

However, such enthusiasm is not universal. Any programme for new teachers in higher education, particularly as programmes have moved from being voluntary to mandatory, can expect to encounter a variety of reactions. These courses are the site of resistance and conflict between subject-based lecturers and those whom they perceive to be advocating a set of generic teaching competences (Taylor *et al.* 2002). This response is part of a more general reaction against the influence of the 'educational development movement' both within institutions and at a national policy level (Malcolm and Zukas 2001; Morley 2003a; Lindsay 2004).

Unfortunately much of the vocal opposition to these courses is based on stereotype rather than reality. Although courses are generic in the sense that academic staff from any discipline can participate in them, most that have been reported in the literature, from Andresen (1995) to Cooper (2004), are clear that addressing teachers' practice within the discipline is an essential feature of the course, and there is a growing volume of discipline-literature for courses to draw on (Higher Education Academy 2004). But that does not mean that disciplinary teaching practices are regarded as sacrosanct. Rather, as Cooper suggests, successful programmes offer

> analytic tools and activities whereby existing and alternative practices and assumptions can be illuminated, rationalised and tested in an open and neutral environment away from the department where such misgivings can be shared and critically examined for their significance.
>
> (Cooper 2004: 62)

If, as Gibbs and Coffey (2004: 98) suggest, 'the training programme provided a kind of "alternative culture" that counter-balanced the negative influences of the culture of teachers' departments', then this may help to explain the antagonism of some towards such courses. Fanghanel (2004: 584) has reported that course participants' positioning towards such courses was 'seen to be oscillating on a continuum between alignment with and disjunction from concepts expounded in the course'. If initial professional development courses are to be effective they need to focus on reducing the possibility of confrontation between the ethos of such courses and that of teaching departments.

Griffiths (1996) and Bamber (2002) found considerable variation in the nature and content of the courses. Many are based on the 'reflective practitioner' model (Schon 1987), some explicitly desire to create opportunities for genuine peer dialogue along Habermassian principles (Gosling 2000), while others are 'explicitly orientated towards developing teachers' teaching skills, especially their classroom practice' (Gibbs and Coffey 2004: 89). They vary in the extent to which they have a negotiated or a fixed curriculum, the extent to which they require attendance at face-to-face sessions and on their identified learning outcomes (Bourner *et al.* 2003).

The support for these courses appears to be high in the majority of institutions, although there is a sizeable minority where it is variable (Bamber 2002). There is evidence that the majority of staff who have undertaken these courses value what they have learned (Rust 2000), and that they are likely to be more effective, student-focused teachers (Gibbs and Coffey 2004). However, the evaluation of the impact of professional development on new lecturers teaching remains somewhat weak (Bamber 2003). It has been suggested that there are a variety of factors which determine the effectiveness of new teacher courses for each individual teacher relating to the teacher's role, presage factors such as existing approach to teaching, the nature of the programme, disciplinary background, departmental culture and the programme's institutional context (Cooper 2003).

From the perspective of contributing to the university as a learning organization, the critical features of initial professional development courses are that they need (a) to encourage participants to become curious about their teaching and foster habits of critical enquiry into teaching and learning, (b) to assist new teachers to develop a vocabulary to talk about teaching in a scholarly way, and (c) to provide a forum for discussion of a range of teaching and assessment practices.

Other courses for professional development

As we pointed out, echoing Elton, too heavy a focus on new academics leaves large numbers of academic staff without any professional development in teaching and learning. In the UK there has been a considerable growth in the numbers of diploma and masters programmes available, although the total number of academic staff who have taken advantage of these is unknown.

We agree with Rowland (2004) who has argued that such masters programmes should

> have many of the characteristics of a research forum, rather than those of a traditional 'taught' Master's course. The principle of collegiality and the processes of negotiation and collaboration, therefore, are central aspects of the programme. Participants will be encouraged to take an enquiry-based approach to the themes of the modules, to collaborate

in identifying appropriate subjects and methods for enquiry and to assist one another in the development of analyses and interpretations and in the evaluation of work in progress.

We suggest that it is important that those undertaking a higher-level course should be able to relate their learning to their own professional practice and use enquiry in ways which have utility for themselves and their colleagues. We endorse the principles adumbrated by O'Reilly (1996: 74):

- People learn best if they are encouraged to take responsibility for their learning.
- Deep learning arises from people's own interests, needs and desires located in a community of experience.
- For professionals, the workplace is the prime learning environment.
- The process of learning is as important as the content.

To actualize these principles means providing flexible, responsive and supportive programmes, which break away from the tradition of the individual engaging in an isolated activity of research and embraces activity involving peer groups of professionals. In this way the learning of a group of academic staff can be enhanced through the research activity of the course member. By promoting research that engages with the work environment of the individual teacher, advanced-level courses can support critical questioning of the teaching methods, interactions with students, and the social context of learning within the department. If the course participants are encouraged to use an explicit theoretical framework to analyse or investigate their practice (for example activity theory, complexity theory, discourse analysis), then it becomes possible to move beyond 'reflective practice' to new forms of articulation and understanding of professional thought and action and develop a community of scholars of teaching and learning.

Conclusion

In this chapter we have considered how ideas about academic identity impact on professional development. We have argued that because of the centrality of the discipline in the majority of academics' sense of self, professional development needs to respect disciplinary differences and accept that the conceptions of knowledge embedded in disciplinary identity shape conceptions of teaching and student learning. However, we have also suggested that it is necessary to promote a critical evaluation of the assumptions and practices of the discipline in order for new learning to occur. This can best be achieved with cross-disciplinary groups that can promote dialogue that allows new ways of thinking to emerge.

This chapter has discussed some examples of potential ways in which professional development can be promoted. We return to the importance of providing opportunities to develop a scholarly approach to teaching in Chapter 7 when we consider the scholarship of teaching and learning.

Note

1. Accreditation at this time was carried out by the Institute for Learning and Teaching in Higher Education (ILTHE), which since 2004 has been incorporated in the UK Higher Education Academy.

4

Creating Inclusive Learning Communities

> Working class participants and non-participants engage emotionally with negotiations around HE participation, which are grounded within gendered, racialised, classed and sexual identities.
>
> Archer and Leathwood 2003: 191

All members of a learning university, whether academic, manager, support staff or student, should be able to enjoy the opportunity to pursue the learning appropriate to their goals. This is a simple principle, and yet it can sound impossibly idealistic, because of the evidence that shows that students' opportunity to succeed in their studies is far from being equal. In this chapter we focus on the learning needs of students and look at the barriers to achieving equity and inclusivity in order to suggest a framework for addressing the causes of inequality in student success in their learning.

When dealing with change, universities and colleges need to take issues of equity seriously. We believe that this means looking at students' self-perception, constructions of identity, negotiation of meaning and modes of belonging. How students understand their relationship to their programme of study, to their home department and the wider institution is critical. Issues of identity and belonging are central to the creation of 'inclusive learning communities'.

As more diverse student populations negotiate their way through a multitude of programmes of study, it becomes more important to examine the implications of this diversity for a whole range of aspects of higher education: access and admissions, induction/orientation, course design, teaching and learning methods, assessment and employability. In order to take effective action to achieve the goals discussed in Chapter 1, attention needs to be paid to the transformation of students' understanding of themselves, the democratization of knowledge, inclusivity and social responsibility.

Learning is a social, as well as an individual, process. Consequently, improving teaching and learning is not just about an individual student's approach to study. It requires attention to the social context in which that learning is taking place and the impact of the 'learning community' on individual performance.

Equity and inclusivity

The argument about who has a right of access to universities and who can benefit from it has a long history. It has been accepted, for well over a century now, that the education of children in primary and secondary education (or 'K through 12'), is a general social good which should be open and available to all. Higher (or tertiary) education has been viewed differently. It has been assumed that, firstly, only a minority of the population can benefit from higher-level learning; secondly, that many people would not want to go to university even if they could; and thirdly, the country does not need everyone to go to university.

The provision of university education, whether privately or publicly funded has, therefore, always been limited.[1] This means that the distribution of higher education as a social good and as a benefit to the individuals who receive it, is a matter of distributive justice. Meritocratic principles for admission have, in general terms, taken precedence over the ability to pay for a university education, although the impact of wealth on access to higher education continues to be an issue (Hutchings 2003) and there continues to be a debate about whether all those who could benefit from higher education are doing so. On the basis of Trow's (1973) definition of a mass or universal system, that is when 40 per cent of the eligible age group are enrolled, higher education in the United States became a mass system in the 1950s when the postwar GI Bill was enacted for the benefit of soldiers coming back from the Second World War. Elsewhere in the world the transition from elite to mass systems has happened more recently or is continuing to happen today.

In the UK, the development of a mass system is relatively new and is still creating tensions. Between 1987 and 1992 the participation of students from the traditional age cohorts almost doubled from 14.6 per cent to 27.8 per cent. Since that time the participation rate has gradually risen to 41 per cent (HEFCE 2001). But despite the recent huge growth of student numbers to approximately 1.8 million, there continues to be 'a strong and relatively unchanging link between participation and social class, with extremely low numbers of students from the lower socio-economic groups being accepted onto university courses' (Gilchrist *et al.* 2003: 81).

This is clearly demonstrated in the different participation rates in higher education in England. This varies from less than 5 per cent to more than 70 per cent for differing groups of neighbourhoods (HEFCE 2001),[2] and while participation in higher education by students from families with professional and non-manual backgrounds is now about 50 per cent, it remains only 19 per cent with respect to the lower socio-economic groups (DfES 2003a). The persistence of inequality in higher education, not just in the UK but across the globe, reflects pervasive structures of class, race and gender inequality. Universities and colleges are not neutral institutions, but function 'in the context of political, cultural and social inequalities and play a role in maintaining and legitimating those inequalities' (Rushing 2001: 32).

The link between social class and access to higher education has become a matter of political concern because, in the first place, it is believed that the systematic disadvantaging of students from particular sections of society is inherently unfair. Secondly, it is seen as an economic issue because of a concern that the education system is failing to maximize the potential achievement of the workforce available to the economy (Wolf 2002).

The principle of 'inclusivity' differs from either of these grounds for widening access to higher education because it derives not from individual rights to equality of opportunity or from national economic interests, but from principles about the nature of educational communities. We can distinguish a weak and strong sense of inclusivity. In the weak sense it means that individuals wishing to participate in higher education have the right to fair treatment in being admitted into an institution. Inclusion in this sense merely grants access to higher education, but inclusivity in a stronger sense means having a sense of belonging to and being recognized as a full member of that community.

This is more than an equal opportunity to take advantage of what is made available by others on their terms. It implies that positive steps will be taken within the higher education institution to welcome, incorporate and respect all of its members irrespective of their personal characteristics: age, gender, race, ethnicity, religion, sexual orientation and so forth. An inclusive institution will take active steps to ensure that none of its members are excluded by virtue of their membership of these groups. As a kind of 'social contract', it also implies that members of the organization, students and faculty/staff will make the contribution to the institution expected of them without hindering the right of others to be similarly included.

The UK government strategy for widening participation (DfES 2003c) supports inclusivity in the weaker sense of equality of access. Four priority areas have been identified: attainment, aspiration, application and admissions. The first two concerns, attainment and aspiration, place the burden of responsibility on the failures of the individual non-participant and their schooling. The other priorities, application and admissions, only deal with point of entry issues and do not address matters of course content, teaching and learning, assessment and the broader issue of the unique culture of higher education.

Placing the burden of responsibility on schools and individual students does not tackle the question whether higher education institutions are doing enough to include working-class students. We suggest that the failure of many higher education institutions to change practices that have exclusionary effects, particularly in higher-status universities, calls into question whether there is currently a desire to operate on inclusive principles and advance greater social diversity. The clear association in the UK of high-status institutions with high proportions of students from the private secondary education sector and the low percentage of students from low socio-economic class (HEFCE 2001) attests to the continuation of the trend noted by Giddens (1973) over thirty years ago. He argued that the continued dominance of particular elite routes by the wealthy middle classes ensures the reproduction of class privilege within an expanded system.

Scott argued that 'British higher education still feels much more like an elite than a universal system' (Scott 1995: 3) and that there remains considerable nostalgia in the UK for a past time in which there was a common language with which students and academic staff could communicate. Arora would agree.

> While the rhetoric has indeed changed in some places, deeply entrenched assumptions and philosophies remain in place. These cannot be countered by good will alone; it needs a systematic deconstruction of attitudes, behaviour and procedures.
>
> (Arora 1995: 32)

The challenge to create an inclusive learning community, now that students are being drawn from up to the 50th percentile of the population, and higher education no longer comprises an elite with a relatively homogeneous cultural background, is considerable. But whose responsibility is it to change? Is it the student who must be transformed in order to be assimilated into a relatively unchanging higher education? Or is it higher education that must be transformed to accommodate the needs of the students? Or is it that the sector will divide between those institutions into which diverse students are assimilated and others that will accommodate diverse students?

The response of universities to these questions can be represented by four categories suggested by King (2003).

- There are universities that have changed neither entry criteria nor teaching methods, but offer scholarships and bursaries to students from the lower socio-economic groups to help them through college, provided they have met the entry criteria.
- The second group have widened the socio-economic profile of their students by creating access routes within their region. However, virtually everything else about the university remains unchanged; it is only the entry routes that have been opened up.
- The third group of universities have indeed widened participation by changing their entry requirements and are taking larger and more diverse cohorts. But they continue to teach and assess in much the same way, though with bigger groups, more use of virtual learning environments and with some additional support for English, mathematics and study skills for students who are in danger of failing.
- The fourth group are those that have the most flexible admission policies. They have also changed teaching methods, course design and assessment, particularly at the first level of undergraduate study, to take account of the

> different student profile. Their regulations are also likely to be more flexible and encourage the use of credit accumulation to allow greater flexibility in students' programmes.

King argued that only this last model takes seriously the needs of students recruited as a result of widening participation, and in our terms could be regarded as inclusive. The consequence of taking this approach is, according to King, that 'the very nature of the university is changed'. The university must 'meet its students where they are . . . [and recognize] that what people come out with, rather than what they come in with, is what matters'. Flexibility of the educational experience on offer is also key: 'We have to look again at when we open, where we teach, what we teach, what skills for employment and life we aim to give' (King 2003: 12).

If the change is so significant, does this mean that such institutions are no longer universities? There are those who argue that universities must accept the need for a 'redefinition of higher education' (Stuart 2001). With an increasing proportion of higher education taking place in other types of institutions (in the UK 15 per cent of all higher education takes place in further education colleges – 25 per cent in Scotland – and this proportion is set to grow), higher education cannot be equated with universities. In these institutions the traditional coexistence of teaching and research no longer obtains, which some have argued is an essential feature of a university. The differentials between universities in their cultures, mission, the balance between research and teaching, in income and wealth, are so wide that it has been said that the UK has a 'two-tier system which actively discriminates against students from working class and ethnic minority backgrounds' (Cohen 1995: 4).

An example of how this differentiation occurs relates to the impact of working while studying. Whereas in the USA there has been a long tradition of students working their way through university, in the UK it is only since the recent abolition of personal grants to students that large numbers of students have needed to work while studying. In the USA, studies indicate that working full-time or part-time off campus, has been found to have a uniformly negative effect on student attainment (Astin 1993). Evidence in the UK suggests that there are significant differences in proportions of students studying part-time and the hours worked at different types of institutions (Metcalf 2003). In the universities with low entry requirements, 60 per cent of students were found to be working in term-time compared with 27 per cent in a university with high entry requirements, and the students from the low-status institutions were working, on average, longer hours. Students reported that working not only reduced their study time but also led to less sleep, both detrimental to study. The conclusion Metcalf draws is that

> not only are students from non-higher education families less likely to enter higher education but, once there, they are more likely to be employed during the term-time and thus to benefit less from the education provided.
>
> (Metcalf 2003: 325)

Universities that are responding to the reality of their students' life have made adjustments such as scheduling classes at different times, recording lectures and making them available over a virtual learning environment (VLE), extending opening hours of all educational facilities and ensuring flexibility over the pacing of learning and work deadlines. The students who have the most difficulty are the ones working longer part-time hours at a traditional university where none of the adjustments have been made. Metcalf (2003) points out how a vicious circle is operating which has the effect of segregating students from less well-off homes without a tradition of higher education from high-status institutions. Those who expect to work will be more likely to go to the universities that facilitate term-time working, thus reinforcing the need for such policies in only some universities.

The quandary faced by those institutions which make the adjustments that King (2003) refers to in admission policies, teaching, the curriculum and the organization of learning, is that in doing so they are perceived by the wider society, and by many academics, as confirming their lower status. As Cohen has pointed out, they are caught in a dilemma.

> They do not want to be the poor relations of the traditional universities with whom they cannot possibly compete in terms of prestige or resources, but nor do they want to embrace a form of modernisation which condemns them and their students to second class citizenship.
> (Cohen 1995: 4)

In these ways, structural inequalities are reinforced and perpetuated. Recent evidence in Scotland (SHEFC 2004) indicates that the proportion of students from the poorer social groups attending the 'ancient' universities has actually declined, although overall the numbers have increased. The growth is occurring in further education, not in the elite universities.

These differentials between institutions impact on students' self-image, achievement and employability. Students are only too aware of the differences in status between universities. Ainley quotes one student in a former UK polytechnic who said: 'Let's face it, nobody comes to (Inner City) unless they're desperate' (Ainley 1994: 65). This is a realistic assessment of the public perception of institutions that have done most to widen participation and the impact this is likely to have on students' career prospects. For this reason, few institutions in the UK declare themselves as 'access' universities, although one does claim to be'the most socially inclusive HEI in England' with a vision to being the leading access institution in higher education.

What is at issue here is how much the culture of higher education can change. The strategy of inclusion and access cannot be operated effectively without addressing the wider concerns of academic culture and expectations. This is because, in general, 'the culture of the university has been one that has ignored the multiple narratives, histories, and voices of culturally and politically subordinated groups' (Giroux 1996:100). The dominant culture defines excellence in an exclusionary way, since 'the essence of excellence in higher education, unlike compulsory education, lies in the inability of the vast majority of the population to achieve its standards' (Williams 1997: 32). Buttressed by powerful notions of tradition and power that are deeply ingrained in national cultures, elite universities are celebrated as the ideal, despite the fact that the majority of higher education institutions cannot match their resources or their status.

What does it mean to be an inclusive higher education community?

The idea that universities should be 'inclusive' learning communities could be regarded as a platitude or as a demand for radical action. It is a platitude if it simply means that universities act in the ways characterized by the first three categories in King's typology. Virtually all institutions could say that they have achieved this much already. But we wish to suggest that being inclusive represents a potentially more challenging idea and a far more contested one.

Being an inclusive learning community demands a shift from an assimilationist model, 'students must fit in to what we provide', to one that incorporates greater responsiveness to the needs of students. Institutions need to be responsive to more variability in educational background and qualifications; more mature students; more students with disabilities who need particular forms of learning support; more students from different ethnic, national and religious groups; more students whose motivation to learn does not match their teachers' expectations; more students working part-time; more students studying at a distance; more students who exhibit greater diversity of language skills.

There is no doubt that many of these students present challenges to the traditional ways in which higher education has operated. Some students have disabilities that create multiple disadvantages in their studies; some have to balance the demands of their studies with family responsibilities; many have to work long hours to earn money to live. Yet the extent to which institutions have adapted to take account of the needs of such students varies considerably (Riddell *et al.* 2003).

Higher education institutions can no longer assume that there is a common understanding by students of the purposes of higher education or of the nature of studying at higher levels (Simpson 1996). Students now being recruited into higher education are coming from backgrounds without the 'cultural capital' (Bourdieu 1988) that was once taken for granted within higher education. Nor do they have access to the 'social capital' (Schuller 2002), the networks of interpersonal social relationships, to which middle-class students have access. As a result, many bring with them low self-esteem, low self-confidence and a sense of their 'otherness' or detachment from the dominant culture of higher education (Ainley 1994; Archer and Leathwood 2003; Longden 2004). There is a concern that many of these students enter higher education but do not achieve their aimed-for degree. Attention in the

UK has been drawn to this concern since 1996 when the Higher Education Funding Council for England (HEFCE) commissioned a study into how many students were leaving higher education before completing their studies (Yorke 1999). Annual data on the rate of non-completion following one year of entry shows an enormous variation between institutions, from only 3 per cent in the highly selective, high-status universities to approaching 30 per cent in inner-city universities with a widening access mission (HEFCE 2002). If the desire to improve the chances of success for these least advantaged students is taken seriously, then King's call for significant change in higher education must be attended to.

A theoretical framework

Because the largest threat to student continuation occurs within the first year of study, we focus here on the period of transition to higher education. Tinto (1993) provides the most commonly used model for understanding this period in the experience of students. It is based on interactionist theory and posits that the critical factor for student retention is the level of academic and social interaction achieved by the student. Other studies, such as Astin's (1993), also point to the importance of student 'academic involvement'. But a number of recent studies have focused on the importance of students' prior state of tacit knowledge and 'cultural capital' on entry to higher education (Reay 1998; Thomas 2001; Archer *et al.* 2003; Longden 2004).

We will build on these studies by focusing on the process of transition that students undergo. We do so because we wish to go beyond explaining differences in students' staying-on rates by reference to factors beyond the students' and universities' control, such as social class and level of social capital. This will enable us to suggest a basis for a constructive improvement strategy.

The theoretical framework we consider here has been provided by Lave and Wenger (1991).[3] They view learning as a 'situated activity', that is, a social rather than an individual process, which is defined by the specific set of beliefs, practices and values into which the learner is being introduced. They argue that knowledge is relational in character and that learning is a matter of negotiating meaning through the 'concerned (engaged, dilemma driven) nature of learning activity for the people involved' (Lave and Wenger 1991: 33). A central and defining characteristic of the process is what they have called 'legitimate peripheral participation'. By using this concept, Lave and Wenger draw attention to the point that 'learners inevitably participate in communities of practitioners and that the mastery of knowledge and skill requires newcomers to move toward full participation in socio-cultural practices of the community' (1991: 29).

Students at the beginning of their studies are undertaking a 'cognitive apprenticeship' during which they need to negotiate meanings, acquire skills and knowledge as relative newcomers to the discourse and practices that define the pedagogical community (Bernstein 2000) that they are joining. They are metaphorically moving from the 'periphery' of a subject to becoming proficient in it.

In contrast to the purely individualistic cognitive understandings of knowledge and approaches to study that have dominated recent discussions of learning and teaching, Lave and Wenger emphasize that learning involves the whole person. Rather than 'receiving' a body of factual knowledge about the world, the student is understood as an agent actively negotiating their way in the world in which 'that agent, activity, and the world mutually constitute each other' (1991: 33). This understanding is within a long tradition of social theories of knowledge (see, for example, Berger and Luckman 1967), which suggest that knowledge is 'constructed' rather than simply received. The nature of the negotiation will thus depend on the existing beliefs and conceptual frameworks the student brings to the process. Some students, who have already been introduced to practices and understandings in their previous education that are consistent with the expectation of their teachers in higher education, will find the process relatively easy. Others, as Archer and Leathwood (2003) have described, find themselves negotiating in a new world, not only with respect to new knowledge but also with respect to different ways of speaking, different assumptions about what is inherently desirable or inherently normal (Lawler 2000), and different attitudes to knowing. This is challenging on many levels, personal and emotional, as well as intellectual. It also means that what the students learn is not necessarily what the teacher believes they are teaching.

> This viewpoint makes a fundamental distinction between learning and intentional instruction. Such decoupling does not deny that learning can take place where there is teaching, but does not take intentional instruction to be in itself the source or cause of learning and thus does not blunt the claim 'that what gets learnt is problematic with respect to what is taught'.
>
> (Lave and Wenger 1991: 41)

Some of the key ideas that emerge in Lave and Wenger's study of apprenticeships are: (a) as peripheral participants, learners nevertheless had a view of what the whole enterprise was about and what was to be learned, this created 'strong goals for learning'; (b) the apprentices achieved much of their learning by being engaged in the practices of their community, which led Lave and Wenger (1991: 93) to comment: 'engaging in practice rather than being its object may well be a condition for the effectiveness of learning'; (c) the mode of learning was 'decentred', that is, it was not through the teaching of the 'master' but rather 'through the organisation of the community of practice of which the master is a part'. The implication of this view of learning is that

> The master's effectiveness at producing learning is not dependent on her ability to inculcate the students with her own conceptual

> representations. Rather it depends on her ability to manage effectively a division of participation that provides for growth on the part of the student.
>
> (Hanks 1991: 21)

As a model of the process of becoming initiated into an academic discipline or professional area, Lave and Wenger's account contains much that is useful to aid our thinking about students' transition to higher education. The idea of 'communities of practice' helps to understand how identities are formed, and how rules for appropriate action are formulated and acted upon. But there are limitations that also need to be recognized. Firstly, by using the spatial metaphor of the 'periphery', Lave and Wenger also imply that there is a 'centre', but this is misleading if it implies an essentialist understanding of academic disciplines. The knowledge and practices that form a 'discipline' are not 'monist' but an array of knowledges and practices that can be more contradictory and fragmentary than the idea of a community of practice suggests.

Secondly, the novice is not simply absorbed into a community of practice unchanged by the experience. The process of negotiating meaning also alters it. As Engestrom and Miettinem (1999: 12) have said: 'What seems to be missing is movement outward and in unexpected directions: questioning of authority, criticism, innovation, initiation of change.'

Particularly in the context of an academic community, it is vital that we encourage novices also to be critical of the ideas and processes that they are being taught. For example, as we discuss later in this chapter, students from minority groups have been critical of the assumptions embedded in a Eurocentric curriculum. We expect students not simply to be passive in the acquisition of a set of skills, but also to be agents in defining the meaning and use of those skills for their own purposes.

Despite these points of criticisms there is much that we can use in the approach of Lave and Wenger and other activity theorists who have developed the ideas of 'situated cognition' and 'constructivist' theories of learning.

It is important that apprentices in pedagogical communities are able to get a vision of the whole subject and what it can achieve. Introductory courses which restrict students to a narrow and limited conception of the subject, 'because that is all they can cope with', will be counterproductive. Students must be allowed to become 'engaged' with the subject and to be active in participating in its activities and purposes, for example in placements and work-related learning, or research projects. The role of the teacher in this process is not principally to instruct or to attempt to control students' conceptions; rather it is to arrange for students to engage in productive learning. 'Being a good teacher is very much about being a good designer of tasks and a sensitive facilitator of student engagement with them' (Knight 2002: 124).

This 'decentred' pedagogy nevertheless requires careful management. A decentred approach does not imply a 'sink or swim' abandonment of students, but rather a structured programme of learning that works from the current state of knowledge held by the students. This can only be achieved if teachers have a good understanding of their students' conceptualization of the discipline by testing the understanding students have at the outset of their course (Entwistle *et al.* 1992). Although getting to know students is difficult with large classes, it is essential that there is a strategy to build on students' existing starting points.

When planning students' programmes, account must be taken of the situated nature of academic discourses. Students experience a variety of different types of 'situatedness', some of which may easily conflict. This variety can assist the students' negotiation of meaning, for as Bowden and Marton (1998) emphasize, variation of experience plays an important role in learning, but it can also be confusing. Learners need to achieve 'focal differentiation', that is, ways of centring on what is relevant to achieve the task at hand. Too much unplanned and conflicting variation prevents this, and students can feel lost. For example, students can encounter difficulties with the conflicting requirements for written work by different disciplines (Lea and Street 1998), and teacher feedback using generic terms such as 'structure' and 'analysis' have different epistemological connotations that may be hidden from the student (Warren 2003).

Teachers in higher education need to recognize the time it takes for students to negotiate the meaning of the activities they are engaging with, and allow alternative meanings and interpretations to emerge, and be discussed. This requires careful management of group learning to build students' confidence and trust in each other (Feito 2003). In the early phases of programmes it is essential that there are learning strategies that enable students to test out their understanding of the subject in a risk-free environment. Structured group work with peers is a useful way in which this process can be supported.

Learning development

The framework we have discussed sees students entering higher education having to negotiate the transition into a new set of institutional and disciplinary cultures. Students do not have all the 'pre-formed' cognitive and linguistic capacities they need to succeed on their course. Furthermore, some students, those lacking 'social capital', will be a considerable distance away from being able to respond in the way that is expected of them. This is likely to be class related (Knight and Yorke 2003), through lack of information and contact with higher education (Hutchings 2003), lack of preparation by further education colleges (Roberts and Allen 1997), and lack of family experience of higher education (Connor *et al.* 2001). Cultural and language difficulties are also more likely to be associated with students for whom English is not their first language.

Students are not merely learning to use a new vocabulary, they have to adopt different attitudes to knowledge itself. Perry (1999) has suggested that there is a fairly common pattern of cognitive development that students go through in their college/university years, starting with an absolutist (right or wrong) stage moving through uncertainty to a relativist stage which, with maturity, grows into a stable set of personal commitments. The principal objection raised against Perry's analysis is that it does not take enough account of the variation between academic cultures that students encounter (Webster 2002). The extent to which these cultures are perceived to be novel will vary between students. There are a number of types of novelty that are relevant:

- the subject of study may be new;
- a new approach to a subject the student is already familiar with;
- different epistemological assumptions and values employed;
- teaching methods employed may be different from those encountered to date;
- the expectation of student study methods may be very different from that encountered previously;
- the language of instruction and assessment may not be the student's home and/or first language;
- the academic literacy required may be different from the students' previous experience.

The potential strangeness of becoming an apprentice in their subject goes deeper. Students can find the requirements of 'argument' in an academic sense quite bizarre. Words like 'contend', 'hypothesize', 'refute', 'contradict' can appear pretentious and alien (Gardner 1991). The apparently counter-intuitive nature of what is a problem in an academic sense itself creates a difficulty. 'Academics not only cultivate problems that are not recognised as such, they like to invent problems that most people are not aware of or look for new ways to describe already recognised problems' (Graff 2002: 29).

Students see finding problems where they do not appear to exist as part of the 'relentless negativism and oppositionality' (Graff 2002: 35) that they find strange and even repugnant. Students are expected to express and discuss these problems using what Bernstein has characterized as an 'elaborated code', which might from other perspectives be thought pedantic and bombastic. Students also have to learn when it is appropriate and necessary to use references and what will count as plagiarism if they fail to reference accurately. From our experience, we know that large numbers of novice students have difficulty in using references, but this is not a simple matter of learning a technique and a set of conventions. The process of learning how to reference goes to the heart of what is academic knowledge and how it is produced and reproduced. The ability to use ideas from sources and to reference is 'essential to the construction of knowledge in the university' (Hendricks and Quinn 2000: 448).

> Students are able to develop their writing when a lecture focuses on referencing problems not as surface errors, but as problems connected

> to a deeper understanding of multi-voiced texts and the construction of knowledge.
>
> (Hendricks and Quinn 2000: 456)

Equally the question 'what is plagiarism?' is not simply a matter of cheating (although there is plenty of evidence of that too), it is about discipline-specific understandings of originality, the accumulation of knowledge, and intellectual property rights.

Students are coping with all these forms of novelty in their studies as well as adjusting to a new institution. This is a difficult process for almost everybody, but for some it creates a complex cocktail of emotions of loss and expectation, fear and hope (Percy 2001). The anxiety felt can be high. Brown *et al.* (2000 cited in Leach 2002) found that 49 per cent of students suffered emotional health problems that affected their daily functioning. Recent evidence confirms that financial and other difficulties have increased British students' levels of anxiety and depression and that financial difficulties and depression affect academic performance (Andrews and Wilding 2004). Creating a community that is welcoming to the new student and one that provides opportunities for discussion of emotional aspects of the transition to higher education, are essential parts of an inclusive community. It is also necessary to ensure that there is specialist counselling for students with clinical levels of anxiety and depression.

The diversity of the student body requires all teaching programmes to be more explicit about the expectations it has of students. 'Time on task' is the single best predictor of student success (Astin 1993). However, in the USA the National Survey of Student Expectations (NSSE) found that only 14 per cent of full-time students spent more than 25 hours a week on study (NSSE 2002: 7). There is clearly a need for greater clarity about the time students are expected to be studying.

More explicit instruction on matters that fall within the umbrella term 'academic literacy' is a critical part of adopting a more inclusive approach. Academic literacy has been defined as 'the complex of linguistic, conceptual and skills resources for analysing, constructing, and communicating knowledge in the subject area' (Warren 2003: 46). This includes the nature of argument, searching out information, judging the worth of texts and websites, and principles and practice of academic referencing. Learning academic literacy is one of the keys to the process of moving from the periphery to engaging in a pedagogical community, because encoded in the disciplinary discourses is a range of assumptions about what can and cannot be said, how knowledge claims are substantiated, the appropriate tone to be adopted in writing, whether personal experience counts or not, the acceptable range of writing genres and many other considerations. Students without previous experience of the kinds of writing required by higher education need practice in writing for different purposes in a relatively risk-free environment with plenty of feedback.

It is common to adopt a deficit model to explain why some students are 'under-prepared' for study in higher education (Ozga and Sukhnandan 1998). The difficulty with this model is that (a) it implies the responsibility for the problem lies entirely with the student, and (b) it stigmatizes certain groups and individuals. The mismatch between students' current capabilities and the manner in which they are expected to perform is as much the failure of the teaching, curriculum and assessment as it is of the students. 'Higher education institutions have a moral and educational responsibility to ensure that they have effective programmes in place to meet the teaching and learning needs of the students they admit' (Department of Education 1997: para 2.3.3). This implies that once students have been admitted, the responsibility for matching their learning needs lies with the institution. This does not of course remove the responsibility from the student to make best use of the learning programme.

We need to think not only in terms of 'students at risk' (Entwistle *et al.* 1992) but also in terms of teachers' practices which can put students at risk: what has been called the 'institutional practice of mystery' that surrounds acquisition of academic literacy (Lillis quoted in Mitchell and Riddle 2000: 10).

Our proposal for the appropriate way for higher education to respond to these issues is based on two principles that relate to the university as a learning organization. First is the principle of 'learner development'. Rather than regard students as 'deficient' in the skills they need and provide 'remedial' programmes, we believe that the right approach is a 'learning development model' (Simpson 1996; Cottrell 2001; D'Andrea and Gosling 2001; Gosling 2003). A learning development model is predicated on the assumption that all students, indeed all people, have ongoing learning development needs. It is our view that this can best be achieved by creating an environment in which it is recognized that all members of the university are actively engaged in learning.

Because of the discipline-centred nature of much of 'academic literacy', the second principle is that all staff with teaching or learning support roles have a responsibility for the development of students' academic literacy. The link between academic literacy and the subject is an intrinsic one that cannot be dodged, but it does require subject teachers to become more conscious of the links between writing and the epistemology of the subject and to incorporate reference to the nature of academic argument in the discipline in their teaching.

Supporting the transition to higher education

The process of negotiating a set of conventions that is neither obvious nor simple begins before entering higher education. Communication and liaison with local secondary education institutions can help to clarify what the higher education courses demand of students and what they can expect to be doing. Having realistic expectations is an important factor in helping students stay 'on course', since students' perception that they are on the 'wrong programme' ranked highest in reasons for leaving university (Yorke 1999). A mismatch between students' experience of a discipline and their preferred learning goals can have a significant effect on their motivation (Breen 2002), and some have unrealistic expectations of the workload required (Rickinson and Rutherford 1996; Seymour and Hewitt 1997). For the same reason, pre-entry advice should be available for all students, either before they arrive or during the induction/orientation period. Course documentation needs to be transparent about the course requirements and anticipated workload for students. Students transferring into a course from another institution or from another programme also need a structured programme to support the transition. They need to be encouraged to identify any special needs, not just at enrolment but also later in their course since some are reluctant to disclose a difficulty they may have. Parker (1998) suggests that self-identification needs to be prompted at application and at enrolment and during study through publicity about the university special needs/disabilities and dyslexia support service. A rapid response to students' self-identification is reassuring to the student who may be anxious about their ability to cope with higher education, followed by an appointment for an assessment of the students' additional needs.

The initial contact with the university is important to set the tone of the relationship and to establish the expectations that students and staff have of each other. In the UK the traditional welcoming week or induction is typically a mix of orientation to the university, its geography and services, the necessary official registration and enrolment processes, and supporting social and academic integration. Structured events that enable students to mix socially with faculty/staff and students, using peer facilitators (Frame 2001) are essential. Group-based project work which engenders the idea of a learning community is an effective way to introduce students to the subject and to find their way around the library and information technology (IT) services (Ash 2001).

Once students have started their course of study it is important to find ways of creating a sense of belonging to a purposeful community of learners. In a large, alien environment when students feel they know no one and have no support to turn to, they are less likely to persist with their studies if they face difficulties. A group identity needs to be cultivated with both face-to-face meetings and electronic contact via email and shared areas in the virtual learning environment. There is a cost to providing this level of contact. But since it is in the first year that the students have the most difficulty, adjustments need to be made where help can make the greatest impact on both feelings of self-confidence and progression rates. This investment in students' future is well worth making (Astin 1993; Yorke 1999).

A subject-embedded approach to supporting students' transition to higher education means that study skills cannot be devolved to a specialist department. Displacing responsibility on to a separate study/key skills course and on to support staff charged with amending students' writing difficulties was an inhibiting factor for the effective development of students' understanding of academic argument (Mitchell and Riddle 2000: 13). The alternative approach requires staff to 'focus on making the rules and conventions of academic thinking, valuing, acting, speaking, reading and writing overt to students using the mainstream curriculum' (Boughey 2002: 306). This does not mean that there is no role for learning support specialists. Analysing the linguistic problems of students and diagnosing dyslexia are specialist tasks, and students can be the victims of amateurish efforts to support their English (Boughey 2002). The specialist needs to work alongside the subject teachers, so that students see the subject-specific relevance of what they are being taught about writing styles (Warren 2003).

The learning support services, including library and IT staff, studio and laboratory technicians, also have a role to play. They are often the first point of contact for students when teachers are not available. Librarians help students to learn how to access information effectively, how to make judgements about relevance, currency and authority of the texts they access, and how to select what they need from the vast array of resources available on any topic. Developing these skills is essential for the successful student, and all students will need to learn them not only at an introductory level but also as they progress to more sophisticated literature searches for dissertations and theses. Information technology skills are equally important. Although more students enter higher education with advanced IT skills, this is not true for all, and many older students and those from developing countries will initially have more to learn. A diagnostic test run by IT staff can reveal which students need this extra support.

Other support services – counselling, child-care facilities, health services, specialist support for students with disabilities, residential services, financial advice – all play an essential role in supporting students to become full members of the learning community and prevent certain groups of students being excluded for reasons that have nothing to do with their capacity to benefit from their course of study. These services provide support that academics do not normally have the skills, or the time, to provide. They do, however, need to be embedded in the organizational strategy of support for students if they are to be effective and proactive (Layer 1995; Rowley 1996).

That students have a variety of motivations for being a student, not all of them to do with learning, is nothing new. A common distinction derived from Dweck (1999) is between students who have performance goals and those with learning goals. As we discussed in Chapter 1, distinctions can be made between vocational, academic, personal and social goals, each associated with different aims: to get a job, intellectual interest, self-improvement and having a good time (Beaty *et al.* 1997). Of course, individuals can have more than one aim, although, when they conflict, students are forced to prioritize them. Variations in motivation can have a significant effect on student performance and their approach to study (Ramsden 1992; Prosser and Trigwell 1999). In the UK, the personal development planning (PDP) process is a vehicle for assisting students to reflect on their priorities and improve the organization of their work (Jackson and Ward 2001; Gosling 2003).

The range of students' motivations and the disparity between student and faculty/staff aspirations and expectations is a potential difficulty. This calls for sensitivity to differences in students' motivation and orientation to their course and a requirement to devise strategies that are appropriate to the needs and aspirations of different students and different programmes (Rustin 2001). Ways of demonstrating this kind of sensitivity include relating academic theory to authentic work-related situations, providing opportunities for students to use their preferred learning style, valuing students' own experience where possible, utilizing experiential learning, for example through community-based projects, and paying attention to developing students' employability.

We know that students who are alienated from the environment in which they are required to study are less likely to succeed. Students who fail repeatedly are likely to become alienated and discouraged. Students with low self-esteem will be less effective as learners (Bandura 1986). There are a number of strategies that teachers can adopt to address these difficulties. A helpful strategy is the use of student-collaborative learning such as peer-led action learning sets, supplemental instruction or peer-assisted learning (Fleming and Capstick 2003). Encouraging students to have more control over their work is another strategy. For example, students can be encouraged to consider and set their own goals, use learning contracts to define their own projects and learning outcomes (Stephenson and Laycock 1993), and employ self-assessment and self-reflective writing tasks to become more aware of their own approaches to study (Cottrell 2001).

Providing feedback to students

The idea of teachers and students working together to create a learning community requires that students receive feedback on their progress from their teachers. We know that receiving feedback is important in any learning process. Research has shown that formative feedback does improve learning and, what is more, the gains in achievement are 'among the largest ever reported for educational achievements' (Black and Wiliam cited in Knight 2002: 150).

In his study of feedback to history students, Hyland (2000) found that while students' valued feedback, many were disappointed with the feedback they received. Comments focused on the negative aspects of their performance and often gave little indication of how students could improve their work. Teachers reported that as many as one in six students left course work uncollected: but if the experience of reading the feedback is so dispiriting, this is perhaps not so surprising (Hyland 2000). Again, the NSSE study in the USA found that only just over half students 'received prompt feedback from faculty' (NSSE 2002).

The work of Knight and Yorke (2003) and Hounsell (2003) reflects the experience of many when they argue that university teachers find it difficult to provide formative feedback to students within a semester time frame. Feedback at the end of a module/course is often 'received too late for students' subsequent choice of study . . . and may also be insufficient, if only given as a mark, or grade, for learning on subsequent modules' (Knight and Yorke 2003: 35).

The importance of formative feedback is that it connects directly to the emotional and attitudinal factors relating to students' self-esteem, beliefs about self-efficacy, motivation and engagement (Bandura 1986). Knight and Yorke (2003) utilize the work of Dweck (1999) to suggest that the extent to which students believe that their efforts can make a difference to their success is an important factor in their motivation. Students 'best placed to develop are those who tend to see practical intelligence as malleable, not fixed' (Yorke and Knight 2004: 28). Students who believe they can succeed, principally by their own efforts, will be more encouraged to work hard than those who believe their success or failure is determined by factors outside their control. The teacher should, wherever possible, provide opportunities for students to succeed, even if by small incremental steps, and to demonstrate how their own efforts brought about this success.

Hounsell (2003) has identified three trends in improving student feedback: (a) more explicit criteria and the use of assignment proformas; (b) greater student involvement using self- and peer assessment; and (c) greater use of collaborative assignments, presentations and posters which all have the effect of bringing assessment and feedback into a more public domain. Knight (2002) suggests that feedback needs to be interactive, purposeful, relative to criteria, developmentally useful, understood, timely and appropriate to students' conceptions.

How, then, can more effective formative feedback, within the tight time constraints of semesters, be achieved? Here are some ideas:

- Keep assignments, exercises, or tests, short, and administer them and provide feedback within class time.
- Use the virtual learning environment or email to receive and comment on work.
- Use multiple choice tests, which can be provided online, to test breadth of knowledge.
- Employ classroom assessment (Angelo and Cross 1993).
- Have students mark each other's work; you only need to mark a sample.
- Use the assignment as part of preparation for the next class session; for example, 'prepare a presentation'.
- Have the students display their work on posters instead of collecting work to mark. All students assess the posters against agreed criteria.
- Use computer-based assessment. Some packages will provide the students with feedback on how well they have done without any marking by the teacher.

When the curriculum is fragmented into courses or modules it is important that students have an opportunity to review their overall progress and to record their achievements. This is another function of personal development planning which has been shown to be effective as a way of promoting a dialogue with students about their learning achievements, provided it is supported by academic staff and introduced with careful planning (Jackson and Ward 2001; Gosling 2003).

Ethnicity and inclusive learning communities

Recognition of greater cultural and ethnic diversity is an important dimension of the modern university. In the USA, the debate about multiculturalism, affirmative action and 'Eurocentrism' has been a feature of the higher education system since the 1960s (Chism 2002). By comparison, in the UK, the debate has been less prominent and rarely features in the literature on higher education. This is despite the fact that the number of students from 'ethnic minority groups' is now significant (14 per cent) and continuing to grow. There are two reasons for this growth. Firstly, the composition of the student body is reflecting the racial and ethnic diversity of an increasingly multicultural society, and secondly, a globalized higher education attracts many international students to universities in the developed world. These national, cultural and ethnic differences make particular demands on higher education institutions, but also provide opportunities.[4]

What does building an inclusive learning community require in this context? Firstly, the curriculum is one area that needs examination to ensure that it is more representative of writers who are outside the 'Eurocentric' paradigm. Secondly, deeply ingrained forms of 'institutional racism' need to be challenged (Law *et al.* 2004). Thirdly, it means democratizing decision-making and consultation processes. We recognize that achieving change of this kind is difficult. We therefore suggest some directions rather than arrival points. We do, however, believe that any attempt to improve teaching and learning across an institution must take account of the diversity of students and staff and find ways of ensuring that the marginalized groups are not excluded, whether this is an intended or unintended consequence of decisions taken for other reasons.

There are a number of reasons why approaches of this type are controversial. The traditional liberal position has emphasized the universal values of rights, duties and responsibilities and plays down cultural and other forms of 'difference'. It favours a 'colour-blind' or 'neutrality paradigm' (Ofori-Dankwa and Lane 2000) approach in which all students are treated 'equally', ignoring ethnicity, religious, sexual orientation and other forms of self-avowed identities. Taking this view, the only obligation on universities is to ensure that no student is overtly disadvantaged by any act of unfair discrimination or individual prejudice. It places responsibility on individual academic staff or students to bring complaints that identify instances of unfair discrimination. The norms in admissions policies, teaching and assessing are assumed to be operating in favour of all students until proved otherwise. The prevalence of this view explains why 'there has been very little evidence of systematic attempts concerned with addressing racism and cultural and religious diversity in higher education' (Law 2003: 519).

All of the classifications used in this debate are themselves contested, terms such as 'ethnic minorities', 'people of colour', 'multiculturalism', 'racism', 'harassment' and 'discrimination'. The challenge of recognizing cultural difference and individual uniqueness without also abandoning all commitments to universal values of respect and equality of rights, for example, appears, in the words of Hall, to have 'outrun our current political vocabularies' (cited in McLennan 2001: 989).

A recent trend in the UK has been the emergence of 'patterns of ethnic segregation and segmentation' (Law 2003) in higher education. The great majority of UK students from minority ethnic groups are to be found in a relatively small number of institutions (Connor *et al.* 2004). The dominance of the 'majoritarian' culture in most institutions means that issues of inclusivity are rarely raised, and yet recent research found wide-ranging institutional racism and experiences of everyday racism among staff and students (Law *et al.* 2002). In this research, over 20 per cent of academic staff and students surveyed across 20 departments reported experiences of racism, although these instances were rarely brought to the surface through institutional procedures. Adia (1996: 56) also found that 32 per cent of 'ethnic minority' and 23 per cent of white students agreed or strongly agreed that 'there is racism and stereotyping within my university/college'. The consequences, as one senior academic put it, is that 'it is difficult for in-comers to feel connected to their values'.

'Racism is not overt but subtle in its manifestations – assumptions made and language used in documentation and professional dialogue. Women in the university face the same dilemmas' (Law 2003: 9). The same might be said of other minority groups such as students with disabilities and gay students, but here we consider actions that can be taken to address issues of ethnicity, religion and nationality. Many of the same principles apply in creating equality for all disadvantaged groups. A necessary first step is to ensure that there are policies and guidelines that make clear the university's stance on equal opportunities and anti-harassment. As a minimum, students and academic staff need to have a formal complaints procedure in order to seek redress when they feel that they have suffered unfair discrimination. They must feel confident that they can raise issues without penalty, and that also relies on creating the right ethos across the institution. Students making use of the anti-harassment procedures may need specialist advice and guidance.

If there is to be a serious attempt to change the culture of the institution, it must deal with issues in the organization of teaching and learning. A difficult but essential part of the process is to initiate a debate about the possibility of racism, or other kinds of prejudice, in the curriculum. Within the framework of multiculturalism the apparently 'neutral' or 'universal' values of modernity are thought to be 'heavily marked by specifically Western prejudices . . .' (McLennan 2001: 986). The consequences are that cultures that do not conform to western forms of 'reason, science and liberalism' are perceived as inferior. This debate continues and the implications for the curriculum have to be a matter for each subject area to decide.

What is at issue here is 'the politics of recognition'. 'Enlarging and changing the curriculum is essential not so much in the name of a broader culture for everyone as in order to give due recognition to the hitherto excluded' (Taylor 1995: 65). Inclusivity requires that we examine the curriculum specifically to ensure that the histories of minorities are not being excluded. It has been argued that much of higher education is racist because of the omission of values from other cultures.

Some would go further than this and argue that more positive steps should be taken to address the question of students' cultural identity. On this view students need to be informed about their histories, including the experience of slavery and colonialism, current issues of inequality, and of positive role models in order to build a strong sense of their group identity.

An inclusive university that takes seriously the idea of democratizing knowledge, which we discussed in Chapter 1, should ensure that there are opportunities for students to explore these ideas. For the majority of students, what is more important is that a range of actions are taken which ensure that recognition is given to all cultures, races, ethnicities and disadvantaged groups. Some ideas for taking this forward are:

- ensure that diverse perspectives are encouraged and valued in discussion and writing;
- encourage students to talk to others different from themselves within classroom activities;
- ensure that bibliographies reflect a range of perspectives;
- use teaching methods that encourage students from all groups to participate;
- ensure that placements and work-based learning do not subject students to discrimination;
- monitor assessment and results to check that fairness to all groups is demonstrated;
- ensure the university calendar recognizes major cultural and religious holidays;
- ensure that university publications do not contain assumptions about the ethnicity of the readers;
- provide specialist counselling, advice and support services;
- provide places for all faiths to carry out acts of worship.

Carter *et al.* (1999) argued that, to counter institutional racism in higher education, institutions needed commitment from the top down and recognition that racism is an issue for everyone and not simply the concern of black and minority ethnic academic staff and students. Attention needs to be given to the composition of interview panels for appointments and promotions, and panel members should receive training on fair interview techniques. The outcomes of processes like this need to be carefully monitored to provide information to the institution on whether its processes are being operated in a non-discriminatory manner.

An aspect of democratization and inclusivity that is often missing is the opportunity for students and staff from all groups to be consulted and to be heard. We have shown in Chapter 2 how learning communities, learning sets and networks play a vital role in developing the learning university. These can be used specifically to promote debate between students and staff on matters such as a Eurocentric curriculum. In this way, difficult issues are shown to be open to debate and student views, ideas and opinions from all groups are being recognized and valued.

Evaluation and monitoring

Any institution that is committed to becoming more inclusive must be willing to put resources into adequate collection of data on student entry, progression and achievement. The purposes of tracking students are to identify trends at several levels:

- within programmes of study (or degrees);
- within individual modules and courses by cohorts;
- within categories of students: full-time, part-time, face-to-face and distance learners, age on entry, previous educational experience and qualifications, sex, ethnicity.

Tracking needs also to operate at the level of the individual student so that those responsible for academic guidance can have easy access to information on each student's progress.

Conclusion: A framework for creating inclusive learning communities

We conclude with a framework for creating inclusive learning communities which summarizes the discussion in this chapter. The framework has six categories of activity: student engagement, flexibility of provision, quality of teaching and assessment, learning development, personal support, and equity in processes and relationships.

- *Student engagement.* Student engagement is not only a characteristic of an inclusive learning environment but also the best predictor of student success. The single biggest factor influencing students' success is the time students devote to educationally purposeful activity. Involvement in studying, attending class and other educationally related activities enhances student academic and personal development. Institutions need to have multiple strategies for maximizing students' sense of belonging, recognizing and respecting them as individuals and as members of groups, and encouraging interaction among students and with academic staff. Students will only feel they belong if their personal histories and identities are valued and used as the reference point for their learning and their relationship with the institution.

- *Flexibility of provision.* As students' lives become more complex, balancing home, work and study, there needs to be flexibility in their relationship with the institution: flexibility in modes of attendance, pace of study, time allowed to complete programmes of study, possibilities to interrupt and return to study; flexibility in place, by using open and distance learning methods, recognizing learning that takes place outside the university, for example in the workplace; flexibility in admissions processes, recognizing alternative routes to learning and valuing a variety of experience and the opportunity for students to accumulate credit for learning that has been achieved wherever it occurred (see discussion in Chapter 5).
- *Quality of teaching and assessment.* The characteristics of good teaching make a critical contribution to achieving inclusivity. Features of good teaching include building on students' experience, starting from where the students are, encouraging student's use of collaborative learning and enquiry-based learning through group work, supporting students to become autonomous learners, providing timely and useful formative feedback, being clear about the goals of the learning expected, aligning teaching and assessment with the stated goals. The seven principles of good practice provide a good basis for determining teaching quality. They include: encourage contact between staff and students; develop reciprocity and cooperation among students; use active learning techniques; give prompt feedback; emphasize time on task; communicate high expectations; respect diverse talents and ways of learning (Chickering and Ehrmann 1996; see discussion in Chapter 6). Inclusivity does not imply any lowering of standards; on the contrary, challenging students is an important aspect of good teaching.
- *Learning development.* All students have learning development needs, and inclusive institutions must be proactive in anticipating these needs and providing a structured and supportive environment for them to be met. This approach rejects the idea of a 'remedial' service detached from departments. A learning development approach is best achieved from within each students' subject or professional area, but supported through using the advice of specialist staff.
- *Personal support.* Students' personal circumstances can, and do, become a barrier to their successful inclusion in study. A supportive campus

environment, or online services for distance students, is essential. Students need guidance and advice to give them the best chance of succeeding, from pre-entry, through the entry process, on course and on exit.

Adequate services can be a critical factor in enabling students to stay on course such as, support for students with disabilities, health, counselling, careers, child-care and financial management.

- *Equity in processes and relationships.* Inclusivity implies fairness. Nothing alienates marginal groups more quickly than if they feel they have been treated unfairly by being ignored, denigrated or discriminated against. Transparent processes in admissions, assessment, application of rules and procedures best demonstrate equity. Teachers need to be alert to unintentional ways in which unfairness might be perceived, for example in giving and receiving attention in class, allowing some students to miss deadlines, by ignoring differences in students' past educational experience, in language used and examples given. Fairness is also about ensuring that students are taught in ways that recognize their learning development needs.

In this chapter we have suggested that improving teaching and learning across an institution requires attention to the ways in which students are made to feel included within their programme of study. We have also noted that this requires going beyond 'fair access' to applying principles of inclusivity. This implies taking a proactive approach to anticipating the learning development needs of all students, whatever their previous educational experience or their social group. Minority groups rightly demand to be recognized and to be included in the curriculum. Students lacking the 'cultural and social capital' to make the transition into higher education deserve to be given the support that will increase their opportunity to succeed. There is an increasing need to pay attention to students' learning development as they make the transition from novice to membership of their chosen community of practice. Becoming more inclusive is the responsibility of everyone in the university.

Notes

1. In the UK, the government took responsibility for full funding of universities between 1946 and 1979 (Jarvis 2001: 31), and in the USA there has long been a wider tradition of private colleges and universities.
2. Students' home 'neighbourhood' was identified by HEFCE using their home postcode. These data were used to identify low participation neighbourhoods.
3. Lave and Wenger developed their theoretical standpoint from studies of 'apprenticeships' in a variety of social contexts across the world, including tailors in Liberia, midwives of the Yucatan Mayan people in Mexico, navy quartermasters in the USA, butchers in the USA and people attending Alcoholics Anonymous.

4. In the UK, the recent application of the Race Relations (Amendment) Act 2000 to higher education places obligations on institutions to have an active policy to promote good race relations and ensure that no student is disadvantaged or suffers harassment or discrimination because of his or her race or ethnicity.

5

Supporting Change in Course Design

> Those who can understand the informal yet structured, experiential yet social, character of learning – and can translate their insight into designs in the service of learning – will be the architects of our tomorrow.
>
> Wenger 1998: 225

In this chapter we examine some of the issues involved in developing course design across the institution.[1] We define course design as the creation of a connected series of structured experiences intended to achieve learning. In this definition, designing teaching and assessment methods are included within 'course design' as well as the formulation of aims and/or learning outcomes, course content, and the design of an environment to foster learning.

We begin by considering some of the influences on the selection, organization, delivery and assessment of the curriculum. These contextual factors frame the thinking of teachers in higher education and are sometimes perceived as barriers to change. We consider three broad theoretical grounds for improving course design and the levers for change in respect of the curriculum and how it is taught and assessed. Finally we discuss how changing course design can be supported.

What are the principal influences on course design?

There are many factors that influence how a subject is taught, what is taught and how it is assessed. A useful way to conceptualize the factors that influence course design is to think of them as being at three levels: the macro, meso and micro. At the macro level are the factors that impact nationally and international, such as the trends we discussed in Chapter 1, for example massification, globalization and marketization. At this level are the broad political, social and economic influences that impact on higher education.

The meso level is constituted by influences deriving from the department and the institution. These include, for example, the culture of the department, the physical location, the student profile and institutional policies. At the micro level are the influences on individual academics, including their personal theories of teaching, their beliefs about the subject and their professional knowledge. We will be examining how these factors impact in more detail later in this chapter. Various attempts to summarize the complex interrelationship between all these factors have been made: see, for example, Tooey (1999); Entwistle (2000); Light and Cox (2001).

Entwistle (2000) conceptualizes the teaching–learning process as a relationship between:

- Student's characteristics:
  - approach to learning: prior knowledge, intellectual abilities, learning style, personality
  - approach to studying: attitudes to course, motivation, work habits and study skills
- Teaching characteristics:
  - approach to teaching: level, pace, structure, clarity, explanation, enthusiasm, empathy, teaching methods
  - selection of teaching methods: lectures, discussion groups, practicals
  - selection of content
- Departmental characteristics:
  - policy on teaching: study skills support, workload, freedom of choice, assessment procedure, feedback to students
  - course design objectives, learning materials, library provision.

Other important influences on course design include: external pressures from employers, professional bodies, accreditation and quality agencies; internal policy drivers relating to employability and widening access; and political commitments, such as inclusivity and learner emancipation.

Biggs (1999) has also proposed an interactive systems approach which identifies influences at three points of time: the factors that impact before learning takes place (presage factors), the process during learning, and the product or outcome of learning (see Figure 5.1).

What are the perceived constraints on improving course design?

Given the complexity of the influences on course design, it is not surprising that bringing about change in this area of the university is difficult. Attempting to improve course design is further complicated by the perception that many of these influencing factors are fixed and immovable barriers that prevent the possibility of any significant development.

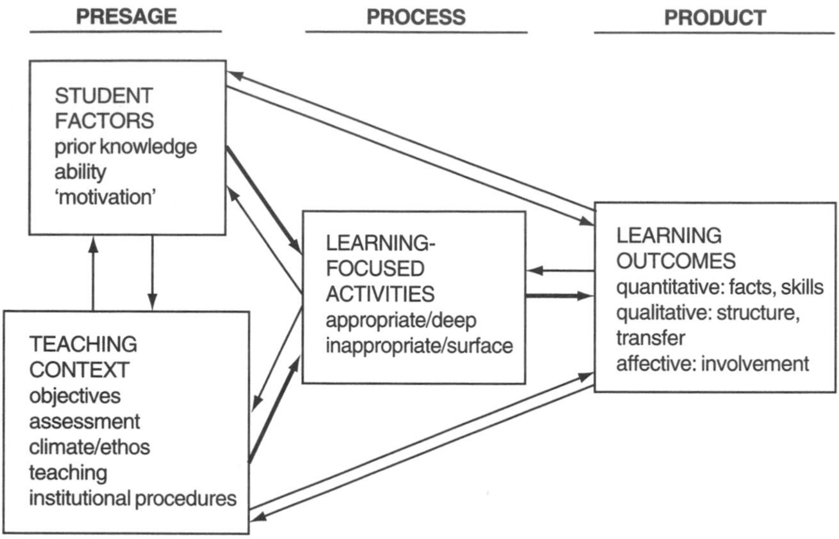

Figure 5.1 The 3P model of teaching and learning

Let us begin to unpack these complexities by considering a hierarchy of structural influences, ranging from the international context through to local political structures (see Table 5.1). The agents of the political authority exercise varying levels of control that reflect historical and legal relationships between the state and higher education. Within the institution there will be influences deriving from its mission, its distinctive values and culture (Schein 1992; McNay 1995), and power relations between different levels of the executive and the constituent parts of the institution. As we saw in Chapter 3, the notion of a subject or discipline identity is mediated through a department, faculty or school, which will have its own character and subculture (Moore 2003). But departments are not homogenous or monolithic structures. There are often subsections within a department which may be demarcated by different programmes of study or sub-disciplines (Becher and Trowler 2001) which will influence the parameters within which decisions about course design will be taken. At the lowest level of course/module the individual teacher or a team of teachers can have the most apparent autonomy, although influenced by the hierarchy above it.

The formal structures of higher education, as represented in a general way in Table 5.1, create in both explicit and implicit ways assumptions about the nature and purpose of higher education and tend to shape what is taken for granted about how to teach and what assessment methods to use. Features that are peculiar to a particular system are taken for granted as beyond challenge. For a long time, for example, the three-hour, unseen essay type examination had this status in the UK, whereas in other countries assessment might be equally unchallenged but quite different, such as multiple-choice

Table 5.1 Hierarchy of contexts for curriculum design

Curriculum design context	*Influences*
International context	Global market, international agreements (e.g. the Bologna Agreement)
State or national framework	Government or state policy, national quality agency (e.g. QAAHE[a]), funding councils, legal framework
Institutional level	Institutional mission and culture, registry/quality assurance department, learning and teaching strategy
Subject/professional area	Subject associations, professional bodies, subject benchmarking statements
Programme of study/award	Professional bodies, programme specification, peer review, student demand
Module	Course design, validation requirements, level descriptors, student feedback

[a] Quality Assurance Agency for Higher Education.
Source: Gosling and Moon (2003). Copyright © SEEC.

tests in the USA or oral examination in Italy or Russia. The honours degree classification in the UK is another example of a system-specific idiosyncrasy that has been taken to be sacrosanct and is only now being challenged. When these taken-for-granted assumptions are not made explicit, they often remain unquestioned. As we shall see, one strategy for bringing about change in the curriculum is to make these assumptions explicit and therefore open them up to debate and discussion (Mann 2003; Sharpe 2004).

There are a number of formal structures that influence course design in most national contexts. The principal relevant structures are, typically:

- *National qualifications framework (NQF).* NQFs are designed to define the levels of degrees in terms of what students are expected to achieve. They are typically outcomes-based and require assessment criteria to be specified for each unit of learning. Most NQFs include a structure for the award of credit(s). In some countries, a single framework controls the whole range of programmes, from basic literacy through to postdoctoral degrees. In others, as in the UK, there are separate but interrelated qualification frameworks for schools, further education and higher education.
- *International agreements.* In an increasingly global market for higher education there have been moves towards attempting to recognize international equivalencies. For example, the Bologna Declaration of June 1999 is an attempt to achieve closer comparability between levels of qualifications within the European Community, but the wide variation between the traditions and cultures of higher education in the national systems of European countries are significant obstacles to implementing the details of the Declaration (Corbett 2003).

- *Credit frameworks.* Most of the curriculum structures developed in tertiary education over the years have assumed that the student will follow a particular route towards a specific qualification at a single institution. Modular programmes, already common in the USA, began to be introduced in the UK in the 1970s using credit accumulation and have begun to challenge the traditional 'supply model' by something closer to a 'demand model' (Robertson 1994; Allen and Layer 1995). Although modular frameworks create the opportunity for greater choice to students, institution-wide or faculty-wide, programmes typically impose some restrictions on course design. Each unit of learning has to be assigned a volume of learning at a given academic level, normally using an outcomes-based credit framework. This means that course design must be described within a template that allows the number of credits and level to be judged. Institutional regulations governing the length and size of modules/courses tend to impose greater restrictions on courses operating within a modular framework than the requirements of a credit framework per se, although the two tend to be associated in the minds of some academics (Allen and Layer 1995).
- *Professional associations.* The professional associations that control entry to professions such as law, medicine and engineering, are another influence on course design and are often seen as significant constraints on what is possible in innovation in course design. Academics in subjects geared to achieving professional accreditation refer to the requirements of professional bodies as a reason for denying the value or the feasibility of innovation in course design. But no formal description of a course, whether it be of input (curriculum) or output (learning outcomes), can completely specify every aspect of course design. In an output design there will be alternative ways of reaching the specified learning outcomes. In externally examined systems there are different ways of preparing students for the examination. In an input specification there can be different ways of teaching and examining the syllabus.
- *Quality assurance and accreditation systems.* The extent of the influence of national or regional bodies on course design varies among national systems, but in all cases the influence is exercised through both formal and informal systems. The formal or regulatory system will set parameters that will limit what can and cannot be done for a course to be approved. But there are also informal limitations which are determined by the norms of the academic community, for example through peer review processes such as the external examiner system in the UK and the institutional accreditation process in the USA. Institutional quality assurance regimes can sometimes be more restrictive than the national system requires and can be experienced as a significant barrier to change and innovation. According to Morley (2003a), the bureaucratic requirements of quality assurance systems are serving a disciplinary function, creating a culture of compliance and negativity that is damaging to academic culture. As Foucault has argued, the twin processes of 'normalization' and 'surveillance' constitute

two main instruments of disciplinary power (Olssen *et al.* 2004), and both have been employed to enforce norms in teaching and learning. We return to this issue in Chapter 8.

- *Political–legal framework*. Each higher education system operates within a specific political and legal framework which can determine curriculum content and even methods of teaching. Typically, the political influence operates through two main mechanisms: legislation that imposes obligations on universities, and funding processes. Legal requirements, for example to make provision for disabled students or to establish a race equality policy, are potentially enforceable through the courts, whereas funding regimes can exercise a more direct influence. The development of specific subject curricula can be determined by making funding available for some subjects and not others, although funding can influence university behaviour in many more subtle ways (Barnes 1999).

There are informal influences on course design that operate through political debate about higher education, its goals and function. The political rhetoric is often backed up by funding initiatives which create incentives for universities to behave in particular ways. For example, in recent years in the UK, programmes to develop the employability of undergraduates have been supported by a number of funding incentives, such as Enterprise in Higher Education (Jones and Little 1999). There has been an enormous increase in courses which either explicitly or implicitly teach and assess skills believed to enhance student employability (Gordon 2004) while others have argued that much of the existing curriculum has the potential to develop employability skills (Knight and Yorke 2003). Coupled with this concern with employability has been the growth of work experience placements and internships in courses which had not traditionally been linked to the workplace, such as cultural studies, fine art and politics. These trends, or fashions, penetrate to particular subjects and topics within those subjects. Sometimes these trends are driven by student demand or, at least, academics' perception of what will attract students. Sometimes the trends reflect shifts in the profession or research communities.

Discipline cultures and course design

Academic staff are sometimes portrayed as being unwilling to contemplate change in course design not only because of the constraints we have been considering but also because of assumptions created through the socialization process through which teachers have been introduced to the subject in their undergraduate and postgraduate studies. The culture of the subject is reproduced through many social practices, as we have seen in Chapter 3. The particularities of the cultural reproduction of subject identity are strongly influenced by the dominance of a small number of elite institutions that undertake the majority of postgraduate research supervision. Indeed, it has been said that 25 per cent of all academics entering the profession in the UK have received their postgraduate training at one institution: Oxford University (Gibbs, personal communication, 2004). If the other three or four major research universities are included, then it can be seen how the cultural identity of subjects is being reproduced through a small number of universities who are the providers of new academics for the university sector.

The assumptions embedded in subject cultures impact on and shape course design in many hidden ways. They often determine what academics think is possible and what can and cannot be done with curriculum. The 'professional knowledge', as discussed in Chapter 1, that individual academics hold about course design is derived largely from their individual experience. Here is an academic speaking about course design:

> I think if people are very experienced they're probably redesigning a course, or designing a course, based on a great deal of experience and probably doing something that is very good not informed by theories or models but because they're intelligent analytical people with a great deal of experience.
>
> It sounds quite arrogant really. I didn't feel I needed to draw on outside things. I could see there were really quite predictable problems that were likely to surface very soon and I had taught on pioneering, but quite different excellent courses of this kind, but I'd also read the course documentation, wider variety so I felt very familiar with the type of course and type of issues at different institutions already.
>
> (Oliver and Plewes 2002: 8)

Although it would be wrong to generalize from the limited sample derived from one elite institution in the Oliver and Plewes study, it is striking that academics do not see a need to refer to research into student learning or any pedagogical theory to inform their choice of teaching or assessment methods. Indeed, there is a clear preference for prioritizing the authority of personal experience over any such theorizing. Any change process in relation to course design must start from and respect the highly situated experiential knowledge base of individual academics (Shay 2004).

There is some evidence that younger academics who have participated in a course of initial professional development are more willing to take account of research into teaching and learning (Henkel 2000), and also evidence that they have, as a consequence, better teaching skills (Gibbs and Coffey 2004). According to Rust (2000: 256): 'Of the skills they most appreciated having learnt on the course, the skills of planning and course design were the most valued.'

However, another limitation on the capacity of universities to undertake change in course design that affect both experienced and new teachers is the conflicting demands of teaching and research. The pressures of seeking funding for and undertaking research limit the time and energy available to devote to innovating in the curriculum.

> The changing student intake has placed an emphasis on the need for pedagogical and curriculum change and, consequently, on the professional identity of the university teacher as teacher, capable of developing and marketing innovative programmes. At the same time, however, the changing conditions of academic work have placed a premium on the professional identity of the university teacher as researcher, capable of attracting external funds within an increasingly competitive research culture.
>
> (Nixon *et al.* 2001: 232)

The impact of this role conflict is very significant. There is a real fear among many very good teachers, who are also active researchers with a reputation to maintain, that to devote large amounts of time to curriculum innovation is a distraction that could have a negative impact on their careers. This largely explains the reluctance of many academic staff with a strong interest in teaching to apply for funding or awards which could take them away from their research.

There does seem to have been some considerable variation between disciplines in the extent to which they are open to change. The explanation for this lies with the notion of pedagogical community and 'pedagogic identity' (Bernstein 2000). Bernstein characterizes some pedagogical communities as having what he calls a 'restricted identity' (RI) which is shaped by grand narratives of the past.

> These narratives are appropriately recontextualised to stabilise that past in the future . . . The bias, focus and management here leads to a tight control over discursive *inputs* of education, that is its content, *not* over its *outputs*. R.I.'s are formed by hierarchically ordered, strongly bounded, explicitly stratified and sequenced discourses and practices.
>
> (Bernstein 2000: 66–7)

Some subjects are more 'decentred', have much less tightly drawn boundaries and are more future orientated. Examples of these might be geography and health studies. They will be less resistant to change and more open to ideas from a variety of sources.

The general conclusion is that it is wrong to think that any change to course design will impact in the same way on different pedagogical communities. Where the pedagogical identity of the subject, such as philosophy, theology and classics, is formed by beliefs about the past, any change that threatens to destabilize the narrative of the past will be regarded with suspicion. Ideas about change, perceived to be originating from outside the pedagogical community, will be resisted and regarded as alien. Also, the tight management over inputs means that routes of access into the community are limited, partly because they are hierarchically controlled, partly because definitions of a person acceptable to the community are very narrowly drawn. Credibility, another word for legitimacy, is therefore hard to win without being 'one of us'. Even someone who is, or who has been, a teacher within the pedagogical community will be regarded with suspicion if they take on an alternative identity defined by something regarded as external to the subject.

There is equally tight control over acceptable discourses. This means that terms and idioms drawn from discourses deriving from outside the pedagogical community, for example 'learning outcomes' or 'benchmarking', will be received with hostility irrespective of any merit they may or may not have in other contexts. Sensitivity to cues in the language that give away their external origin will be heightened. The anxiety that the subject is being colonized by an external discourse will provoke a variety of strategies: outright resistance, subversion or passive acquiescence (Henkel 2001). Those engaging in these strategies will be regarded as 'loyal' and will be supported strongly by colleagues, even when it would appear to be against their own interests, for example leading to the closure of a department.

Institutions, and the departments within them, also exert a powerful influence on course design. Formally, universities exert their power over the curriculum through the process of validation or initial approval. Informally, influence occurs through conversations and peer networks that maintain social norms about what is allowable and what is approved. The exercise of this informal power can create 'a serious loss of personal identity' when academics feel themselves 'forced to fit into some mould' (Walker 2001a: 53). Sometimes academics can only introduce the course they want to teach by moving to another institution that either favours their preferred approach or is more tolerant of different approaches. For change to occur in the face of a dominant culture which is opposed to innovation requires a combination of individuals willing to challenge their socialization in a subject and an institutional and departmental context that supports, or at least allows, the possibility of innovation (Hannan and Silver 2000; Knight and Trowler 2001). We consider how this supportive context can be developed later in this chapter.

We have seen that there is a complex set of forces, some structural and some cultural, which impact on course design. Some of these forces will operate in a conservative way, tending to reinforce the status quo. Others, such as legislative change or shifts in funding, can be powerful forces for change. However, before we proceed with a discussion of supporting change to bring about improvements in course design, we need to examine what constitutes improvement in this context. There needs to be good grounds for believing that it is necessary to rethink the traditional approach to subject teaching and course design.

Challenges to traditional forms of course design

Traditional forms of teaching led by subject content continue to dominate in higher education. This has been challenged in three ways. The first challenge derives from consideration of the epistemology of the subject, the second from considerations about theories of teaching, and the third from ideas about course design. We briefly review each of these three challenges.

Each discipline has some distinctive conceptions about what constitutes appropriate discourse, what is 'knowing', and what is skilled performance. As we saw in Chapter 4, what counts as adequate evidence in support of a knowledge claim also varies and, typically, there are discourses that are characteristic of its approach to creating and verifying knowledge. These discourses, as Foucault has argued, 'assume certain historical forms in which specific groups and ideologies have dominance' (quoted in Taylor *et al.* 2002). Students have to learn through the curriculum within their subject area the unwritten rules of these discourses: how to make statements that carry conviction, if not certainty. As they journey from the subject periphery to become members of a community of practice an important lesson for students to learn is how these epistemological variations impact on conceptions of 'truth', 'argument' and 'research'.

Epistemology influences course design by the extent to which these knowledge claims are hierarchically organized and in the assumptions made about what students need to know, or be able to do, before they can proceed to the next level of knowledge or performance. Sometimes these assumptions are based on the belief that a given area of propositional knowledge is a logical prerequisite for some other area of knowledge, but in other cases it is merely assumed that some sorts of knowledge and understanding are foundational within that subject. This also applies to the skills that students are required to develop within different subject areas. Skills can be ordered in a variety of ways, for example in terms of level of complexity, difficulty of application, or ability to be employed autonomously by the student (SEEC 2003).

Barnett (2000) has argued that the challenges to traditional conceptions of knowledge have led to the situation that he calls 'supercomplexity'. In a postmodern world, Barnett suggests, we can be less confident that expert knowledge assertions cannot be challenged. Alternative structures of thought and of ideologies may entail quite different conclusions even when starting from similar or the same evidence. The extent of 'radical unknowability' (Curzon-Hobson 2002) is a matter of dispute, but whatever position is taken, there is an obligation on teachers in higher education to help students attain the ability to use self-reflective critique about the knowledge they claim to acquire. Knowing is not just about uttering a statement which is true or thought to be true, but also about understanding the evidence which supports the knowledge claim and why that evidence provides appropriate support. It is also about understanding the limitations of our knowledge and appreciating the provisionality of theories and explanations.

When knowledge is understood in this way, the two principal assumptions of the so-called transmission model (Kember and Gow 1994) become untenable: firstly, that knowledge has a determinate reality, and secondly, that knowledge can be transmitted from teacher to students. But many academic staff continue to see their role as 'inputting information' (Murray and

MacDonald 1997) and, as we shall see in more detail in Chapter 6, the use of learning technologies is often founded on a limited understanding of 'delivering learning' (Brown and Duguid 2000). Following our earlier discussion of Lave and Wenger (1991), we have understood learning as a process of an individual interacting in a social context, negotiating and constructing an understanding which necessarily has features in common with others, but which is also uniquely influenced by the individual's own experience and history. It is for this reason that it is a fundamental principle of good course design that the plan for students' learning should relate to and build on the students' existing knowledge, experience and levels of understanding. It is also the reason why students' creating new knowledge is possible. When the discourses of western higher education are opened to new influences of feminism, for example, or from outside the Eurocentric tradition, the elitist assumptions of traditional cultural transmission are challenged and the university can become 'one of the major sites of cultural deconstruction' (Delanty 2001: 63).

The challenge to traditional conceptions of knowledge transmission has serious implications for teaching, the curriculum and assessment. The goal of a higher education curriculum cannot be understood in terms of acquiring a predetermined set of skills and a body of knowledge. It must also be about learning the means to be able to critique existing knowledge claims from a variety of perspectives. It is our view that this aspect, above all others, distinguishes higher from other levels of education.

The second challenge to traditional models of teaching in higher education has derived from work on theories of teaching. Fox (1983) describes 'personal theories of teaching' using the metaphors of 'transfer' and 'shaping' to describe what he regards as 'simple' theories of teaching, and 'travelling' and 'growth' for more 'developed theories'. Similarly, 'presenting information' and 'teaching as transmitting information' are regarded as a less complete conception of teaching by Dall'Alba (1991 cited in Prosser and Trigwell 1999: 143). For Martin and Ramsden (1993), an 'expanding awareness' of teaching requires the teachers to move from an understanding of only themselves and what they are doing, to one in which the content of what is being taught, and students' understanding of that content, are also included. Kember and Gow (1994) make a similar distinction between 'learning facilitation' and 'knowledge transmission'. The schema developed by Trigwell and Prosser (1996) relates conceptions of learning to conceptions of teaching (see also Biggs 1999; Prosser and Trigwell 1999).

These later theories have all been strongly influenced by the 'approaches to learning' literature originally discussed in the 1970s (Marton and Saljo 1976) and further developed by Entwistle and others (see Marton *et al.* 1997). According to this view, whether a student takes a 'surface' or 'deep' approach to study is significantly influenced by the teaching method used. The contention is that a teacher who uses a transmission model of teaching will tend to produce in students a surface approach to study. In their research, and supporting the findings of Kember and Gow (1994), Prosser and Trigwell (1999: 159) found that 'the way university teachers approach their teaching in a range of large first year classes in higher education is associated with the way their students approach their learning in those classes'.

Meanwhile in the USA, working within a different tradition, Barr and Tagg (1995) posited a 'new paradigm for undergraduate education'. The traditional and dominant paradigm they called the Instructional Paradigm. This is centred on the input of the teacher who delivers instruction, offers courses, gives lectures or leads discussions. The object is to 'cover material', namely the content predetermined by the teacher. Assessments are set and graded, privately, by the teacher. Knowledge is assumed to exist 'out there' and is 'delivered' to students who must acquire and retain it. The teacher's expertise is judged by their knowledge of subject content.

In contrast, their new paradigm is the Learning Paradigm, where the purpose shifts from input to output, namely the learning of students. The teacher's role becomes one of creating learning environments and using learning technologies, and the goal one of improving the quality of students' learning. The criteria for success depend not on the quality of the lecture or the teacher but on the quality of the outputs. All academic staff that contribute to students' learning work together with students to 'empower learning'. The Learning Paradigm frames learning holistically, recognizing that the chief agent in the process is the learner. Thus students must be 'active discoverers and constructors of their own knowledge' (Barr and Tagg 1995: 21).

The third challenge to traditional forms of teaching has come from the increasingly influential ideas about outcomes-based curricula, which have a direct conceptual link with the Learning Paradigm and the prioritizing of outcomes over input. Barr and Tagg (1995: 25) speculated that 'if we begin to talk about "learning outcomes" we'll experience frustration at our nearly complete ignorance of what those outcomes are'. Although, in some ways this is a surprising claim, since the 'educational objectives' movement goes back in the American debate to Ralph Tyler in the 1940s, higher education had largely ignored the need to specify outcomes of learning. In more recent times, in the UK, there is a growing consensus that it is the responsibility of the teacher to determine the outcomes the students will achieve and set appropriate assessment to determine whether the outcomes have been met. This is demonstrated through government statements, the requirements of quality agencies, the national qualification framework, and theoretical justifications by Biggs and others.

The objective of good course design in this model is what Biggs (1999) has called 'constructive alignment'. Achieving course alignment means that the three key elements of course design are:

- the planned learning outcomes of a course;
- the learning activities designed to achieve those outcomes; and
- the assessment to determine whether those outcomes have been achieved.

The design should ensure that (a) the assessment methods chosen will measure in a reliable and valid way the extent to which students have achieved the predetermined outcomes, and (b) teaching methods are chosen which will assist students to achieve those outcomes. 'If students are to learn *desired outcomes* in a *reasonably effective manner*, then the teacher's fundamental task is to get students to *engage in learning activities* that are likely to result in their achieving those outcomes' (Shuell 1986: 429).

In addition to these three elements – curriculum objectives, assessment procedures and teaching methods – two other factors are important: the climate that we create in our interactions with the students, and the institutional climate around the rules and procedures we have to follow (Biggs 1999: 25).

This model of instructional design has been called the 'systematic approach to course planning' (D'Andrea 2003: 31). It is based on a five-step approach:

1. Plan intended learning outcomes.
2. Assess students' existing knowledge, personal characteristics, goals, learning styles, reasons for enrolling and motivation.
3. Design teaching/learning units (i.e. subsections of the course).
4. Implement learning/teaching strategies that are geared to the outcomes.
5. Assess whether outcomes have been met.

These steps are set out diagrammatically in Figure 5.2 which includes as a sixth step a revision cycle in which the activities of step 3 (designing the teaching/learning units) may be modified following assessment of the outcomes in step 5.

In addition to the argument that this is a coherent approach to planning teaching, an outcomes-based approach also encourages teachers to make explicit the outcomes of their teaching that would otherwise be implicit. This not only encourages teachers to think more carefully about what they are trying to achieve and to plan their teaching to better achieve those objectives, but also makes the outcomes transparent to the learner and avoids the students having to guess what it is that they are supposed to be learning (D'Andrea 2003). This supports what we said in the previous chapter about demystifying expectations of study in higher education, particularly with respect to students who are not familiar with these.

Learning outcomes, defined as 'statements of what a learner is expected to know, understand and/or be able to demonstrate after completion of a process of learning', (Gosling and Moon 2003) are also an essential part of a credit-based framework. Credit is awarded to students who have successfully demonstrated that they have achieved the learning outcomes and thereby completed the course at a given level of learning. This facilitates the process of credit accumulation and transfer by making the outcomes of learning transparent. This separates assessment from teaching because the student is judged by the learning that has been achieved rather than by how it was achieved. The implication of this is that the student can arrive at the destination by a variety of routes, for example by a mixture of university-based, work-based, full-time and part-time or distance learning. The student might

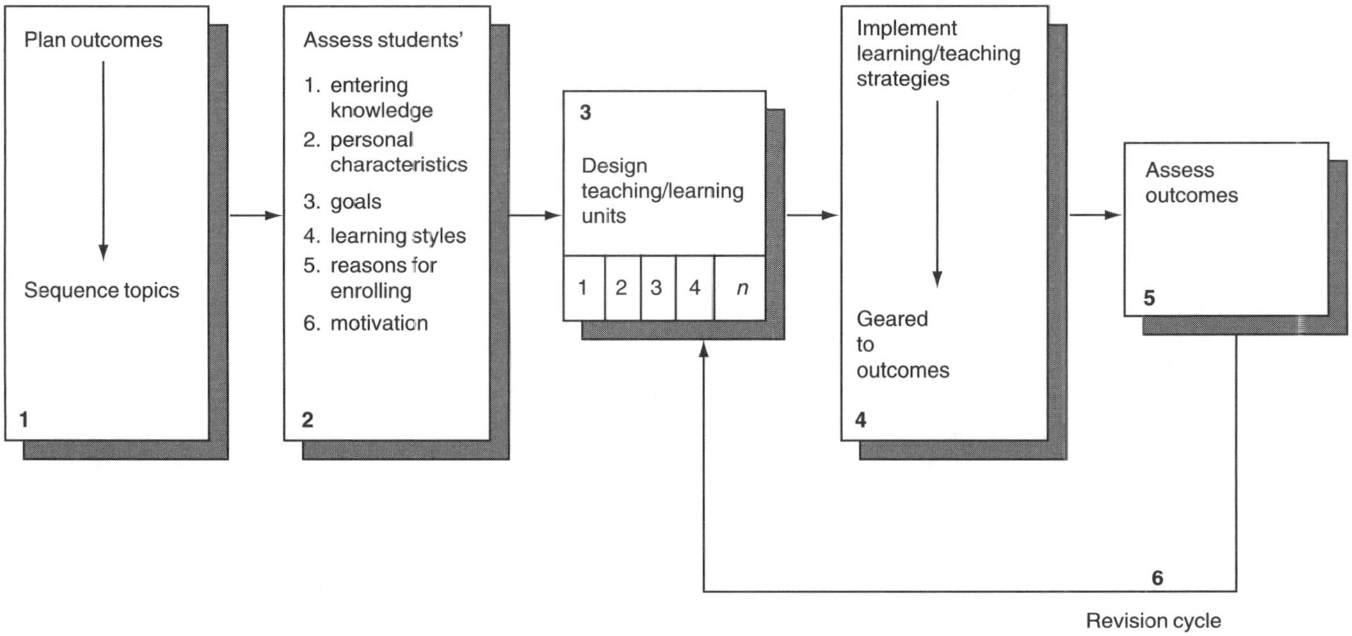

Figure 5.2 Systematic approach to course/module planning
Source: Adapted from Davis (1976) and Wagenaar (1978).

be able to demonstrate that they have already achieved the outcomes and can ask for this learning to be assessed through the Accreditation of Prior or Experiential Learning.

The specification of learning outcomes also creates the possibility of independent and negotiated learning; it allows students to take different routes to the achievement of their degree than by the traditional full-time attendance at a university; and it gives greater control to the student to determine their own pattern of learning (Gosling 2001a). Increasing student choice and flexibility of study can be seen in two ways. The autonomous student exercising choice can be seen as consistent with the ideals of the free independent citizen and it can also be seen as exemplifying the presuppositions of the capitalistic economy that values individualism, enterprise and entrepreneurialism. On this second view, education becomes another form of consumption and knowledge another commodity (Usher *et al.* 1997).

In the older tradition of collegiality, teachers and students have 'intellectual equality' in the search for truth or at least a better understanding of the subject of the course.

> The presumption of intellectual equality has implications for the kind of teaching a university ought to do and the attitude it ought to seek to invoke in students even if they are not, and do not wish to be, prospective research students. It should treat them not as dependants but as intellectual equals who happen to be beginners.
>
> (Evans 1999:10)

The difficulty within a mass higher education system is that the 'presumption of intellectual equality', as Evans calls it, sits uneasily with the experience of teachers teaching large classes of students who have little understanding of the expectations of a university. Furthermore, many students do not see themselves as engaging in the pursuit of intellectual goals but rather as consumers of a system that will provide them with a qualification and consequently the opening into a career outside of academe.

The focus on the pre-specified outcomes of learning rather than on the teaching process is a major reason why this approach is disliked by many academics. For Rowland, teaching should be tolerant of ambiguity, create opportunities rather than determine outcomes. Specifying the outcomes of learning is reductionist and the language positivist, and the transparency of outcomes is a smoke screen for controlling students' learning. 'Reflecting on and writing about learning should preserve or create an openness, which is fundamental part of the practice of learning, rather than the closure of categorisation, which has more to do with oppression and control' (Rowland 2000: 82).

Against this view are the many areas of education where it is entirely appropriate to specify precisely what it is students are expected to be able to know or do and this is not a matter of 'oppression and control' but of acquiring professional expertise. Process rather than product outcomes can be used where more open-ended enquiry is desirable, and where alternative endings should be determined by students themselves and not dictated by the teacher. Process outcomes include, for example, 'being able to use logical argument to defend a position'; 'illustrate an example of oppression through the use of drama'; or 'specify a hypothesis to be tested'.

It is an irony of this debate that both sides claim to be standing for the freedom of the student. The challenge is to find ways of preserving the core values of higher education that we discussed in Chapter 1 while simultaneously opening the opportunities that higher education offers to those groups in society that the selective tradition has systematically excluded.

How is change in course design initiated?

One of the reasons why people have difficulty with the outcomes-based approach to curriculum design and 'constructive alignment' is that neither approach matches the reality of how teachers approach course design. It is rare that course design proceeds by identifying programme outcomes then working back to how they should be assessed and then to how students can be assisted to do the learning to achieve those outcomes. Although this may be rational, it does not reflect the typical pressures that drive changes in course design. 'The fallacy of rationalism is the assumption that the social world can be altered by seemingly rational argument' (Fullan 2001). There are, in practice, many starting points for course design: the experience of students, changes to professional requirements, restructuring of departments, declining student demand, a desire to incorporate the use of learning technologies, among others (D'Andrea 2003).

Typically, change in course design occurs when there is a perceived problem that needs to be addressed. The course design described by Wilkinson (2001) starts from the difficulty that many engineering students have with the mathematical 'concepts and technical skills required in order to reach the level of confidence and ability they need as engineers'. Although Wilkinson has a clear conception of the learning outcomes that students need to acquire, it is the means to achieve these outcomes which is seen as problematical and drives change. In the case study described by Moore (2003), the impulse for changing the curriculum derived from two previously separate departments being brought together and the need to avoid duplication in the various programmes which had previously been taught separately. Some other typical starting points for changes to course design are:

- the head of departments requires changes to a core course that is unpopular with students and has a high failure rate;
- a new teacher takes over an existing course and believes it needs updating to reflect recent changes in the subject;
- the course team now includes, for example, a scholar with a new theoretical perspective who wants to incorporate this approach into the course/module;

- the accreditation or quality assurance panel has criticized an existing course/module, so something has to change;
- student feedback has revealed dissatisfaction with aspects of a course that has declining student numbers;
- the university requires the course to be provided in part-time mode using a virtual learning environment.

What is happening in these examples? It seems that, typically, there needs to be some catalyst or pressure that provokes reconsideration of what already exists. The catalyst or pressure may be:

- from government agencies such as those which control funding, accreditation, quality assurance, student numbers and set the legal framework within which higher education institutions operate; new degrees; new qualification frameworks;
- from students, through student feedback; student success/failure rates; student retention; changes in the composition of student profile, for example growing numbers of international students; changes to students' previous education as a result of opening up access or changes to the school curriculum; student demand for aspects of the subject previously not covered;
- competitive forces between universities for students, research funding and reputation;
- strategic alliances such as partnerships with business, employers, research agencies, other educational institutions such as feeder schools and partner colleges, and professional bodies;
- internal drivers such as the vision of leaders; university mission and sense of its own history and culture; repositioning or restructuring; reduction in resources or new resources made available; new quality assurance requirements;
- changes within the subject or profession, perhaps the emergence of a new theory, a new approach, a new ideological slant; new professional requirements; new methods based on changes to technology; emergence of new sub-fields;
- changes to individuals as a result of shifting personal goals, for example to help students become more involved in their local community; a desire to use new technologies or to incorporate problem-based learning.

Although it often takes pressure to initiate change, it does not follow that all change is for the better. Improving course design, on the other hand, implies some changes to existing practice that are believed to enhance the achievement of chosen goals. As we suggested in The Introduction, the notion of improvements cannot be understood outside of some value framework. There is no one approach that will always constitute an improvement, since the improvement must be designed to achieve an agreed goal within a specific context. Table 5.2 provides some examples of modifications that might be aimed at making improvements towards what we called 'outcome

Table 5.2 Examples of the influence of outcome goals on course design

Subject	*Outcome goal*	*Change to course design*
Psychology	Prepare students for new careers in psychology	Introduce options on forensic psychology, and occupational psychology
Philosophy	Improve employability attributes of graduates	Introduce PDP, including personal skills audit and reflections on skills acquired. Introduce greater diversity of writing required of students
Medicine	Improve students' awareness of disability issues	Adopt problem-based learning approach in which trainee medics are required to interact with people with disabilities
Architecture	Improve alignment between programme goals and assessment methods	Modify assessment to include wider variety of forms of assessment, including group projects and oral presentations
Computer sciences	Reduce plagiarism	Introduce more in-class assessment; vary exercises from year to year, require early drafts to be submitted with final assignment
Literature	Create stronger connections between literature and political values	Students undertake social research and undertake street theatre project
Economics	Students have enhanced ethical awareness about global issues	Internationalize the curriculum; introduce modules on sustainability and factors influencing global poverty

goals' (see discussion in Chapter 1). These are no more than indicative changes though they are based on actual examples. The point here is that real improvement is best achieved when the change is related to an agreed aim that is believed to be important. On the other hand, where course design is being driven simply by a need for compliance with a regulatory change, for example requiring all modules to have learning outcomes, the result is often superficial and does not impact on the students' learning experience. Unless there is a full understanding of the rationale for the change and a significant attempt to engage teachers in a dialogue about its implications then little real improvement is likely to be achieved (Trowler 1998).

How is change in course design supported?

Some of the key features of support for improving course design include:

- *Leadership*: a head of department or course leader who not only supports the change but is also active in bringing others into conversations about improving course design, making time available and providing resources to enable the design process to occur.
- *Institutional culture*: an ethos that encourages dialogue on teaching and learning, and which rewards innovation and does not punish risk taking.
- A *departmental culture* of open debate among the academic team to listen to those with ideas and cooperate with them.
- *Sufficient knowledge and expertise* among members of the team, or access to those with the appropriate experience, so that the repertoire of possible alternative approaches to teaching and assessing the course is known.
- *Technical support* where the changes include learning technologies.
- *A quality assurance regime* which is sufficiently flexible to allow alternative models of teaching and assessment to flourish, including the understanding of any external examiners or reviewers.

Since, as we have seen, many academics consider they have sufficient knowledge of the possible approaches to designing a curriculum, the knowledge requirement may be overlooked. Indeed, the subject specialist knowledge content and ownership of the curriculum development must rest with the teachers who will be implementing the new design. But, as we saw when we considered the professional knowledge that teachers have, much of this expertise is tacit rather than explicit. There is a role here for academics with knowledge of the literature of higher education and practical experience in processes to facilitate change. These academics often have an educational development responsibility within institutions. In this capacity they can promote discussion, creating an environment in which ideas can be exchanged and developed within a critical framework (Walker 2001a). Their role can include collecting relevant data, proposing possible ways of responding to an identified problem and supporting the development that has been initiated from within the departments (Shrives and Bond 2003). They can also act as consultant to curriculum change projects and advise on project management (Segal 2003). Sometimes, specific expertise is required, for example in learning technology or distance learning to advise or provide services such as setting up interactive websites or designing distance learning materials.

Collaboration between individual teachers attempting to bring about change on the one hand, and the educational development staff on the other, can be invaluable, provided there is authentic participation built on trust rather than compliance. This requires clarity on both sides about what the 'consultant' to the departmental development is expected to contribute. Because educational development staff typically have a cross-institutional role they can help to create collaborative networks which foster discussion between academics across subject networks. These are usually internal to institutions but sometimes can include others from outside with specific expertise. For example, a department moving over to problem-based learning (PBL) may find no one within the institution with experience of PBL, but can make contact through national higher education organizations to find others who have experience of implementing this approach to learning. It is important in these cross-disciplinary conversations that participants do not feel they are being dictated to, but rather are being supported to develop their ideas grounded in their own experience and subject context (Walker 2001a).

Attention needs to be paid to reward structures that give positive encouragement through promotions for those academics who take risks and develop new courses or new ways of teaching. For academic staff who devote considerable energy and time to developing new courses, or recasting their courses in radical ways, there is an inevitable impact on the time they have available for research. If promotion panels always favour research outputs over course innovation, it will only be a small minority of academics who will be willing to risk the impact of working on teaching. Academic staff will be quick to realize that a reward structure that on paper says it will recognize and promote those engaged in course development, but which rarely does so, is only paying lip service to the importance of teaching. This was the most common complaint in a survey of 50,000 faculty in the USA (Diamond and Adam 2004). The findings suggested that the rhetoric about rewarding staff is not yet matched by the reality.

Funding to support curriculum innovation is also useful although not always critical. Undoubtedly the existence of money to support innovation projects can be a big assistance. Such funding can release academic staff from other duties while they concentrate on redesigning courses, linking into networks, developing new course materials, buying staff with particular expertise in, say, web design or distributed learning. There are many good examples in England of curriculum innovations that have been significantly enhanced by national funding (Baume *et al.* 2002) or by institutional innovation funds (Laycock 1997; Gibbs *et al.* 2002).

On the other hand, such funding is not essential when the motivation of the academics is sufficiently strong to bring about change. Pratt (1997), discussing the experience of the polytechnics in the UK in the 1970s and 1980s, charts the development of student-centred learning, independent study, work-based learning, self-learning packages, modular degrees, flexible programmes to allow student choice and variable pace of learning, skills development related to employment, and many other developments that were innovative in the context of the UK at the time. This was also during a period when funding was being reduced, student–teacher ratios were increasing and polytechnics were subject to external validation procedures. Nevertheless, the drive to change was sufficiently powerful, partly because there were those who held strong convictions about how higher education should change, and partly because the political and institutional climate fostered innovation, that change occurred despite the lack of funding.

> The most innovative courses were those where polytechnics designed from first principles, and innovation was encouraged when existing assumptions were questioned. Often there was no experience from the past to draw on. In the most innovative cases, the polytechnics decided what they thought they should do and just did it.
>
> (Pratt 1997: 155)

A key factor in the success of the management of improvement in course design is the manner in which the change relates to the identity of the academic involved. As we saw in Chapter 3, subject identity is a strong feature of many academics' self-perception. Change that is consonant with this sense of self or group identity can be sustained better than change that is outside or is simply perceived to be alien to the culture of the discipline identity. For example, let us suppose the university has decided that key skills should be embedded in the curriculum to improve student employability. Any attempts to introduce entirely generic skills that are content-free are not only difficult to make meaningful to students but also run up against the subject identity of the academics. Evans (2002: 41) has voiced the concern of many academics when she argues that teaching key skills 'substitutes for the teaching of subjects, in which the content is deemed to be important in itself and mastered only by acquiring and practising the skills, an attempt to teach the skills themselves in comparative isolation'.

Instead of introducing generic, subject-free skills, the solution is to find ways of introducing key skills through the subject framework as we discussed in relation to academic literacy in Chapter 4. This will allow the specifics of the subject discourse to dictate the precise form in which the change is interpreted and implemented. Over-prescription from agents outside the department or subject structures is likely to create resistance which from the perspective of the individuals undertaking the resistance will be seen as a rational response to a threat to values held dear within the disciplinary pedagogical community.

This explains why innovations that depend on individual 'buy-in' by 'early adopters' but without the full support of the whole department are often doomed to failure. Some kinds of innovation can survive within individual courses, for example the use of particular learning technologies, but when the change is designed to have a more widespread impact on students' approaches to learning, for example to encourage them to be more independent (Baume 1994), develop attributes to enhance their employability (Knight and Yorke 2003), or to use research methods in enquiry-based learning (Jenkins *et al.* 2003), then an individual teacher cannot achieve this on their own. Indeed, the isolated innovation may even be counter-productive because, if it fails, this failure is used as a reason for making no further attempt to introduce the innovation. The whole department programme-wide approach has many advantages, as Wright argues in relation to one curriculum development project 'Skills-plus':

> Departmental structure is well established in academe. And university students tend to quickly identify themselves with an academic specialisation. The most promising way to make a positive impact on the educational experience of the undergraduate is to reform his or her programme. Skills-plus encourages academic staff to fine-tune, to tinker, to enhance and, in some cases, to rethink aspects of the total departmental offerings. Given the often entrenched positions of various faculty members, even the 'fine-tuning' of a given course of studies can present huge obstacles.
>
> (Wright 2001: 7)

Sometimes these obstacles relate to the phenomenon we discussed earlier, what Bernstein calls subjects with 'restricted identity'. In these kinds of departments, where disciplinary identities are particularly strong, any improvement, even if emanating from within that department, will only be given legitimacy if it is perceived as being consistent with the values of the pedagogical community. Key individuals who command respect will need to have ownership of the change and therefore must be brought 'on board' to further the aims of change. Inevitably there will be those who do not implement the change in ways envisaged by those initiating the innovation. Berg and Ostergren (1977: 126) suggest that 'the system must tolerate those who deviate from it and let them influence the development' rather than attempt to force compliance. Attention needs also to be given to those who 'resist' because they feel personally threatened by the proposed change.

> For the implementers of the innovation, the risks of loss should be minimised and the potential of gains maximised. This means, for instance, that selective financial support should be available. Attention should also be given to the potential for security and self-realisation.
>
> (Berg and Ostergren 1977: 126)

This kind of strategy illustrates the more general point we have been making, that improving teaching and learning must be tailored to the specific characteristics of the pedagogical community it is aiming to engage. The dialogue that is needed to bring about change can be a time-consuming business. Clegg (2003) makes the point that there is often a tension between the time within which a centrally initiated change is expected to be introduced and the time it takes for academic staff to undertake the necessary discussion to be persuaded and to begin to implement any change. When institutional managers are leading changes, this factor is often neglected. 'Differing experiences of time underpin periphery/centre tensions in relation to learning and teaching' (Clegg 2003: 817)

Time is clearly critical. Perhaps the single most valuable action that managers can take to improve the quality of course design is to give it the appropriate priority when planning academic workloads by recognizing the time it takes to introduce a new approach to course design. When courses are designed, they require discussion with colleagues, new written materials, new reading lists and other resources, and these materials often have to be made available through the virtual learning environment or website.

In order to promote debate for improving course design it can be useful to hold events in which all teachers in a department, or all those involved in a programme of study, are invited to consider a particular aspect of the curriculum. These events require academic staff to devote a minimum of a day to examining and reviewing the existing curriculum. Four examples of the kinds of exercises that can provoke this kind of reconsideration are given here:

- *Skills audit.* Teachers of each course or module are invited to identify the different kinds of skills being developed within the courses for which they are responsible. The categorization of skills being used needs to be discussed and agreed, for example cognitive or intellectual skills, generic transferable skills, subject specific skills (SEEC 2003). The audit might suggest that teachers identify skills that are implicitly developed, those that are explicitly taught and those that are assessed. The skills developed within each individual course or module can then be placed in a map of the whole programme in order to consider whether there are skills that are not receiving sufficient attention in teaching, whether there are some that are being over-taught and over-assessed, how skills are being assessed, and how students record their skills development, for example, through a form of personal development planning. In order to answer these questions, academic staff will need to debate the skills they expect the programme should develop. This debate will need to relate directly to the goals of the programme, its values and its function for the development and careers of the students studying within it. The exercise can be made more specific by focusing on certain sorts of skills such as employability skills or research skills.
- *Assessment audit.* There are a number of key issues regarding assessment that can only be understood by examining the total range of assessment tasks undertaken by a student. Is the total volume of assessment appropriate and comparable with other programmes? Do the assessment tasks provide a valid and reliable test of students' achievements? Do the assessment tasks allow students to demonstrate their achievement of the outcomes expected of a student undertaking the programme? Are there sufficient opportunities for formative assessment that will enable students to learn from undertaking them?
- *Mapping levels and learning outcomes.* As we have seen, the idea of learning outcomes is controversial and not always well understood. An opportunity to consider what is meant by learning outcomes and what function they can serve within an outcomes-based curriculum can be very valuable. A challenging exercise is to consider (a) how the learning outcomes of individual modules relate to the overall intended outcomes for the whole programme, (b) whether the outcomes are appropriate to the academic

level of the course, and (c) how the outcomes are being assessed. The relationship between learning outcomes and assessment criteria is also important to consider (Gosling and Moon 2003).

- *Mapping development of academic literacy*. In Chapter 4 we noted that the development of academic literacy is an essential element in the response of an inclusive university to the widening diversity of students in higher education. If this development is to occur across the whole curriculum then there needs to be agreement between all teachers of a programme about where different aspects of academic literacy are being developed and where they are being assessed. Opportunities to practise skills and reinforce student success require a cross-programme planning.

Exercises of this kind require communication between teachers. In departments where there has not been a tradition of discussing teaching, these opportunities for debate can reveal divisions and disagreements that may not have been visible previously. Resolving or finding an accommodation for these differences of opinion can take time, but the difficulties involved should not inhibit this kind of debate. We have emphasized the importance of finding ways of constructing the university as a learning community that promotes conversations about teaching and learning. It is only through discussions of this kind that the questions of what needs improving and how improvement is to be achieved can be addressed.

Conclusion: Guidelines for improving course design across the whole institution

We conclude this chapter by suggesting some general guidelines for those charged with responsibility to bring about improvements in course design across the whole institution. These are derived from the work of Fullan (2001), Eckel *et al.* (1998, 1999) and Berg and Ostergren (1977).

- Ensure that there is clear leadership from those with power and authority.
- State clearly the objectives to be achieved and the rationale.
- Confer with representatives from all interested areas.
- Create meta-learning communities to consider proposals for curriculum change.
- Recognize and respect academic control over teaching.
- Recognize the time that will be needed and allow a timetable which leaves time for consultation and implementation.
- Devote time to explaining the reasons for the change to all staff concerned.
- Acknowledge the validity of critical debate and allow adequate time for discussion to occur.
- Be ready to deal with unintended consequences of the change being implemented.
- Use pilots to test out innovations before implementing them across the whole institution.

- Build on strengths and past experience where possible.
- Use multiple approaches such as: validation/approval and review processes, professional development events, publications to publicize successes.
- Be flexible, open to suggestions, but keep the overall goal in mind.

Notes

1. We use the term 'course' as a generic term to mean any unit of structured learning within a programme of study.

6

Impact of Learning Technologies on Institutional Change

> Today's world relies upon rapidly changing computer technology in almost every phase of life. That creates a breakneck pace of change for the academy . . . Ironically the solution is not move faster. Nor does it work to follow our instincts about what will work and what will fail. Instead, this time we need to study 40 years of past failures and successes. This time, we need to get it right . . . In order to have a hope of using technology to improve educational activities and their outcomes, institutions need more than just . . . technology.
>
> Ehrmann 2002b: 25, 15

One of the most ubiquitous major recent changes in higher education has been the expansion of the application of technology to approaches in teaching and learning. Learning technologies have been around higher education in one form or another for hundreds of years, if we count the development of the printing press as one of the first of these. When this occurred, students no longer needed to take the role of a 'medieval scribe', and teachers could stop reading from the few books available. When the roles changed, pedagogical activities and learning did too. Similarly, when the chalkboard was first used, it also changed the way that education was approached.

> In the winter of 1813–1814 . . . I attended a mathematical school kept in Boston . . . we were struck at the appearance of an ample Blackboard suspended on the wall, with lumps of chalk on a ledge below, and cloths hanging at either side. I had never heard of such a thing before.
>
> (May cited in Anderson cited in Rocklin 2001:1)

Once ideas could be instantly visible to learner and teacher the learning and teaching process again changed, and in this instance knowledge became more accessible, more immediate and more connected to the learning experience. The distance between ideas and their development lessened and the outcomes of learning changed.

When a new technological approach to learning and teaching has been introduced, debates have ensued about their projected impact, positive or negative, on the learning of students.[1] There is really little that is new about the arguments related to the introduction of learning technologies. Yet, there is a dimension to the latest range of technological innovations being proposed and employed in higher education around the world today. This key dimension, the one thing that makes these learning technologies so powerful in their impact, is the speed at which they are developing and changing. As one leading proponent of learning technologies has put it: 'one year is the equivalent of 5 technology years' (Day 1999; see also Sekers 2000). Keeping up with this pace of change is a major challenge facing modern educators, and it is the speed of change that some see creating a step change in pedagogical developments (Bateson and Bass 1996; J.S. Brown 2000).

This chapter reviews the key issues surrounding the implementation of learning technologies in higher education in order to progress the debates surrounding their use and development a little further. It is our view that, despite the acceleration in technological developments, the debates around their application to the improvement of teaching and learning remain virtually the same as they have for the history of educational innovations and definitive answers remain difficult to find. We begin to unpack these deliberations by considering what can be learned from previous introductions of learning technologies and how these are different from or similar to the current changes. We ask questions about the pedagogical issues surrounding technological change and apply pedagogical principles to the development of learning technologies in higher education. We review the potential and limitations of these technologies for improving learning and end with a section on how to use them as a lever for change.

Learning technologies: something old and something new

Those of us who have experience of learning technologies, as students and/or teachers, recognize that many of the observations about new technologies are quite familiar. Ehrmann (2002b: 18), reminds us of this history.

> Research showed decades ago that self-paced instruction has the power to improve and accelerate learning by about one-third, compared with lectures and conventional assignments on the same topic . . . [However,] interactive self-paced courseware . . . only works well in areas where learning can be organised into chunks, and sequences of chunks, and where answers can be predicted and marked right/wrong.

One of the authors has personal experience of this learning scenario, having learned educational statistics though a self-paced computer-mediated course nearly thirty years ago. This statistics course fits Ehrmann's description exactly. Statistics as a subject can be divided into distinct chunks [frequency distributions: mode, median, mean; measures of variability: range, variance, standard deviation, probability; statistical errors: sampling error, Type I and Type II errors; statistical tests: analysis of variance: correlations, regressions and chi-square and so on], and there are right and wrong answers. The experience of learning statistics in this way, as compared with a conventional lecture or set of assignments, was illuminating and intellectually freeing in all kinds of ways. The process of working through a computer-based package at my own pace allowed me to take the time I needed to learn a subject, for which I had an unwarranted fear, by making mistakes, learning from them and becoming proficient in using statistical methods without losing face in front of my teacher or other students.

What is remarkable is that this method did not become more frequently employed in similar subjects in higher education during the ensuing thirty years. And, as noted by Ehrmann and others, it clearly has its limitations.

> Courses that teach critical and conceptual thinking don't seem to work very well outside the traditional classroom . . . the computer offers no adequate substitute for real-world interaction between professors and students, real field trips, real objects of interest . . . real libraries with real books . . . and real extracurricula activities.
>
> (Graham 2001: 11–12)

Nevertheless, the good news is that in certain subjects there is thirty years' experience of computer-based self-paced learning that we can draw from to deal with the rapid changes occurring as new technologies are introduced to higher education. The lessons from the past are a useful place to start while recognizing that there are new and different issues to address as well.

Before we consider some of the knowledge and evidence available from past implementations of learning technologies, it might be useful to define how we will use the various terms that refer to these changes in learning and teaching. Currently, the term 'e-learning' has become common shorthand for a wide range of technological innovations in teaching and learning and consequently it lacks definitional precision. Some have limited the use of the term to electronic distance learning, also known as distributed learning. When universities embrace whole systems of distributed learning they are often called virtual universities.

Others have limited the term 'e-learning' to computer-mediated communication (CMC) via intranet or internet – synchronous or asynchronous, including uses of the World Wide Web and networked learning, whereas still others include any learning that is assisted electronically, including overhead projectors, film/videos, CD-ROMs, radio and television, audio and video, and print media (Barker *et al.* 1997; Day 1999). It is, however, the internet-related activities that are seen as the impetus for the step-change in higher education that we alluded to earlier. Studies suggest:

> The Internet *is* revolutionizing higher education. But that's not the same thing as saying that the Internet is revolutionizing *learning*. It isn't. What the Internet won't change is the nature of human cognition and social interaction – and therefore of learning. Study after study . . . has demonstrated that the medium of instruction has little if any effect on the nature or amount of learning that takes place. So the Internet will, on the one hand, change everything and, on the other hand change nothing.
>
> (Rocklin 2001: 1–2)

Thus, we are inclined to use the most inclusive definition of e-learning. In fact, we would suggest that, as discussed in the Dearing Report (1997),[2] what is really under consideration is communication and information technology (C&IT), with the emphasis on communication in all its varied forms and in particular its application to learning and teaching. If the focus is placed on communication as the conceptual driver, instead of on information technology, these technologies '[offer] the opportunities for the potential of more creative uses of communication yet [remain] part of the wider human experience, part of everyday life and therefore part of everyday higher education' (D'Andrea 1997: 29).[3] A change in communication processes is more familiar in an academic environment and less likely to produce barriers to change than if the focus is on information technology or technologies in general.

Another element we would add to this definitional debate is the difference between what is a technologically based approach to teaching and learning and a technologically mediated approach. It is our view that the former is about an overarching paradigm for teaching and learning whereas the latter is more about teaching and learning methods. A technologically mediated approach is about finding a tool to achieve the aims and outcomes of learning. There are many ways that learning is mediated: one of them is through e-learning; others include more traditional methods such a lectures and library work. A technologically based approach to learning and teaching is more than that part of course design which selects the teaching methods, it is the paradigmatic basis for learning and teaching. In this case, learning technologies are a driver of learning and can shift the way that learning and teaching are conceptualized as well as the way they are carried out. Both are part of the current debate surrounding e-learning and we come back to this in our final section when we discuss how learning technologies can be a lever for change in learning and teaching. The statistics course mentioned earlier is an example of a technologically mediated approach. It was not a technologically based pedagogical paradigm. It did not shift the conceptualization of learning and teaching in higher education. It did not become a hotly debated issue concerning the delivery of higher education.

Unlike what occurred with previous introductions of learning technologies where they were added on to the already existing learning and teaching approaches, the new learning technologies set the agenda for their implementation themselves. They are, in effect, defining a new pedagogical paradigm and a set of expectations associated with them about how students learn and how teachers will teach. Bateson and Bass (1996) add that the digital revolution does not simply facilitate the communication of existing ways of thinking but is actually altering the way we think, manage knowledge and communicate.

Another issue that often comes up when a new learning technology is being introduced into higher education is whether it will be pedagogically or technologically led. This concern represents an important power struggle within higher education institutions over control of the curriculum, teaching and learning methods, student learning and knowledge production. It is the feeling of many academics that the views of the technologists will inappropriately impact what they see as their rightful domain: the structure and delivery of the student's learning experience. For example, when one of the authors was introducing a video term paper option into an introductory sociology course in the mid-1970s, the IT staff who helped to support this initiative very often would argue against a pedagogically important component of the process in favour of a technological innovation, or against standard academic practice in favour of technological convention. For example, when the teacher suggested that the video the students produced had to include academic references as well as the traditional 'film/video' credits, this was resisted as non-standard for film/video productions, too time consuming to create (lots of text which in the 1970s could not be done electronically) and therefore unnecessary. The compromise was to have the students prepare a paper-based programme to accompany the film, as is often done in art shows, with a complete set of references included as part of the programme information. The technological limits required thinking outside the technological paradigm to meet the expected academic standards.

Similarly, pedagogical principles of assessment had to be addressed. How would the technological components of developing a video term paper fit a standard assessment format? In this case the technological advice was to assess the technical dimensions of the format (such as clean technical edits, use of visual techniques like dissolves between scenes and similar devices), whereas the academic concern was about the video's argumentation and organization of the conceptual themes. Again, the latter could not be compromised since they were both defined as outcomes for the course. The point here is that when academics work with technologists there is a tension around the core focus of the work which each contributes to the process. A current equivalent example – and this does not mean that similar debates around the use of video do not still occur – with computer-mediated learning is the oftentimes technological imperative to simply get things on to the web, often lots of text, instead of how the technology can assist in meeting the course outcomes. 'Using the new technologies in education can tempt some to conflate what is essentially a delivery system into an educational philosophy' (Helm 1997: 45).

> These differences between the technologists and academics are often further exacerbated by the internal organisational structures of academic institutions. Many higher education institutions, in the interests of economies of scale or rationalising central services, have frequently consolidated information technology services with support for learning and teaching into a centralised office that is usually headed up by a non-academic. When curriculum change and teaching and learning innovations are coordinated from a central IT service they are more likely to be technologically led rather than pedagogically led. This presents a number of dilemmas in bringing about changes related to various educational practices.
>
> (D'Andrea *et al.* 2001)

One solution has been to create educational/faculty development centres to lead on ICT. These centres are oftentimes led by academics who have added an expertise in teaching and learning to the knowledge of their subject. There is generally a closer link to the work introduced or carried out by these centres with the approach taken by the academics themselves because the work is being academically and pedagogically led.

Are academic, pedagogically led centres a helpful structure for implementing learning technologies? A study conducted in the UK of the approach taken by eight universities to introducing and implementing learning technologies has suggested that those institutions that supported a combined and integrated educational development and IT approach to developing learning technologies have a higher chance of succeeding in engaging faculty/staff with learning technologies (D'Andrea *et al.* 2001). In light of our discussion of academic identities in Chapter 3, it is not difficult to see why this is the case.

A second important determinant for academic use of learning technologies for improving teaching and learning is whether the technologies are understood to add value to achieving the learning outcomes that academic staff determine for their courses. Various claims about new learning opportunities appear throughout the vast literature on modern learning technologies. Among the specific features cited are:

- greater interactivity with learning materials (with or without a teacher);
- asynchronous learning from multiple sites;
- increased flexibility in location of learning;
- greater opportunity to provide realistic and managed simulations;
- greater opportunity to provide access and experience of large data sets;
- increased access to a wide range of search tools and resources for learning;
- greater student autonomy and independence;
- a student-centred approach.

If these match the aims of the specified learning outcomes, learning technologies are more likely to be used.

Asynchronous and independent learning approaches are not as new as we might think. Students had library assignments and group work activities long before e-learning was introduced. Most histories of distance learning set its start date as the mid-nineteenth century. Examples of asynchronous feedback have been in use since at least the early 1980s. In the USA, one of the authors developed a method of providing audio-taped feedback on students' written work. Gibbs (personal communication, 1993) reports a similar approach in the UK around the same time. According to Gilbert (1997), 'most education has long been a combination of face-to-face meetings (ranging from tutorials to large lectures), asynchronous telecommunications (written assignments) and guided independent work (reading, laboratory experiments').

Although many e-learning activities are not necessarily new, one UK study (Huxley n.d.) identified three major aggregate areas of information and communication technology (ICT) application activities: (a) virtual and managed learning environments (VLEs and MLEs), (b) digital gateways or portals, and (c) e-books. These three have the potential to impact teaching and learning significantly. As this report goes on to state: 'In many ways e-learning in higher education is still an emerging concept . . .' (Huxley n.d.: 1). It appears that variations of e-learning will continue to be emergent for some time to come, as will the debates surrounding their application and implementation. What needs to be understood throughout these developments is how to decide which of the new technological options to use while ensuring the student learning experience is central to the choices made. Reminding ourselves of the history of technological developments can be a useful mechanism for doing this.

Pedagogical implications and issues

As we noted earlier, the locus of leadership for bringing a new learning technology into higher education has been highly contested, with both those with pedagogical expertise and technological expertise vying for centre stage. Although new collaborative work is taking place between these two areas of work, universities often separate these two activities in unhelpful ways. In this context, the question of where to start a learning technology initiative needs to be answered.

> It makes sense to begin the process not by buying technology but by considering what educational goals you would like to achieve. Second, ask what barriers currently prevent that kind of educational excellence. Third, begin lowering those barriers. That's key to making sure that, as technology becomes available, it is used the right way, right away.
>
> (Ehrmann 2000: 8)

Friedlander (2000: 3) adds a practical guiding question to this process: '[Can] the learning outcome . . . be improved by integrating the design of the spatial and technological support system with pedagogical innovation [?]'

Building on our earlier work on course planning, and as discussed in Chapter 5, we would approach this question by reflecting systematically on the educational purposes for selecting and using learning technologies in higher education courses of study. The process of choosing whether or not and which learning technologies to use is what some would see as part of the third stage of the systematic planning model (D'Andrea 1999, 2003). Learning technologies remain a means to an end and need to be linked to the aims and outcomes of any teaching and learning experience (D'Andrea 1999, 2003; Gosling and Moon 2003).

Ehrmann's (2000) Triad planning model, when combined with his ranking system,[4] provides a useful device for addressing both the purpose and the priority of using learning technologies because they combine both choices in an interlinked and integrated systematic planning model (see Figure 6.1). The Triad approach to planning can be used as a method both for curriculum planning and institutional decision making on support for learning

Triad			Importance of this triad for our programme institution	Value added if technology were used
Goal	Activity	Role of technology		
Graduates are prepared to work in many cultures	Curriculum includes multicultural content	Use of the web for communication between intercultural teams	3	3
Students graduate with team skills	Collaborative learning is significant part of all course work	Support for online collaborative problem solving	1	1
Students able to master difficult concepts	Lectures are more clear and vivid	Use more visuals and animations	2	4
Students graduate with new degree in e-business	Established a new academic programme	Business software and web for referencing	4	2

Figure 6.1 Triad programme/course planning model
Source: Adapted from Ehrmann (2000: 9).

technologies, as well as any other types of learning support. It is a simple guide to aligning the purpose of the educational programme with students' goals. It is also an application of Biggs' (1999) constructive alignment. We like to call this process purposeful planning and as we have noted it complements the course design activities that we outlined in Chapter 5.

The Triad planning model as illustrated in Figure 6.1 demonstrates how to ensure that pedagogical principles and learning outcomes lead the development of implementing learning technologies in institutions. Using the model to plan this implementation helps to prevent an overenthusiastic response to potential technological fads by focusing attention on the purpose of the educational experience. The model functions as a helpful guide for taking these decisions.

Work at Staffordshire University in the UK suggests that taking a course planning approach has positive outcomes in developing learning technologies, in this case choosing a virtual learning environment.

> All the evidence shows that it is COURSE DESIGN and SUPPORT that has the biggest impact on the quality of the student learning experience using VLEs. Best advice, therefore is: Design your course, select learning strategies, identify indicative resources, and THEN choose which VLE will help you achieve your goals best.
>
> (Stiles 2000: 10)

Other important pedagogical principles have also been applied to the process of selecting learning technologies in higher education. Chickering and Ehrmann (1996) have updated the *Seven Principles of Good Practice* originally developed in 1987 to allow for 'the power of the learning technologies to be fully realised'. They have shown how each of the seven principles can be addressed through the implementation of learning technologies. We summarize their analysis below. When considered alongside a systematic planning process, such as the Triad model, these provide additional useful guidance for making appropriate choices to achieve a university's educational goals.

Good practice and learning technologies: some examples

Applying principles of good practice to the use of learning technologies is a useful exercise in defining their learning benefits. The following examples can be used to prompt further thinking about the relationship between improving teaching and learning with technologies.

1. *Encourages contacts between students and teachers*
   - *Learning constraints*: increasing numbers of students find it difficult to have personal contact with their teachers due to having to leave immediately after class to meet family and work obligations.

- *Technological solution*: students are provided with opportunities for interaction with the teacher through online discussion groups.

2. *Develops reciprocity and cooperation among students*
   - *Learning constraints*: again, time restrictions limit opportunities for students to work collaboratively.
   - *Technological solution*: computer-based tools encourage spontaneous student collaboration, this was one of the earliest surprises about computer-enhanced learning.
3. *Uses active learning techniques*
   - *Learning constraints*: active learning techniques take up too much class time.
   - *Technological solution*: the range of technological possibilities includes simulations and problem-solving scenarios, time-delayed exchanges and real-time seminar discussions, all available outside of class.
4. *Gives prompt feedback*
   - *Learning constraints*: hand-marked text requires additional student time to edit, and feedback comments are separated from revised work making it difficult to quickly review what changes were made and why they were suggested.
   - *Technological solution*: use of the hidden text option in word processors provides feedback that can be used by the student and then turned off so that only the revised text is visible.
5. *Emphasizes time on task*
   - *Learning constraints*: increasing demands on students' time as noted earlier.
   - *Technological solution*: 'Today's technologies can increase students' effective time on task by reducing the amount of time they spend on task components from which they learn little or nothing . . . (e.g. walking to the library and searching through volume after volume of some printed periodical index which has little to do with learning)' (Rocklin 2001: 2).
6. *Communicates high expectations*
   - *Learning constraints*: class-based activities such as lectures do not always demand a high level of student engagement.
   - *Technological solution*: significant real-life problems provided through web-based course materials challenge students to acquire information and sharpen skills of analysis, synthesis, application and evaluation.
7. *Respects diverse talents and ways of learning*
   - *Learning constraints*: face-to-face shared work is limited to the times when several students can meet.
   - *Technological solution*: aided by technologies, students with similar motives and talents can work in cohort study groups without the constraints of time and place.

These examples provide a glimpse of how learning technologies can address principles of good practice. They also indicate how learning technologies can impact on other aspects of the learning–teaching process as well. One of these is the role that students and teachers play both in and out of the classroom. Three examples of where roles are or could be changing include: online collaboration, student autonomy and independence, and online learning communities. We look at each of these briefly to illustrate this dimension of learning technologies.

Mayes (2001: 16) has suggested that 'the most effective way of using online technology . . . is to focus on supporting the learner's involvement in collaboration, authentic tasks, reflection and dialogue, and to do so in a way which addresses identity and community'. Online collaboration is frequently cited as a major benefit of learning technologies that supports a learner-centred approach to teaching and learning. If this were the case we would expect to see evidence that the approach has features that promote student-centred learning such as those suggested by Barr and Tagg (1995) and the Lotus Institute (1996).

Using Alley's (1996) summary of Barr and Tagg's learner-centred pedagogical activities we have checked to see if learning technologies match many of the criteria. In learner-centred teaching and learning the role of the students moves from passive recipient to one of learning initiator and the role of teacher moves from 'sage on the stage' to 'guide on the side', a learning facilitator. We have identified several ways in which this is evident in online pedagogies, a few examples of these are: continuous course assessment can be done via online daily quizzes marked instantly electronically; student driven learning episodes are similar to online discussion groups, etc.

Learning technologies also have the potential to encourage the shift to greater student autonomy and independence. This is evident in the examples included in the discussion on the seven principles of good practice. However, it is important to understand how students engage with the learning process. A report in the USA indicated only 30–40 per cent of the students actually buy the books required for their courses. The researcher concluded that this meant that students expect more from their teachers than from themselves (Gilbert 1999). This would suggest that although autonomy and independence are encouraged and possible when using learning technologies, students would not necessarily expect the traditional roles of teachers and students to change. Their role expectations then often militate against achieving the aims of independent and autonomous learning.

As we discussed in Chapter 2, the use of learning communities can be an important pedagogical tool, and when combined with learning technologies can become even more significant for student learning (Jonassen *et al.* 1999; Chang 2003). In this situation, the principles of democratic participation that are central to these learning structures shift students and teachers into the same role, as co-learners.

Most learning technologies have the capacity to address the key components of learning communities: 'communication, attention to differences, a shared culture, adaptation, dialogue and access to information and resources' (Jonassen *et al.* cited in Chang 2003: 28). Nevertheless, these characteristics alone do not ensure the successful development of online learning communities (Prensky 2002; Chang 2003). Chang suggests that they must be carefully planned in order to achieve their learning goals. So we have come full circle and are back to Ehrmann's Triad planning model, Figure 6.1. Creating learning communities could be added to the table as a goal of a university and listed in the first column, and specific learning technologies could be listed in the third column. How much a priority this would be in any particular university would be up to local needs to determine. In any case, there is the potential for added value to learning communities when learning technologies are included to support their structures and functions.

The potential and limitations of learning technologies for improving teaching and learning

It is tempting to end this chapter with lists of the pros and cons of using learning technologies. Numerous authors have created these lists in an attempt to help teachers new to learning technologies, to make good choices when selecting among them to improve their teaching and students' learning. However, these lists usually provoke an 'either/or' debate among academics about whether or not to use learning technologies at all. Rather than offering yet another version of this debate, which remains ongoing and continuous, we would like to make a few observations related to it and its relationship to the central concern of this book to improve teaching and learning. We then close the chapter with a summary of ways to use learning technologies as a lever for change.

Our experience of working with faculty/staff suggests that pedagogical changes linked to the learning technologies remain closely connected to the transmission model of teaching and learning. Rather than seeing radical change in pedagogy, as might be expected with innovative approaches, the practice remains conservative. For example, a cursory look at what is mounted on the web reveals that content consists mainly of traditional lecture notes. Another example is the inclusion of question-and-answer worksheets that only require rote learning. How are these different from the standard one-way communication classroom experience of most students? Learning technologies are only as innovative as the activities and materials developed to be used with them. 'The single most powerful determinant of the successful use of new technologies in education will be the creativity of individual teachers and the strength of their desire to improve their courses' (Helm 1997: 46).

Thomas *et al.* (1998) suggest that to integrate new technology effectively into education, we need 'an understanding of the whole education pro-

> cess and a critical examination of its functions'. If the learning and teaching processes are not considered and if staff simply continue to apply traditional modes of teaching to the new delivery systems and e-learning environments then 'we cancel out their potential innovation dimensions'.
>
> (MacKnight cited in Bennett and Marsh 2002: 14)

For teaching and learning to improve, it would be sensible to support the creativity of teachers in developing approaches to using learning technologies along with supporting their understanding of the broader system-wide implications of using them.

One issue that remains problematical no matter how creative teachers are in developing online learning technologies is that there is a strong inclination by students for face-to-face interaction in order to develop a full sense of community. The lack of personal human contact remains the challenge, and to deny this fact is to sabotage efforts to maximize the value of using online learning tools. We are also aware that problems that face-to-face groups experience can occur with electronic groups as well. Without a focus or direction, students will not take groups seriously (D'Andrea and Ewens 1990). Other concerns centre on the quality of the debate and level of the contribution made while participating in the groups. Maintaining a high-level discussion is crucial for student learning when it occurs in real or virtual groups and, as noted above in the principles of good practice, is directly linked to communicating high expectations.

In each instance, teachers must be aware of basic teaching skills, and students must be aware of basic learning skills. Oftentimes neither has had the opportunity to develop these skills in relation to traditional teaching and learning approaches and consequently come to apply them to learning technologies without suitable foundation knowledge of learning and teaching more generally.

There are at least three basic problems that have dogged most attempts to translate technological improvements into educational improvements:

> - Confusing one ingredient (technology) with the whole recipe (educational improvement).
> - Forgetting that the lifespan of many new technologies is far shorter than the time it takes to implement that recipe for improving educational outcomes.
> - Ignoring the fact that one of those educational recipes – large-scale reliance on interactive, self-paced, cost-effective courseware – has been tried with almost every new technology for the last four decades.
>
> (Ehrmann 2002b: 14–15)

Whatever the potential of new learning technologies, their use is limited by barriers both visible and invisible. One significant barrier for most universities, no matter what their financial situation, is the enormous investment that accompanies the implementation of new learning technologies. Unlike many other innovations in teaching and learning, this one hits the institutional budget hard, so resource implications must be considered when taking forward improvements in teaching and learning that use learning technologies.

Resource considerations

This section briefly considers resource implications of using learning technologies, sketching out the basic considerations that are useful to keep in mind when planning to improve teaching and learning through learning technologies.

The two key resources needed for implementing learning technologies are time – academic staff time and student time – and money. Both are currently in short supply in higher education. But in spite of the extraordinary financial resources required, time remains the pivotal resource for the successful use of learning technologies. We discuss the importance of time to academics in greater detail in Chapter 7 (see also Gilbert 1999; Ehrmann 2000b, 2002).

> There are two kinds of resources that faculty need which goes beyond financial, equipment and software needs. We need sufficient support staff who can work with a variety of technologies from both the hardware and software perspectives. But we also need time – whether in the form of sufficient released time, sabbaticals or reductions in load. Without the resources of staff support and time, incorporating technology into our work can only lead to early burnout.
>
> (Sipress 1997)

Nonetheless the extraordinary financial resources required for the development and implementation of many of the learning technologies cannot be ignored either. These resources represent increased power for those who have the authority to decide on how to use them and less power for those who have little or no access to them, thus offering opportunities for some and challenges for others.

There is also the impact of shifting funding away from departments to central units that are given responsibility for spending the resources for learning technologies. This has resulted in a debate between central institutional controls over these kinds of resource decisions and departmental/school-based devolved decision structures, where they exist. One example of this at a university in the UK was a central decision to use IBM PCs across the university. This took the appropriate pedagogical decision away from academics in subjects such as, art and design, and architecture, where Macs are the more appropriate pedagogical answer owing to the computing capabilities they have for these subjects. This example illustrates how the location of resource decisions can impact on whether teaching and learning might be improved through learning technologies.

In many ways the following summarizes the main issues we have raised throughout this chapter.

> I know a number of ways in which blackboards can make my teaching and my students' learning more efficient, so the blackboard is a candidate technology. In today's environment, the cost of adoption of the blackboard is pretty low. They're relatively inexpensive to install and last a long time. My investment in developing instruction that uses a blackboard isn't at serious risk from changing standards. Although I have to be a little bit concerned about the possibility that blackboards will go away . . . So next semester, I'll be using a blackboard. If only my decisions about computers and the Internet were so straightforward.
>
> (Rocklin 2001: 4)

Learning technologies as levers for change

A recent summary of over 350 research reports that compared technological and conventional approaches to learning and teaching, indicates that there is 'no significant difference between student learning in conventional modes and technology assisted and delivered modes' (O'Hagan 2001: 8–9). This helps to frame the question that Gilbert (2000) asked about learning technologies: Why bother to use them if there is no evidence of a difference in student learning? Gilbert's answer came in two parts; one focused on the literal use of learning technologies for teaching and learning, the second, more interesting one to us, was his list of 'visionary' reasons to do so. The latter include:

- So that we can preserve what matters most while transforming what needs to change.
- So that we can develop and sustain deeper human connections and avoid drowning in a flood of shallow communications.
- So that individual learners, teachers, and related support professionals can connect better to information, ideas and each other via effective combinations of pedagogy and technology – both old and new, on-campus and online.
- So that teachers, learners and academic support professionals have access to adequate RESOURCES and support services; and, consequently, they can believe in their own ability to improve teaching and learning.
- So that teachers, learners, and academic support professionals believe they share RESPONSIBILITY for improving teaching and learning. But they know that those with knowledge, experience, and wisdom – especially the faculty, both individually and collectively – retain the ultimate responsibility for guiding learning.

- So that everyone can teach and everyone can learn throughout their lives, at least once in a while . . .
- So that learners, teachers, and academic support professionals can be well-prepared to find, evaluate, select, and implement instructional options.
- So that they also have frequent opportunities to exchange ideas and information about academic content, skills, knowledge, and understanding; and about educational and technological options; and about communicating face-to-face, via telecommunications, and in all media.
- So that we can find hope in learning and joy in teaching.

(Gilbert 2000: 7)

With its emphasis on academic values and the need for a meaningful learning community, the themes of this book are echoed throughout this vision.

If we accept the argument that there is reason to bother, what can institutions usefully do to make a meaningful transition to an increased use in learning technologies? Conole (2001) has identified a number of specific actions that universities need to do in order to make this change. They include:

- develop a coherent and focused strategy for the use and integration of ICT, especially through combined teaching and information strategies and those at faculty/departmental level;
- carry out a positional audit of the use of ICT;
- expand support for professional development and student support in the use of ICT;
- have a clear position with respect to the balance of innovation in ICT and development of cutting-edge technologies;
- have a clear mechanism for communications about decisions on ICT use;
- develop appropriate recognition/reward for work with learning technologies;
- give greater consideration to evaluation of costs and educational effectiveness;
- have a flexible timetabling system.

(Conole 2001: 7–8)

In addition, in 2003 a UK audit study reported that institutions with nationally recognized expertise in learning technology were all found to have the following:

- good collaborative networks, internally and with other institutions
- targeted support for teaching staff to integrate learning technology into their courses
- departments/service teams with their own local planning to meet strategic aims

- specialist learning technology development teams within computing services
- a requirement on programmes of study to address student ICT skills
- a requirement on departments to demonstrate pedagogical research/scholarship of teaching

(Timmis 2003: 2)

Interestingly, this last list of characteristics ends with the issue we raised earlier about the need for the pedagogical underpinning of any implementation of learning technologies. It suggests the importance of linking a pedagogical research/scholarship of teaching dimension to the process. We look in detail at the research/teaching/scholarship relationship in the next chapter.

However, in the end it is important to remember that 'educational outcomes take far longer to improve than the likely lifespan of a single generation of technology' (Ehrmann 2002: 20). Previous innovative learning technologies such as CD-ROMs were produced by the thousands in the 1990s, as were videos in the 1970s and 1980s. Where are they now? How much were they used? Fitness for purpose remains a key factor when selecting to use learning technologies to improve teaching and learning.

Finally, if the aim of using learning technologies is also linked to the development of learning communities within the university then:

> Whether or not instructional technology is used, students will surely benefit from our joining with them as partners in the learning process. From such a foundation we will find any subsequent transition to instructional technologies to be far more straightforward.
>
> (Alley 1996: 54)

Notes

1. Unfortunately the debates about the blackboard have been lost to history (Rocklin, 2001).
2. This report was the first comprehensive review of higher education in the UK since the early 1960s. It proposed a series of recommendations on a wide range of issues, including information technology. It encouraged higher education to do more (Dearing 1997: para 3.27).
3. In this chapter we have used what seems to have become the conventional ordering of words: information and communication technology (ICT). It would be an interesting and separate study to review how the shift occurred and how information was given the more privileged position instead of communication. In any case, our view remains that the more accurate designation would be C&IT, since communication is the more all-encompassing term and is the process by which information is shared.

7

Research, Teaching and the Scholarship of Teaching and Learning

> All faculty [staff] ought to be scholars in this broader sense, deepening their preferred approaches to knowing but constantly pressing, and being pressed by peers, to enlarge their scholarly capacities and encompass other – often contrary ways – of knowing.
>
> Rice 1992: 126

Understanding how to improve teaching and learning in higher education requires an understanding of the current state of the research/teaching nexus. At the heart of this discussion is the fact that in most western university systems the status of research has traditionally been greater than for teaching and learning. The three 'Rs' – resources, rewards and recognition – are in abundance for research, whereas the opposite has been true for teaching and learning.

> Teaching is more 'exchangeable' in that others can readily take on the course and teach; this is less the case for research. Teaching remains 'fundamentally a local market, interactive, and personal process, while research is open to the wider market, non-interactive, and a public good phenomenon'... Hence those who are less exchangeable are more valuable to a University. The key to resolving the teaching-research nexus is to make the most valuable person across Universities the best researcher and teacher. Academics gain many rewards from the many research grants (esteem, intrinsic and extrinsic rewards), but from teaching mainly gain only intrinsic rewards and a constant debate about workload.
>
> (Hattie and Marsh 2004: 10)

In this chapter we do not rehearse the now well-known and well-trodden debates (D'Andrea and Allan 2002) on whether or not there is an 'enduring myth' that research and teaching are inextricably entwined (Hattie and Marsh 2004). Instead we seek to look at this important debate, surrounding the research–teaching nexus, by exploring the recent deliberations on scholarship and how it relates to this special relationship.

We begin with reference to the ideas we discussed in Chapter 3 on academic identities, the disciplinary research culture and the current role expectations of academics. Next we take an in-depth look at institutional barriers that contribute to the maintenance of the inequality between research and teaching. In this section we are seeking to understand how the research–teaching nexus contributes to maintaining the status quo or, as we would suggest, can be a potential change agent in universities. In this discussion we return to some of the ideas considered in Chapter 2 where we reported on the work of Boyer (in Rice 1992), Elton (2003) and Brew and Boud (1995a, b) who have added the dimension of learning to the understanding of this phenomenon.

Within the scholarship debate we also look at the status and value of pedagogical research and the scholarship of teaching and learning (SoTL). We consider whether SoTL can provide a bridge between research and teaching and we critically examine the idea of scholarship of learning and teaching.

Finally we suggest some ways that the research–teaching nexus can be enhanced through the development of strategies for building capacity and encouraging scholarship of teaching and learning and scholarly teaching. Our aim is to identify strategies for universities to respond to change through transforming the relationship between research and teaching. As Hattie and Marsh (2004: 1) have said: 'The fundamental issue is what we wish the relation to be, and then we need to devise policies to enact this wish.' We would suggest that these policies need to be at all levels in higher education, local departmental and institutional, discipline and national.

By entitling this chapter as we have, we are not directly challenging Andresen's point that 'research, teaching and scholarship' are redundant in and of themselves (2000: 138). Rather, in this chapter we try to understand the relationship among the three as components of an integrated whole.

Research-led higher education

Demands on academics to be research-active come from a variety of sources. There are the requirements of funding regimes in the Research Assessment Exercise (in the UK), market forces (in the USA), intense disciplinary peer pressure for status and prestige of subjects, and/or a speed-up in the academic environment (Fordist ideas), not to mention personal desires for promotions and academic recognition. With all these pressures to focus on research output, is it any wonder that teaching is further down an academic's 'to do' list?

For many academics this creates a serious tension on the job. Scott (1984 cited in Rowland 1996: 9) has observed that 'professionalisation of academic knowledge has made it increasingly difficult to regard teaching and research as harmonious activities'. Yet a decade later: Rowland's interviewees 'thought that teaching and research should co-exist in a balance within any department' (1996: 9; see also Moses 1990), while they also saw 'research as being the more influential in leading to promotion' (Rowland 1996: 9). In the same year as Rowland's work, which was done in the UK, Martin and Ramsden (2000), in Australia, found that the gap between teaching and research had widened (see also Halsey and Trow 1971; Elton and Partington 1993; Henkel 2001). A year later the work of Tang and Chamberlain reported that 'Faculty ... believe that research interferes with teaching and that they should be required to do either teaching or research, but not both' (cited in Kreber 2000a).

This confusion over academic priorities is illustrated in a quote from Elton's interviews of academics in the UK:

> I am a teacher. I am not employed as a teacher, and I do not wish to be a teacher. I am employed as a lecturer, and in my naivety I thought my job was to 'know' my field, contribute to it by research, and to lecture on my specialism.
>
> (Elton 1995a: 2)

Yet, currently the reality

> in our knowledge-intensive society, [is that] we are all both teachers and researchers. The present separation between teaching and research damages both ... You cannot communicate knowledge without adding to it, and you cannot add to knowledge without communicating it. Every act of exposition, every dialogue with a student, has the potential for creating new insights; and all research findings must be communicated (the wider the better).
>
> (Scott 2002: 27)

This fraught relationship is, and has been, the academic's dilemma and a serious tension in academe. We now explore some of the factors that have contributed to this tension and then follow this discussion with ideas on how to decrease it and/or use it as a lever for change within institutions.

Academic identities, roles and rewards

As discussed in Chapter 3, academic identities act as a significant driver to maintaining research dominance in an academic's life (Henkel 2001; Morey 2003). Academic identity is defined by both role expectations and disciplinary cultures. Collectively they exert a powerful motivation for academics to focus their energies on research over teaching.

Moses (in R. Brown 2004c) and Kreber (2000a) have investigated what academics view as academic scholarly work. Keeping in mind the major differences of both studies: purpose, foci, cultural contexts, and informants;

it is remarkable to note the similarity in the lists of academic role expectations. We have taken these lists and rearranged them to illustrate this point (see Table 7.1). We have not chosen any particular ordering, just matched items from Kreber against Moses. If more than one applied to a particular listing, these are combined and numbered for clarity.

Considering the lists in Table 7.1, there would appear to be a reasonable consensus on the range of activities within the academic role, with local variations of emphasis. This consistency would suggest a normative role expectation for most academics in most academic settings. In fact, it is such a dominant paradigm that it appears to be defining more and more fields of study as universities embrace them. Art and design and professional education (medicine/health, law, journalism, engineering etc.), for example, have working patterns within academe that increasingly resemble the range of activities described in this work.

Rice's earlier work on the academic role echoes much of this list too. He notes:

> Clustering around this dominant professorial image were the following basic assumptions:
>
> 1. Research is the central professional endeavour and focus of academic life.
> 2. Quality in the profession is maintained by peer review and professional autonomy.
> 3. Knowledge is pursued for its own sake.
> 4. The pursuit of knowledge is best organized according to discipline (i.e. according to discipline-based departments).
> 5. Reputations are established through national and international professional associations.
> 6. The distinctive task of the academic professional is the pursuit of cognitive truth.
> 7. Professional rewards and mobility accrue to those who persistently accentuate their specializations.
>
> (Rice 1992: 119)

The question of priorities within this list of expectations is at the heart of the tensions within the academic role and at the heart of the research/teaching nexus. Making a choice to focus on one over the other leads to specific outcomes for the individual, the department, the institution and higher education in general. Whatever choice the academic makes, it is made within the context of a highly structured normative role environment.

> As Everett Ladd (1979) points out: 'When a particular norm is ascendant within a group and institutionalized in various ways, it is very hard for a member of a group to deny its claim, even if intellectually he is fully convinced of its serious deficiency.'
>
> (Rice 1992: 126)

Table 7.1 Comparison of lists of academic work

Moses	*Kreber*
Reviewing of articles for a professional journal	Reviewing and evaluating the work of colleagues (manuscripts, grant proposals, etc.)
Keeping up to date with the developments in the subject area taught	Learning about new developments in one's discipline
Engaging in systematic study to gain new knowledge, or to acquire a new research technique	Conducting research
Delivering a conference paper	Off-campus lectures and conference presentations to professional societies
Maintaining professional contact with colleagues met at professional meetings	
Maintaining professional contact with colleagues nationally and internationally	Being a member/participant of professional associations
Joint research projects with colleagues in the department	
	Writing books, articles, monographs, grant proposals etc.
Having a scholarly approach to academic work	
Doing library research to make course content up to date, when a course is being revised	Preparing for teaching
Discussing teaching with colleagues in the department	• Advising/mentoring/assisting colleagues • Networking with colleagues • Informal conversations with colleagues
Examining teaching and assessment matters to see whether they are appropriate, when a course is being revised	Learning about one's teaching
	Formal instruction
Serving as a guest lecturer in a colleague's class	
Participating in staff and postgraduate seminars	
	Counselling students on programme and career issues
	Advising students on assignments, projects and theses
	Preparing and conducting evaluations of students' work

Moses	*Kreber*
	University and departmental committee work
	Public talks, consulting, community service
Development a new course in a subject area	
Developing a new way of dealing with a problem	

Source: Moses (cited in R. Brown 2004c: 7–8, table 1) and Kreber (2000a: 66).

Is this normative structure influenced by the way the roles are rewarded? Would a shift in reward structures be enough to redefine the academic role? In the next section we consider the question of rewards in the context of disciplinary identity and institutional location.

Academic rewards: disciplinary and institutional influences

Two structural variables appear to dominate discussions of academic rewards: disciplinary peers and the university where the academic is employed. As Clark (1983) has said: 'disciplines are the life-blood of higher education: alongside academic institutions, they provide its main organising base' (cited in Becher 1994: 151). Each of these structures acts, in many ways, as a gatekeeper to change through the role it plays in defining and acknowledging what will be rewarded. Equally, however, it is our contention that both can stimulate change in the reward structure as well.

Rice's seventh point above concurs with Clark's observation that, 'certainly for most faculty members the central system of rewards is recognition from their disciplines for their research and scholarly accomplishments' (Clark cited in Morey 2003: 4). As we discussed in Chapter 3, disciplines do matter in the work of academics. The consensus view about this dimension of the academic identity is supported by study after study, and there is little disagreement on this point. Henkel's work has, in fact, suggested how wide-ranging the disciplinary link is in academic work. She says,

> One of the most persistent themes in this study is that academic working lives continued to be centred in their discipline, whether they saw themselves primarily as researchers, teachers, managers or a combination of more than one of those. This generalisation held across the disciplines in the study . . . It also seemed remarkably robust in the face of drives towards multi-disciplinary teaching and research . . . Some academics, particularly in the context of their educational responsibilities, explicitly

> saw sustaining the discipline as an end in itself . . . Many academic values were embedded in concepts of the discipline and often expressed in a language shared by members of the discipline.
>
> (Henkel 2001: 4)

However, if 'the strength of our disciplines is often more political than intellectual' (Rice 1992: 24), then it would seem that disciplines are as susceptible to the same influences and strategies used in other political contexts. And, furthermore, if, as Rorty (1979) indicates, disciplinary peers decide 'what counts as a relevant contribution, what counts as answering a question, what counts as having a good argument for that answer or a good criticism of it (cited in Becher 1989: 26; see also Huber 2002), then it should be possible for the definition of what counts, and more importantly what is rewarded, to be strategically shifted within the disciplinary context. We make some suggestions of how this might be done in the last section of this chapter.

The role of institutions as the second organizational base for establishing academic norms and privileging certain work is an equally significant structural player in potentially creating greater balance between the research and teaching roles. However, returning to Henkel, her findings on academic roles indicate that within the institutional context a new dynamic is occurring which could potentially impact the outcome of both the balance between roles and the ways they are rewarded. She reports that 'there was a powerful sense among academics that theirs was no longer the monopoly or even the dominant culture. They were competing with the cultures of the market, of managerialism and of bureaucracy' (Henkel 2001: 2). It is worth reading more of Henkel's description of how this impacted the daily work of the academics she interviewed.

> There was a decline in informal 'collective academic endeavour' such as reading groups, making 'spaces for political and theoretical discussion' and going to inaugural lectures in other parts of the university . . . Increased interactions with the institution were, for the most part, experienced by academics as limiting their control of the working environment, reducing their status and shifting their own use of time from the academic to the administrative . . . Greater stress on data recording, on procedures and systems . . .; work was more open to scrutiny by administrators as well as by senior academic management and academic's own heads of department. . . . Power relations between the institution and the department changed and were potentially less stable . . . There were more quasi-hierarchical forms of relationship in some departments . . . and more transparent inequalities. Work was more formally organised and individual performance more formally evaluated . . . Individuals were more careful and instrumental in the use of their time.
>
> (Henkel 2001: 2–3)

Predating Henkel's findings, and in a way foreshadowing an ongoing regulatory climate in higher education institutions, Rowland (1996: 13) noted that 'the category distinction between teaching and research may owe more to the demands for accountability than to logical or pedagogical differences between academic roles'. Again we look at some ways of using this change to enhance the relationship of teaching and research later in this chapter.

Rewarding research and teaching

Overall, the message concerning the current circumstance within the higher education community remains no different from previous accounts of academic role structures.

> The present culture of higher education ostensibly values the integration of faculty roles, particularly of teaching and research. However, . . . a message that is typically conveyed is that . . . real responsibilities rest with the research function while teaching (and service) are necessary add-ons.
>
> (Kreber 2000b)

Interrogating this situation further, Kreber found that role integration was stronger for experienced staff than for junior staff. Yet, she also found that 'the university reward structure . . . places undue emphasis on refereed publications' (Kreber 2000b).

Even more interesting to us is that when staff are rewarded for their role as teachers they often remain wedded to their research role as their primary identity. This is best illustrated by the views expressed by a University Teaching Award recipient at a UK university when asked if they were willing to be put forward for a prestigious national teaching award:

> Thanks for the opportunity but my interests lie more in pure research. So my 'spare' time is taken up with [subject field]. I feel I couldn't devote the time (that would undoubtedly be needed) for this kind of project. My interests, and to be honest my skills, lie elsewhere.
>
> (Personal communication 2003)

This response is not uncommon. 'Efforts [in the USA] to reward teaching and learning did result in innovations, but little has changed the research prominence in the reward system' (Lazerson *et al.* cited in Morley 2003: 3; see also Kreber 2000b for a similar observation).

SoTL: bridging the research and teaching divide

The work cited thus far suggests that the reality in higher education today is that research remains dominant in the lives of academics, in terms of their professional identities, professional affiliations and professional location. If teaching were to achieve a similar place in the academic world it would, in our view, need to be identified with research activities in some direct way. This is more or less possible even now in some disciplines and some institutions. Moses' (1990) work illustrated that 'teaching is experienced differently in the different disciplines' and added that in some disciplines teaching and research may be more or less connected. She suggests, as we do, that 'scholarship provides the bridge between both' (Moses 1990: 373) and in a range of disciplinary and institutional contexts.

The long-standing notion of scholarship as an integral part of academic life (see Rice (1992: 118) for a succinct history) has regained topicality in discussions of ways to balance the research–teaching nexus. Boyer (1990), in his fruitful work *Scholarship Reconsidered*, in effect proposed, via his delineation of four forms of scholarship, a mechanism to increase the status of teaching. Before reviewing these four categories of scholarship, and in particular the scholarship of teaching, we begin by reminding ourselves of the various meanings attached to scholarship.

Elton (2003, 2004) has provided what he considers a not wholly adequate translation of the German *wissenschaft* from which the English word 'scholarship' derives its meaning. He has suggested that 'scholarship is defined as a deep understanding of a subject . . . [and] the unceasing process of inquiry' (Elton 2004: 2). In both cases, it is fairly clear that scholarship includes a rigorous investigation of ideas.

Boyer (1990) has suggested a similar definition and links it to the research–teaching nexus through adding the dimension of learning as core to scholarly endeavours (see also Elton 1986; Moses 1990; Blackburn and Lawrence 1995).

> Scholarship is not an esoteric appendage; it is the heart of what the profession is all about. All faculty [staff], throughout their careers, should themselves, remain students. As scholars they must continue to learn and be seriously and continuously engaged in the expanding intellectual world.
>
> (Boyer quoted in Rice 1992: 120)

Others have asked 'whether scholarship is a goal to be attained or a process to be maintained' (Braskamp and Ory 1994: 36).

> Scholarship thus defined would be precisely what scholars do and not only what they produce . . . We might consider expanding our definition of scholarship looking at both process and product, and base our definition of scholarship on the present work experiences of academics.
>
> (Kreber 2000a: 63)

A culturally specific definition of scholarship is illustrated in Rice's reminder that Emerson, in 1837, 'called for a new approach to scholarship, one that would be fully engaged with the needs, realities of, a vibrant, developing democracy' (Rice 1992: 127).

However, the definitions of scholarship that have the most relevance to the discussion of the research–teaching nexus have come from the work on the scholarship of teaching and learning (SoTL) that grew out of the efforts of Boyer and others to redress the balance between teaching and research. Following this brief review of the further elaborations on scholarship by Boyer, we explore why we see value in SoTL as a bridge between research and teaching and a lever for change in higher education.

Categories of scholarship

Boyer (1990) defined four categories of scholarship. We consider each of them below and add some explanatory commentary from Rice who worked closely with Boyer on this project.

- *Scholarship of discovery*. Rice (1992: 123) suggests that 'we should urgently insist that scholarship have as one of its anchor points the discovery of new knowledge – what has traditionally been known as original research'.
- *Scholarship of integration*. Rice (1992: 123) notes that: 'Without the continual effort at reintegration, we have fragmentation. It was also Weber who warned of the possibility of a modern world filled with "specialists without spirit, and sensualists without heart." Scholars are needed with a capacity to synthesize, to look for new relationships between the parts and the whole.'
- *Scholarship of practice*, including the practical application of knowledge. Rice (1992: 124) sees this as very American and linked to the Land Grant Colleges movement. Huber (2002) suggests that at some point between 1994 and 1995 Boyer started to call this the scholarship of engagement, 'by which he meant those activities within any of the four scholarships which connect the academic with people and places outside the campus and which ultimately direct the work of the academy "toward larger, more humane ends" ' (Boyer cited in Huber 2002: 2).
- *Scholarship of teaching*. Rice (1992) suggests that this form of scholarship

  > has an integrity of its own, but is deeply embedded in the other three forms . . . In addition the scholarship of teaching has at last three distinct elements: first the synoptic capacity, the ability to draw the strands of a field together in a way that provides both coherence and meaning . . .; second pedagogical content knowledge . . ., the capacity to represent a subject in ways that transcend the split between intellectual substance and teaching process . . .; third, what we know about learning, scholarly inquiry into how students 'make meaning'.

Rice comments further:

> While we want to treat the four forms of scholarship as individually distinctive, we also want them to be understood as interrelated and

> often overlapping: an independent whole, with each distinctive form encompassing each of the other three. See Figure 7.1.
>
> (Rice 1992: 125)

These categories and the definition of scholarship of teaching, in particular, have been discussed, elaborated and reinterpreted by academics for over a decade and a half (Elton 2000; Healey 2000; P. Hutchings 2000; Kreber and Cranton 2000; Rowland 2000; Trigwell *et al.* 2000; Cambridge 2001; Richlin 2001; M. Hutchings 2002). Out of this discourse and debate, SoTL has emerged as a scholarship in its own right.

In the Higher Education Funding Council for England review report on SoTL, Gordon *et al.* (2003) reviewed the common concepts surrounding SoTL and tried to provide a clearer understanding of their use. Although SoTL was less commonly known in 2000 in the UK, Ped R (pedagogical research) and Ped D (pedagogical development) had become a type of shorthand for two major dimensions of SoTL as it is used currently, and it is important to realize that these two terms (or disciplinary jargon as some would suggest) were an attempt to find a way to understand better what

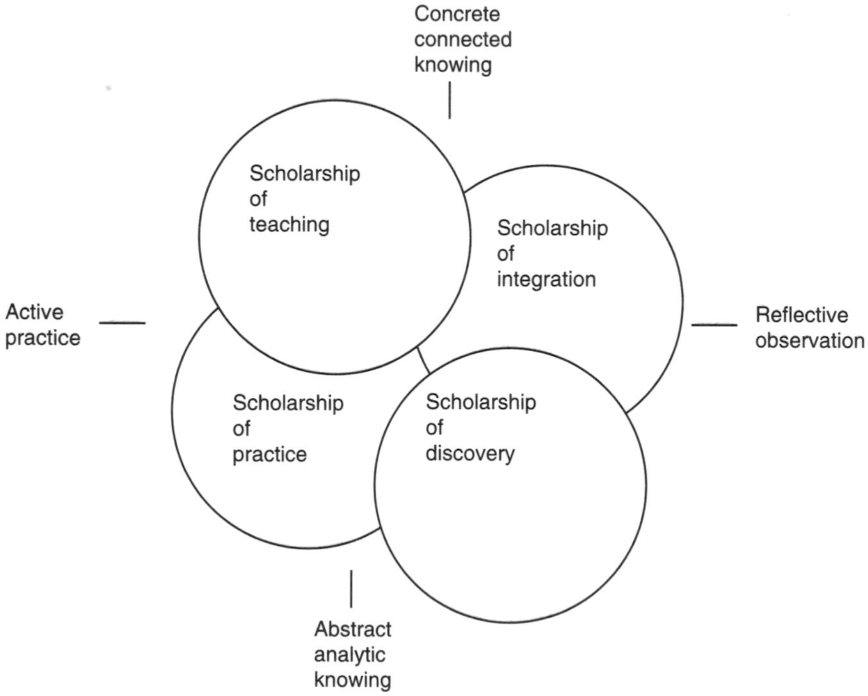

Figure 7.1 An enlarged view of scholarly work
Source: Rice (1992: 128).

Table 7.2 Dimensions of pedagogical development and pedagogical research

	Ped D	*Ped R*
Activity	Aim to improve practice	Aim to describe, analyse, conceptualize
	Informal methodology	Formal research proposal
	Context-specific	Applicable to wider contexts
	Own teaching/own department	Independent of own teaching
	Aimed at local audience	Aimed at national/international audience
	Pragmatic, low theorization	Based on established theory
	Subject-focused or generic	Subject-focused or generic
Outputs	Improvement to practice	Better understanding of practice
	Limited generalizability	Generalizable output
	Non-refereed publication	Peer-reviewed publication
	Guidelines on good practice	Analytical description/ conceptualization
	For own institution use	Results in the public domain
	Website	May be reported on website
	Publication	Publication

Source: Gordon *et al.* (2003).

constituted scholarly work on teaching and learning.[1] The characteristics of these two dimensions are set out in Table 7.2.

Comparison of Ped R and Ped D

The first point to note is that Ped D and Ped R have a common focus. This is the relationship between teaching, the learner and subject matter, within the context of higher education. Both terms can refer either to activities, or to outputs that derive from these activities. There is a considerable overlap between the activities and the outputs. We suggest that the terms may be used to denote different features of enquiry within the broader field of SoTL. Ped D and Ped R represent different characteristics, or different emphases, within what are called 'dimensions of enquiry' (Gordon *et al.* 2003: 24).

The Gordon *et al.* report went on to describe examples for each of the dimensions listed in Table 7.2. Because this work was originally done in 2001 and the debate has moved on considerably since then, we limit the discussion of Ped R/Ped D in this chapter to how they contribute to an understanding of SoTL.

Figure 7.2 illustrates how we see the relationship between these various elements of scholarly work. From our perspective, SoTL overlaps both Ped R and Ped D which in turn are situated in the middle circle of a Venn diagram

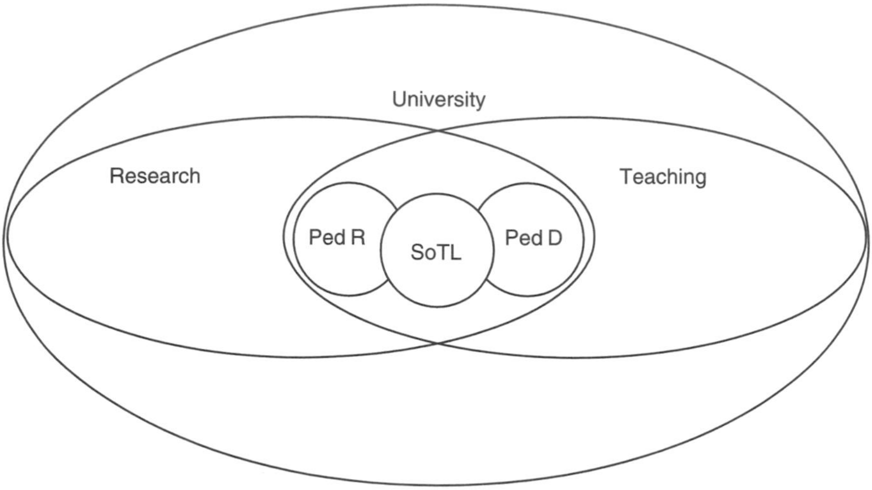

Figure 7.2 The university research–teaching nexus and pedagogical research (Ped R), pedagogical development (Ped D) and SoTL

linking research and teaching. We are suggesting that SoTL is the bridge between research and teaching because it encompasses both Ped R and Ped D.

Kreber has succinctly summarized how this relationship can be demonstrated in practice. She and her co-author Cranton draw on Habermas's notion of three different knowledge domains, as well as his theory of communicative action to

> suggest that acquiring scholarship in teaching is a learning process involving various combinations of instrumental, but primarily, communicative and emancipatory learning processes . . . Professors validate their knowledge about teaching though critical discourse within a community of peers. One could perhaps conclude that learning about one's discipline and learning about teaching are two processes that inform each other and are inextricably intertwined.
>
> (Kreber 2000: 75)

On this topic see also Rowland (1996), Clark (1997), Colbeck (1998) and Jenkins (2000).

Scholarship of teaching and scholarly teaching

Another important discussion which adds to the suggestion that SoTL can be a bridge between research and teaching surrounds the differences between scholarship of teaching and scholarly teaching. When matched against the characteristics of Ped R and Ped D, respectively, there is a striking similarity in the ways in which each is described.

> Hutchings and Shulman (1999) speak about scholarship of teaching as . . . being public, open to critique and evaluation, and in a form that others can build on . . . a kind of 'going meta' in which faculty [staff] frame and systematically investigate questions related to student learning . . . and do so with an eye not only to improving their own classroom but to advancing practice beyond it.
>
> (Cambridge 1999: 2)[2]

Cambridge describes scholarly teachers as:

> Faculty [staff] who wish to explore the challenges in fostering student learning who seek feedback from students through classroom assessment; guidance from local peers through reciprocal visits, joint course development activities, or faculty development workshops; and insight from disciplinary colleagues through reading literature about pedagogy in their field. They become informed teachers who benefit from the scholarship of others.
>
> (Cambridge 1999: 2)

Again we would see both scholarship of teaching and scholarly teaching as key elements of SoTL, overlapping each other at times, distinct from each other at other times but both aimed at a similar purpose: the improvement of student learning through a systematic informed process of investigation. This process has been articulated by the Director of the US National Science Foundation, STEM (Science, Technology, Engineering and Mathematics) Project. He says,

> In fact, the improvement of teaching is . . . a research problem addressing the question 'What have my students learned?' In the STEM projects, STEM scholars engage in . . . conceptual steps in the teaching-as-research process [which] follow the model of most STEM disciplinary research:
>
> 1. Learning foundational knowledge
> 2. Developing goals and ideas (hypotheses) for improved student learning
> 3. Defining measures of success and the required evidence
> 4. Developing and implementing practices within an experimental construct
> 5. Collecting and analysing data
> 6. Reflecting, evaluating and iterating.
>
> (Mathieu 2004: 3)

Mathieu concludes by saying: 'The application of the teaching-as-research is meant to lead participants to an ongoing process of discovery and change, which is the core motivation of all researchers' (Mathieu 2004: 3). We would suggest that what he calls teaching-as-research is SoTL by yet another name. Work like this helps to illustrate that an integrated link between research and teaching is possible.

This process of integration in scholarly work has been described by Brew

(2004) as a type of 'inclusive scholarly community'. She goes on to note that at her university they distinguish

> between the scholarship of teaching and research-led teaching to ensure that research-led teaching, which focuses on disciplinary research and its use in teaching (in every way that implies) is not confused with pedagogical research (referred to in the University of Sydney context as the scholarship of teaching).
>
> (Brew 2004: 5)

We now explore this added distinction before moving on to suggestions on how to engage with SoTL for the improvement of teaching and learning.

Research-led teaching and learning

Griffith (2004) has also considered the question of what constitutes research-led teaching. In his recent work he has suggested three main models of how research and teaching can interrelate. He sees different research approaches linked with specific approaches to pedagogy. These are:

- research-led: the familiar notion of curriculum content being dominated by staff [faculty] research interests, where information transmission is the main teaching mode;
- research-oriented: the curriculum is also about knowledge production and staff [faculty] try to engender a research ethos through their teaching;
- research-based: the curriculum is genuinely inquiry based and the division between teacher and student is minimal.

(Reported in R.B. Brown 2004b: 11)

Using Griffith's categorizations of research-led teaching we not only see ways in which research and teaching can be part of one integrated role but also ways that this link supports the learning experience of students. Brew and Boud (1995b) have also suggested, as we mentioned in Chapter 2, that the link between teaching and research is through learning because both activities are inherently part of a learning process. The two become blurred in a way similar to the blurring that Rowland suggests happens between research and scholarship. As one of his respondents put it: 'the dissemination of research is a pedagogical activity and therefore to separate teaching and research is illogical' (Rowland 1996: 13).

SoTL as a lever for change

It is our view that SoTL provides a unique opportunity to rebalance the research–teaching nexus. Going back to Clark's point about the two key structures of academe, it seems that if SoTL activities are directly connected to these structures there is a greater likelihood that this rebalancing will occur. The process may be slow at first but it is one that could gain momentum if the other factors we have discussed are taken into account as well.

We take our lead for this approach to changing the relationship between research and teaching from two national initiatives – one in the UK and one in the USA – that have SoTL activities embedded within in them. Both have addressed this challenge through a strikingly similar three-pronged approach. Both focus on the individual, disciplinary/subject groups and institutions. Figures 7.3 and 7.4 illustrate these similarities.

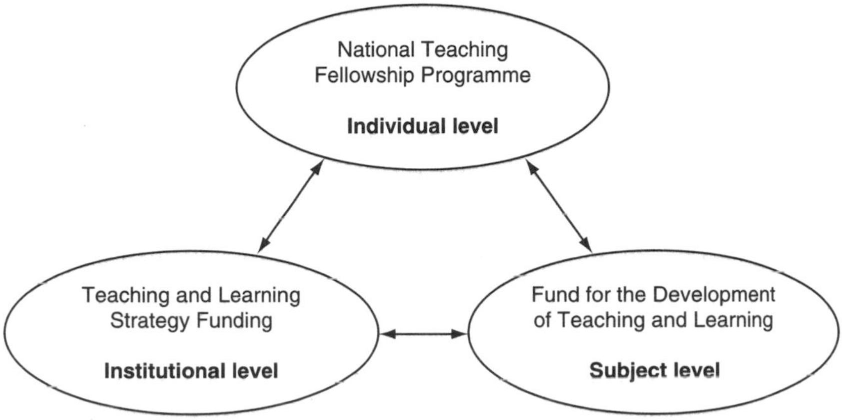

Figure 7.3 Teaching Quality Enhancement Fund (TQEF), England

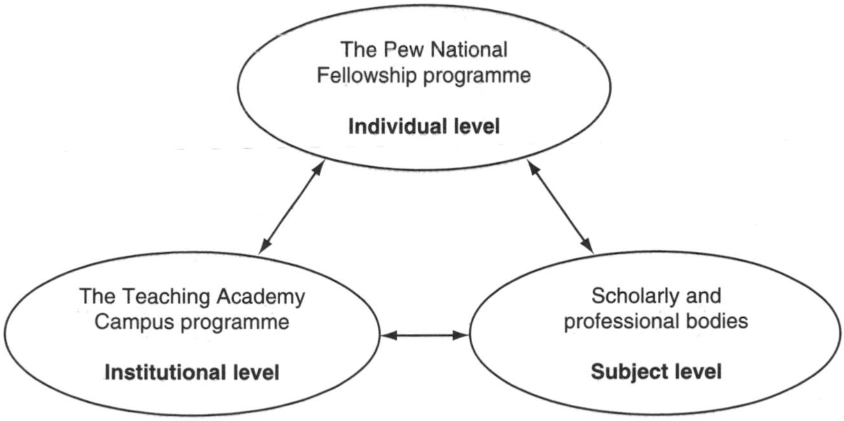

Figure 7.4 CASTL links between teaching and research, USA

National SoTL Developments

The Teaching Quality Enhancement Fund (TQEF) is an initiative of the Higher Education Funding Council for England. This government-led set of programmes is designed to address concerns in the academic community regarding special extra funding available for research activities through the UK-wide Research Assessment Exercise which critics claimed is having an adverse impact on teaching and learning. In England (and Northern Ireland), extra funding is made available to support individuals through a National Teaching Fellowship (NTF) programme and to institutions to support the development and implementation of university-level teaching and learning strategies. The third part of the programme is a programme to support disciplinary/subject-level developments in teaching and learning through a Fund for the Development of Teaching and Learning (FDTL), linked to subject outcomes in a subject-based quality assurance exercise. The individual and disciplinary work focused on SoTL activities in the form of pedagogical projects (see Figure 7.3).

In the USA, the Carnegie Academy for the Scholarship of Teaching and Learning (CASTL) programme, one of the many initiatives of the Carnegie Foundation for the Advancement of Teaching, is engaged in similar activities and for a similar aim. Its purpose is to

> reinvigorate education by renewing the connections between teaching and research. . . . programs seek to foster forms of reflection and inquiry that will raise the level of attention to educational issues throughout American academic life. The long-term goal is to stimulate a fundamental shift in values, cultures and priorities of universities . . . a shift which in turn, makes possible a re-framing of the teaching professions.
>
> (Carnegie Foundation for the Advancement of Teaching 2000: 7)

The CASTL programme also consists of a three-level programme to effect this change. Each programme is aimed at bringing about a change in the status of pedagogical research at different levels of the academic community. The Pew National Fellowships is aimed at the individual faculty/staff members who are known as Carnegie Scholars, although selection until recently has been limited from year to year to designated disciplinary categories. The Campus Academy is aimed at institutional change across disciplinary boundaries, while the work with scholarly and professional organizations is aimed at changing the view of pedagogical research through the subject disciplines (see Figure 7.4).

The strengths of both the UK and US initiatives lie in their attempt to link key structures in the academic community with one another by working to change the status of teaching and pedagogical research at multiple levels. This approach attempts to improve the links between national professional disciplinary groups with those more generic networks at the national level via the Fellows and those within selected institutions. This reinforcing structure is creating interconnected networks of teaching scholars in three contexts:

within their institution, within disciplines and across disciplines. These initiatives applies Clark's key understandings of the importance of disciplinary structures and institutional structures, which we discussed earlier in this chapter, as a double lever for change. In this case, the underlying premise is that scholarship holds the key to the connections. These activities support the ambitious goal to rebalance the research and teaching nexus and, if successful, have the potential for powerful cultural change in higher education.

Disciplinary SoTL developments

Some disciplinary associations have independently and in advance of national initiatives created networks around pedagogical interests. In the USA, one leader in these activities was the American Sociological Association (ASA), which has had a Projects on Teaching initiative since the mid-1970s. It is a prime example of a disciplinary social movement to improve the status of teaching. Partially funded by the Lilly Foundation, a private education charity, and the National Science Foundation (NSF) through the Fund for the Improvement of Postsecondary Education (FIPSE), the ASA Projects on Teaching focused on three specific areas of change: curriculum, faculty/staff development and institutional development programmes. The outcomes include (1) a Teaching Resources Center with a catalogue of materials on a wide range of subject-specific teaching issues such as teaching methods and course syllabi sets, and (2) the Teaching Resources Group (now the Departmental Resources Group) consisting of over 40 sociologists who act as consultants to departments and institutions as well as initially organizing and running a series of national workshops on teaching held throughout the USA in the 1970s and 1980s. Various ASA Projects activities have been maintained over three decades now.

In the UK, the Group for Learning in Art and Design (GLAD) is one example of a subject group with a similar commitment to teaching. Others include the Geography Discipline Network, which has had a teaching journal for over twenty years, the Council for Hospitality Management, and the Council for College and University English (QAAHE 1998).

Another UK-wide disciplinary development has been the creation of the Learning and Teaching Support Network (LTSN) that we discussed in Chapter 3. It was established to promote pedagogical developments through 24 subject/disciplinary organizations. Each of the 24 subject groupings has an educational development centre. These centres engage in a variety of SoTL activities, again including small grants for pedagogical projects either to investigate possible innovations in teaching and learning or to disseminate work that has been acknowledged as outstanding (see www.heacademy.ac.uk). It is through these centres that the opportunity exists to have a direct impact on the influence of pedagogical research at institutional level. This is most likely to occur if the national/disciplinary/subject work is tied to local centres of teaching and learning on individual university campuses.

Institutional SoTL developments

At institutional level, the influence of SoTL will vary considerably depending on the extent to which learning and teaching is supported within the institution. In institutions where there is support from an institutional educational development centre and funding for SoTL activities there is a much stronger likelihood that it could have impact on the research/teaching nexus within the institution.

If SoTL activity is to be valued at a local level, those supporting these centres need to ensure that SoTL activities are related to the dominant academic culture and the mission of the institution, as well as to the ethos of the teaching departments within them. If SoTL projects are perceived as having immediate value and utility to both individual staff members and the institution as a whole, they are more likely to be acknowledged as valuable contributions to the academic enterprise. It is easiest when, as Colbeck has observed: 'The broader the university definition of what counts for research, the more faculty are able to integrate research and classroom-oriented teaching' (cited in R.B. Brown 2004b).

As we mentioned in Chapter 2, institutional-level educational development centres have established a wide range of functions, from support of the full academic role to development of academic policy. More recently, many have had an important role in promoting and co-ordinating SoTL activities. Some institutions take a conscious decision to ensure that the academics within the centres are themselves involved in scholarly projects.

Centres that model scholarly work in this way support and encourage the same activity among faculty/staff across the institution. Centre team members who are SoTL scholars can also partner faculty/staff in schools/departments to investigate teaching and learning. The results are often both traditional SoTL outcomes such as co-authored publications and non-traditional SoTL products (see Gosling and Jiwani 1997; O'Reilly *et al.* 2000 and City University's Educational Development Centre at http://www.city.ac.uk.edc/).

Another common feature for supporting SoTL activities is the provision of a mechanism for small-scale 'seed grant' funding for projects to promote investigation of innovations or evaluation of teaching and learning activities. These projects enable faculty/staff to:

- investigate and evaluate the professional work in which they are already engaged (see http://www.itl.usyd.edu.au/);
- get feedback from the centre's SoTL support staff;
- publish papers internally for dissemination across the institution;
- 'demonstrate a relationship between teaching and research' (Hattie and Marsh 2004: 6);
- create 'pedagogic impact statement(s)' (Gibbs 2001b: 2).

Often, there will be a group of faculty/staff in higher education institutions who are already engaged in SoTL, but no one has named it as such.

They may be isolated within their departments; however, if they can be put in touch with others who have similar interests, together they can create an institutional critical mass that can influence others to become involved in SoTL. Common mechanisms currently used for building and supporting these links among faculty/staff include:

- teaching and learning research clusters designed to provide peer review of work in progress;
- seminars for initial presentation of research results to test out ideas;
- seminars on how to get published and how to upgrade investigations into a published paper;
- one-to-one support from centre academics;
- email/newsletter notification of opportunities for publications and presentation at conferences;
- collaboration with students;
- regular social gatherings (teaching roundtable lunches/dinners);
- a physical place for these gatherings and comfortable communication (Mathieu 2004: 4).

At the University of Sydney, the result of these kinds of activities was a showcase where one hundred presentations by University of Sydney staff were featured. These included:

- reports of scholarly enquiry into teaching and learning;
- examples of teaching that use evidence from research and scholarship on learning;
- examples of using disciplinary research in teaching;
- examples of engaging students in enquiry in teaching and learning;
- discussions on bringing research and teaching together.
  (Brew 2004: 3; see: http://www.itl.usyd.edu.au/RLT)

What is being established through these kinds of activities is a community of peers not dissimilar to those with whom faculty/staff engage when working on disciplinary research. These are all forms of learning communities/communities of practice that we discussed in Chapter 2. Kreber's study of teaching award winners has found supportive evidence for this. She notes that 'learning about teaching and learning about the discipline are associated with interactions with colleagues, which may suggest that these professors conceive of such learning as a communicative process that occurs within a community of peers' (Kreber 2000a: 74).

An extension to this approach is to create an inclusive SoTL community, 'adding students to events, seminars and meetings usually only open to staff [faculty]' (Gibbs 2001b: 2–3). Rowland (1996: 18–19) suggests that students could be more actively involved with classroom research as well. In this case, the faculty/staff member can encourage the students to 'deconstruct' the lecture, allowing for the 'same critical orientation as research and keeps the subject matter of research alive and open to further inquiry' (Rowland 1996: 15).

A further support mechanism for promoting SoTL work at institutional level can be provided through internal publication programmes. Various types of publications can be used to disseminate the results of SoTL work being conducted within institutions. Editorial boards of faculty/staff can be organized to act as peer review panels to referee the publications which, if accepted for publication, can be given an ISBN/ISSN as appropriate. Some examples include:

- a compendium of the teaching and learning project reports on internally funded innovations (see D'Andrea 1996);
- occasional papers which focus on recent issues in higher education (see, for example, University of Glamorgan, Centre for Lifelong Learning);
- an in-house journal (see, for example, London Metropolitan University).

SoTL peer review support can also be applied to publishing in external journals. A SoTL network or learning set, as described in Chapter 2, could be set up with the specific purpose of functioning as a peer review group that would provide supportive formative advice as a critical friend to the author prior to submission for publication. Appendix A to this book provides a list of possible relevant journals for a SoTL publication from the catalogue of just one major publisher. The total list of all journals published that might be interested in SoTL work is far too large to include in its entirety in this book. However, the Carfax list should be sufficient to prompt thinking of other potential publishing options. (See: http://www.city.londonmet.ac.uk/deliberations/journals/index.html for another set of journal lists.) Although some of the titles listed have not published SoTL work to date, it may be worth engaging in a dialogue with the editors about this possibility.

Currently there are two electronic peer reviewed journals that do focus on SoTL specifically. JoSoTL (http://titans.iusb.edu/josotl/) and MountainRise (http://mountainrise.wcu.edu/). Both accept submissions on a regular basis.

To promote broader public discussion and provide an opportunity for pedagogical research to go public, it is important that faculty/staff are encouraged to present SoTL findings at conferences where the results of their enquiries can be discussed and debated. National and international networks exist which provide forums for the debate of SoTL (see Appendix B for list of some of the many relevant conferences).

Another approach to supporting SoTL at institutional level is the appointment of visiting professors and fellows whose responsibility is to lead the SoTL agenda (see http://www.city.ac.uk/edc/). Their role is to provide:

- advice and guidance to faculty/staff;
- deliver a professorial lecture in the area of SoTL to contribute to the credibility of the work;
- assist in the development of proposals for external funding.

In the case of visiting professors in particular, they can bring their experience, reputation and expertise to add weight and credibility to the SoTL development process. In institutions that lack the track record in applying for pedagogic-related grants, the support of visiting professors can be critical to the success of a bid (see http://www.esrc.ac.uk/esrccontent/researchfunding/tlrp_thematicseminarscomp_call.asp).

Institutions might want to consider how SoTL can specifically inform curriculum development activities, including teaching and learning innovations. Gibbs (2001b: 2–3) has suggested a number of ways this could be done:

- Encourage research-only staff to advise on curriculum (books lists, lab exercises, review of course content) and to be guest lecturers or lead special seminar sessions.
- Studio and labs could be designed to address state of the art issues in the field.
- Curriculum development could be linked to researchers' interests and offered as upper-level courses/modules.
- Increase the use of project- and consultancy-driven courses/modules that can exploit expertise and case material derived from faculty/staff consultancy and applied research experience.
- Change the pedagogy to include research activities: projects, dissertations, internships, consultancies and/or research projects, independent study with increased student access to labs, equipment and other resources usually limited to researchers.

Woodhouse (2001) and others have emphasized the opportunities available for institutional developments of SoTL by going back to the original Humboldtian vision of engaging in research with students. This is often described as an enquiry mode of learning and can be initiated as a part of the ongoing curriculum development processes in institutions (Barnett cited in R.B. Brown 2004b; see also Rowland 1996; Barnett 2000; Gibbs 2001b).

An important element in any strategy to promote SoTL is the provision of professional development courses that are based on enquiry and research, as we suggested in Chapter 3. Investigative work undertaken for such courses can provide faculty/staff with their first published paper in SoTL. Through such courses faculty/staff can be encouraged to:

- evaluate teaching and learning using relevant theoretical frameworks, and
- reflect on and analyse their teaching and students' learning.

Another approach can be linked to peer observations, which are becoming more common in higher education. A developmental observation scheme known as 'expeditions to teaching and learning opportunities' has been organized at the University of Wisconsin in the USA (Mathieu 2004). Unlike summative evaluative observation schemes, the specific purpose of this scheme is to encourage SoTL applications in the classroom.

We return now to the first paragraph of this chapter, where we suggested that the three key areas that prompted faculty/staff to focus more on research than on teaching were resources, recognition and rewards. The previous section has explored a variety of ways to resource and recognize SoTL which is aimed at creating the conditions for a greater equilibrium between research and teaching. We have also briefly noted ways to reward these activities. However, it is our view that, for real change to occur, there needs to be recognizable career routes which provide recognition and reward for faculty/staff who are engaged in SoTL. We would like to suggest that putting some or all of the following in place could contribute to this change:

- Promotions within a department, school or faculty which (a) demonstrate that the institution values SoTL and (b) support the faculty/staff member to take on a role to investigate teaching and learning issues within their subject.
- Annual awards which provide public recognition of achievements in the investigation of teaching and learning.
- Nomination for national awards.
- Recognition of the best teacher/researchers (Hattie and Marsh (2004: 6) noted the lack of such awards).
- Temporary appointments (secondments from schools/departments) to educational development centres which support SoTL.

The Scholarship Index at the University of Sydney is another interesting approach to creating a reward structure for SoTL activities. It is, however, a mechanism to reward departments, not individuals, who engage in SoTL. The department's score is based on a set of weighted criteria that are used to calculate the department's score. For example: 'a qualification in university teaching (10 points), a national teaching award (finalist) (5 points), a publication on university teaching – refereed article (2 points)' (Brew 2004: 5–6). This shifts the drive for more critically informed teaching activities to a community of practice – the department – and away from individual innovators, giving this change the momentum and power of a critical mass.

Rowland (1996: 18–19), although not directly addressing SoTL developments, has created a list of development activities that, in many ways, mirrors the major themes in this chapter on using SoTL as a lever for change. We think it is a useful guide for creating the conditions for improving teaching and learning through SoTL. His list includes:

- Creating critical interdisciplinarity to break down unhelpful disciplinary stereotypes and tribalism.
- Encouraging students to express their ideas as part of teaching process and how they are assessed.
- Supporting teaching which is risky and unpredictable.
- Focusing discussions on understanding the curriculum, the research underpinning it and the context within which students exist.
- Encouraging lecturers (faculty/staff) to develop strategies for researching their own and each other's teaching processes.

Table 7.3 summarizes the discussion on possible SoTL initiatives at the institutional and disciplinary levels. It provides a quick checklist for those developing programmes to bridge the research–teaching divide in this way.

In the end, promoting SoTL is all about creating opportunities for teaching

Table 7.3 Possible SoTL initiatives at institutional and disciplinary levels

SoTL developmental activity	*Institutional*	*Disciplinary*
Build on academic culture	✓	✓
Build on institutional mission	✓	
Centre with a cross-institutional role	✓	
Educational development centres		✓
Pump-priming funding	✓	✓
Link to funding opportunities	✓	✓
SoTL peer review	✓	✓
SoTL support networks	✓	✓
Reward and recognition for SoTL activities	✓	✓
External support: SoTL experts	✓	✓
SoTL publications	✓	✓
Other SoTL products	✓	✓
SoTL conferences	✓	✓
Developmental observation	✓	
Professional development courses on teaching and learning in higher education	✓	✓

to 'go public' and be acknowledged as an equal partner with research in the academic world. Although the benefits remain undocumented, they certainly can be inferred from the outcomes to date. However, no matter what the motivation for engaging in specific academic activities, whether as researcher, scholar or teacher, all are short-changed owing to limits of time. And time, as every academic knows, is the scarcest commodity of all. D'Andrea (2001) has suggested that 'value for time' is often more important for the academic than 'value for money'. In this chapter we have focused on finding a balance between the competing demands of research and teaching (see Henkel, 2001). We have also suggested that the SoTL is one way to both bridge and combine these activities.

Notes

1. What is interesting to note is that these terms originated in the UK and no doubt they are linked to the broader discussions on the Research Assessment Exercise (RAE). The Research and Teaching Group (R & T Group) that was started by Professor Roger Brown and a few others interested in policy issues related to the research on the questions concerned with the perceived link between research and teaching, held a conference in January 2000 for UK higher education policy makers and researchers in this field (R.B. Brown 2000b). In order to discuss pedagogical research in the context of current policy in the UK, a distinction was made between pedagogical research (Ped R) which was more like traditional research (RAEable in the UK) and pedagogical development (Ped D) which was more like project work (not RAEable in the UK).
2. Richlin (2001) has added to this discussion by specifying the differences between teaching scholars and scholarly teaching.

8

Quality Development

> Phew, It's 22! If we had got 20, we would have been the worst [subject identity] provision in the country. If we had got 24, the best. So really it is a five-point scale. At eight this morning I had a member of staff in tears, another threatening to resign, and a third threatening physical violence. All to get us on the middle of a five-point scale.
>
> Head of School, Personal communication 2001

The focus of this chapter is on what we are calling the 'new' quality agenda. We take a critical look at how quality issues and debates in higher education are maturing. The quality agenda, whether externally imposed or internally developed, is a major concern that modern universities have to deal with on a regular basis. The impact of quality issues on the functioning of universities has increased significantly in recent years, though in some countries more than others; and has been oftentimes linked to trends in the massification of higher education. Whether this is a real or spurious link is debatable; however, we leave this discussion for another occasion. What we focus on here is the 'quality reality' that institutions worldwide face almost daily.

We begin this chapter by reviewing the quality enhancement (QE)/ quality assurance (QA) debate in higher education. We are concerned to understand how the quality agenda can be reclaimed by the academic community and used developmentally to improve the learning experience of students. In order to do this, we critically analyse both self-regulatory approaches of institutions and those imposed by external regulatory agencies. We consider the effect of the increasing regulatory activities in higher education on academe, academics and the students they serve. We draw on the work of Salter and Tapper (1994) and others who have framed this debate as an 'ideological struggle between the economic view of the purposes of higher education, the traditional liberal ideal, [and] the bureaucratic drive of the state . . . in framing educational policy' (cited in Greatrix 2001: 13).

We conclude the chapter by proposing a quality development (QD) model. This model addresses the tensions between competing models of quality and reflects our discussion in Chapter 2 on building learning communities within universities. We illustrate how learning communities and quality activities are able to complement each other in the task of maintaining continuous quality improvement for student learning.

The (QD) model emphasizes a formative approach to replace what has been primarily a summative process. It applies assessment theory to organizational learning in the same way as it is applied to student learning. There are undoubtedly ways that developments in learning and teaching will be, and should be, reflected in the criteria by which quality is assured in higher education. And similarly, there are quality assurance mechanisms that can be, and should be, part of an integrated process for improving the student's learning experience. As in previous chapters we provide a number of examples of how, in this instance, the quality development model works in practice, along with suggestions on how to put it into practice.

What is meant by quality in higher education?

Frans van Vught (1994) has explored the meaning of quality in higher education by placing the discussion squarely within a definition of higher education itself. He identifies what he calls the intrinsic and extrinsic qualities of higher education. 'The intrinsic qualities are related to the ideals of the search for truth and the pursuit of knowledge. The extrinsic qualities are found in the services higher education institutions provide to society' (Vught 1994: 32).

Vught argues that this same combination should be the basis of an effective system of quality assessment in present-day higher education. We return to this point when we discuss our model of quality development at the end of this chapter.

Vught also suggests that it must be recognized that quality activities in higher education are:

- as elusive as they are pervasive;
- self-contradictory (Pirsig 1974);
- political – linked to far-reaching government policies;
- sensitive – requiring a look at strengths and weaknesses;
- multidimensional and subjective – overvaluing measurable indicators.

Each of these adds an important element to the quality debate. Starting with the political implications of quality systems in higher education: as would be expected, these are dependent on the political system where the higher education activity is situated. In some instances, quality activities are directly tied to policies to extend higher education opportunities through, what in the UK is known as, widening participation, and in other instances they might be more directly linked to national economic growth policies. In any case it is important to recognize when there is a relationship between quality activities in higher education and national policy wherever it exists. It is important because of the impact on higher education and the potential for an imposed national curriculum and other possible constraints on academic freedom.

Sensitivity is an equally important element of a quality system if it is successfully to promote quality outcomes. Looking at strengths and weaknesses of universities is not much different from understanding these in individuals: in both instances, for changes to occur a willingness to change needs to be understood. We discuss this further in the last section of this chapter in relation to the quality development model we propose.

The multidimensionality aspect of quality improvement is an equally powerful inhibitor to improvement if it is poorly understood or ignored. The recent total quality management (TQM) movement and other systems adopted by higher education from business and industry have been introduced to help deal with understanding these complexities of multidimensionality in more concrete terms. However, these approaches to quality management are highly dependent on measurable objectives that can, in effect, complicate things further. We comment on the overvaluing of this approach later in this chapter.

Now back to Vught's first points. When the first one is explored carefully, the second becomes self-evident. The first is probably the most important to the discussion of the meaning of quality activities in higher education and, as has also been noted by others: 'quality' is a seriously ambiguous term (Ellis 1993; Harvey and Green 1993; Gordon 2001) encompassing a range of possible approaches to its use. Several of these include:

- quality as the outstanding ('excellence');
- quality as realization of specific standards ('zero errors');
- quality as relevance ('fitness for purpose');
- quality in relation to inputs ('value for money');
- quality as change ('transformation').

(Harvey and Green 1993 cited in Lauvås, 2000: 3)[1]

If the notion of quality as excellence is used as the basis for judging academic provision, by definition, it limits the number that can actually be identified as 'excellent'. Taking standards as the starting point to define excellence then there are questions about who defines the standards and how they are recognized in the higher education context. 'Fitness for purpose' is also problematical if it defines the standard by which the institution will be judged. The latter can, in effect, allow the institution to be judged against stated goals which it defines for itself.

If the basis for judgement is value for money, then questions arise around the subjective nature of what is valued, who determines these values and whether other values are equally important in academe, such as value for time which we noted in Chapter 7.

Both Henkel (2000) and Newton's (2001) research on the views of academics on the quality agenda found that the process in place since the mid-1990s in the UK was considered highly bureaucratic and burdensome. Henkel (2000: 106) reported that 'academics sought, with difficulty, to articulate and re-assert their own definitions of quality and remained essentially discipline-centred'. We consider this a major driver for the development model we are putting forward and return to this later in the chapter.

Newton's list of lessons for quality activities in higher education, learned from the UK experience of the 1990s, in many ways summarizes the main points made in much of the literature on this topic. His key points are that:

- quality is an essentially contested issue with competing voices and discourses (managers vs front-line academics);
- there is no blueprint for higher education;
- the forces of context and circumstance impact on aspirations of consistency and transformation;
- there is an implementation gap (a difference between planned outcomes of policy and emerging outcomes);
- it is always affected by 'situational factors' and by 'context' which change or subvert the process.

(Newton 2001: 9)

Newton's warnings about the limits of transformation are especially instructive from our standpoint since we are most interested in the transformative dimension of quality processes and focus our attention in this chapter on quality as a mechanism for transformation and change in the educational experience of the students served. We are concerned that improvement of the learning experience is a central outcome of quality activities, and while it can serve other purposes such as meeting a standard or fitness for purpose or value for money, the educational power of engaging in quality reviews is its potential for transformative function. While looking at this dimension as a central theme for this chapter we take account of Newton's points and those of Henkel concerning her findings and the efforts by academics to reclaim quality systems for academic purposes.

To conclude this section on defining quality, we concur with Boyle and Bowden's view that it is futile to try to come up with the definitive definition of quality. As they say:

> In recent years most progressive thinkers and those who are motivated by positive practical outcomes, have moved on from the endless esoteric debates on conceptions of 'quality'. In fact, healthy 'learning organisations' . . . are tending to view the need for having a comprehensive approach to maximising how well things are done as the best reason for adopting a practical meaning for the notion of quality.
>
> (Boyle and Bowden cited in Lauvås 2000: 3)

Thus, we approach 'quality and quality improvement in dynamic, rather than static or absolute terms' (Boyle and Bowden cited in Lauvås 2000: 3).

Internal vs external quality assurance systems

The dynamic characteristic of quality activities as developed in higher education is most evident in the way that their use has evolved in different contexts and settings. As van Vught (1994) has summarized, in the European context, quality activities had two distinct historical approaches, one in France and the other in England. The differences are illustrated in Table 8.1. Both systems were a form of quality assessment. The key difference was the emphasis in England on the internal authority of academics to regulate themselves whereas in France the emphasis was on an external 'inspectorate'.

The problem with self-regulatory systems, which use peer review approaches, are the many challenges they pose to those who also seek to achieve accountability goals as well. The three most common concerns expressed are the possibility for:

- social bias – reputation of institution or members of staff interfere in judgements made;
- intellectual bias – preference of reviewers for particular theories or methods;
- random error – failure of experts to agree on levels of quality leads to low reliability and inconsistency of judgements.

Nevertheless, in his evaluation of these challenges van Vught (1994) is firm in his position that there is no substitute for the peer review process in maintaining quality in higher education. It is our view that peer review is essential to academic freedom and the other intrinsic values core to the higher education enterprise that we outlined in Chapter 1.

'A delicate balance has to be reached between control and autonomy . . . The key is to have a structured, well-founded and disciplined approach to quality, and this must fuel the process of continuous quality improvement' (McGettrick *et al.* 1997: 245, 236). In other words, the day-to-day

Table 8.1 Comparison of traditional higher education quality approaches in England and France

	Quality assessment	*External authority*	*Internal authority*	*Accountability*	*Peer review*	*Intrinsic values*	*Extrinsic values*
English	✓		✓		✓	✓	
French	✓	✓		✓			✓

Source: Based on work by van Vught (1994).

functioning of peer review in academic departments and universities, wherever they are located, should be robust enough to demonstrate a commitment to the ongoing development of their programmes and withstand the test of whatever external system is created and applied to monitoring quality.

In recent years there have been increasing demands for higher education to be made more accountable. As we have noted in previous work,[2] these demands have principally emanated from governments who are concerned that the public investment is adequately monitored. More recently the expansion of the higher education system has also been seen as a possible threat to the quality of higher education owing to the declining resource per student, with the resulting deterioration of faculty/staff to student ratios. All of these have contributed to the demands to increase the external scrutiny of universities.

The response to these demands for quality assurance in Britain[3] has been a considerable growth of quality management processes both within institutions, normally through a quality or standards office, and externally through, first, the Higher Education Quality Council (HEQC between 1993 and 1997), and then the Quality Assurance Agency for Higher Education (QAAHE).[4] The external processes have included departmental subject review, institutional audit, benchmarking, programme specification and performance indicators.

However, as Elton (1996: 97) has noted: 'quality assessment must move from its stress on accountability for past performance to concerns about future performance and that ways must be found to influence *quality enhancement* strategically' (our emphasis). In the UK, the Cooke Report (2002) has focused on how QE can be supported at a national level. Commenting on this report, Mathias (2003) has suggested that QE in the UK:

- is primarily an academic issue;
- involves innovation and risk; and
- is chiefly reactive.

The chief executive of the Quality Assurance Agency for Higher Education (QAAHE) in the UK has added the question:

> Is quality enhancement the new quality assurance? . . . In a mature and reflective institution, the self-knowledge that internal and external review and evaluation provide will lead, inexorably, to the conscious recognition of strengths and weaknesses and the identification of areas for improvement and development.
>
> (Williams 2002: 1)

In contrast to this recent interest in the quality debate is the growth of the 'quality industry' and its impact on all academics and in particular in demands on their time (which we discussed in Chapter 7). This 'industry' has been dominated by what Trow (1994) and others have described as 'managerialism – a manifestation of a more global process of neo-liberal economic and political transformation' (Newton 2001: 2; see also De Vries 1997; Radford *et al.* 1997). De Vries and Radford's critiques of quality systems and approaches also echo Vught's point about their political implications. What is most significant about the managerialist approach is its implied lack of trust of academics and associated academic deprofessionalization (Trow 1994, 1996; Shore and Wright 2000; Newton 2001; Olssen 2001). Trow sees the traditional values of the university under severe threat because of the requirements of the quality assessments.

In our earlier work we have commented on how this situation creates a paradox around QA activities. When universities need to meet increasing demands for bureaucratic reports by the external QA systems, this in turn can affect the quality of the educational experience owing to the decrease in time and energy available for the latter (see also Trow 1996, Olssen 2001).

What is equally paradoxical, and possibly more perplexing, is Smyth's observation that, 'That we [academics] devote so little time to analysing what we do, and how others are increasingly coming to shape that work, must be one of the great unexplained educational issues of our time' (Smyth cited in Newton 2001: 2).

Others have not been silent about the negative effects of these processes, but it seems their warnings have gone unheeded. As early as 1990, Barnett had noted that there were 'ominous signs' of the impact of self-critical evaluations providing less value for higher education. Trowler (1998) has added his account of academic strategies to subvert managerial systems to this discussion. These views confirm long-held beliefs in the academic community that minimal compliance with bureaucratic demands can be achieved without full capitulation to the goals or values underlying them and in effect undermining them, thus making 'accountability . . . a potent force both for and against learning' (Martin 1999: 127).

As Greatrix has noted in reference to the UK quality framework documents,

> its components can be seen to be more to do with control. Control in the interest of enabling government and state to take a stronger grip on steering higher education in the direction of the perceived economic national interest to an extent inconceivable even a few years ago . . . [This] agenda implies not a citizen-led higher education but something more akin to provider servitude at the expense of innovation, enterprise, and indeed, quality. The failure of the sector to respond robustly to the challenges presented by the QAA agenda and to address its flaws merely highlights the extent to which this outcome has already been achieved.
>
> (Greatrix 2001: 12, 16)

The impact of the quality agenda on higher education institutions is not confined to the UK. Martin (1999) has described the impact on teachers in an Australian university, showing the increase on stress, anxiety and defensiveness that intrusive quality management can create. In South Africa the formation of the South African Qualifications Authority has required all departments to register their programmes of study using a learning outcomes approach which was poorly understood and perceived as threatening and inappropriate by most faculty members. By 1998 all European Union countries had QA systems in place (Thune 2002).

In our earlier work we have summarized Horsburgh's (1999) list of claims against current quality management systems in higher education. In brief they range from the overemphasis on documentation to the detriment of teaching and research, meaningless numerical scores with little validity or reliability, methodologies based on values often antithetical to academic culture, and systems at the expense of collegiality. But most damning is that there is little evidence that QA regimes bring about any fundamental changes that can improve the educational experience of students.

If the current quality management systems in higher education do not contribute to the improvement or enhancement of the educational experience or positively impact student learning, then they are an expensive exercise in futility, especially when, in the UK, fewer than 1 per cent of the subjects or institutions reviewed have been found to be of an unacceptable quality and thus not approved (see PAQ Consulting Report in HEFCE 2000a,b). If the key issue is accountability to the taxpayer then it is difficult to defend the value for money spent on the QA process itself (Brown 2004a). Furthermore, QA assumes something is wrong when clearly nearly all provision has been found to be at an acceptable standard or above it. If the process started from the opposite position of 'innocent until proven guilty' it would create an entirely different scenario for the higher education sector and for academic life.

There are examples of systems where the latter is the case and where there is more focus on the QE side of this debate. Scotland has emphasized QE in its approach and asked institutions to include QE strategies in their annual planning documents from 2002. The view of the Scottish Higher Education Funding Council (SHEFC) is that it

> believes that ultimately responsibility for delivery of high quality provision and of quality enhancement lies with institutions. To produce genuine enhancement, and to avoid a 'compliance culture', quality should be clearly 'owned' by the institution . . . QE strategies should be developmental and challenging in the goals which they set for institutions.
>
> (SHEFC 2000: 1, 7)

We strongly agree with this view and later in this chapter we have attempted to elaborate on how a quality development model would work at institutional level.

Another example a little further afield is the work being done in the USA by the North Central Association of Colleges and Schools (a regional accreditation agency). It has established the Academic Quality Improvement Program (AQIP), which is a voluntary alternative to the usual QA processes engaged in with the universities in the region of the USA monitored by the Association. The AQIP approach focuses on assessing and supporting improvement as the main quality driver within institutions. AQIP has the following characteristics:

- It focuses on institutional processes and results rather than resources.
- It focuses on the improvement of teaching and learning.
- It supports institutions to improve students' educational performance.
- It customizes its processes to fit institutional needs and priorities.
- It uses information and communication technology (ICT) to reduce costs.
- It provides useful information for public understanding.
- It is a dynamic process.

(Spangehl 2001)

AQIP's criteria see the education of students as the central focus of any institution, and will not permit a college to 'do quality' while ignoring the processes that shape students' minds. 'The Criteria are not normative, prescriptive, or proscriptive: they do not tell an institution how it should organize or operate itself, nor do they suggest specific inputs or outputs institutions should have' (Spangehl 2001: 3).

The AQIP approach is meant to minimize bureaucratic paperwork while maximizing the institution's efforts to enhance its educational provision. This type of approach to quality has been described as a 'critical friend' process, that is, a process whereby the judgements are formative and assist in improving teaching and learning while avoiding summative sanctions for areas where improvement is needed. Sanctions on their own do not necessarily create the conditions to improve the learning experience of students or bring about needed change.

The preceding discussion in many ways suggests the need for a quality system that performs the multiple functions to improve the quality of the educational experience and provide a developmental function. Before we begin our discussion of our quality development model, we would like to comment briefly on the concept of development.

As we discussed in Chapter 1, we have had strong reservations about the use of the term 'development' in the higher education context because it has been misconstrued by academics as patronizing when applied to change processes and staff development activities. Faculty/staff resent the idea of being told they need to be developed since they have already spent many years preparing for their professional role. When academic staff development activities are focused on the individual staff member through a psychological development model, this can be counterproductive to the improvement of the learning experience for students because of the resistance of faculty/staff to being 'developed'. Shifting to a professional development model that addresses the roles faculty/staff play within institutions, and in the teaching/learning process, places development at a more structural level. Changing structural relationships and role definitions depersonalizes the developmental change and has the potential to make the developmental process more acceptable to staff. In other words, it is not the person who needs changing but the role and role relationships they are playing within the institutional structures.

Despite these reservations concerning the term 'development', we have elected to use it instead of 'improvement' or 'enhancement' because we also understand development to be a process that is not necessarily linked to judgements or deficiencies. The focus of developmental change in this context is proactive and not reactive, and has the potential to be innovative. It is concerned with change, but change that is forward-looking to improvements not backward-looking at a quality assessment score or outcome from a review of research work. In this scenario the quality activities are in effect developmental and not remedial. It is far easier for a person to make changes that are structurally innovative than to make changes that are meant to remedy a problem in themselves simply because the process is less personally threatening.

As educational developers we have worked with hundreds of faculty/staff on a one-to-one basis who have come (or been sent by a manager) because their teaching has been defined as problematical or deficient. Over the years, we have found that by having faculty/staff focus on those aspects of their teaching that both they and their students perceive as working well allows them to understand better what their strengths are which, in turn, allows them to build on these strengths instead of dismantling their weaknesses. This is a process of naming and claiming instead of blaming and shaming. We have further found that this process eventually results in the weaknesses being eliminated by default, since increasing the strengths does not allow room for maintaining the weaknesses.[5] It is this principle of development that we have applied to our quality development model. In this way, improvement and enhancement can then be seen as needed and desirable. If development processes are an integral part of everyone's role as a teacher/scholar, then it is the rule not the exception to work on developing that role and the improvements these developmental changes can bring to the learning experience of students. For QE to contribute to the transformation of the educational experience of students it needs to be a part of the everyday activities built into the role of academics, not a remedial process of staff development or a policy objective.

Quality development as a lever for change

As we discussed in Chapter 5, the underlying principle that informs the work of our quality development (QD) model is the recent paradigm shift in higher education that places the emphasis on learning instead of teaching (Barr and Tagg 1995). Emphasis on learning is interpreted broadly in our model and includes a wide range of activities such as the design of curricula, choice of content and methods, various forms of teacher–student interaction, the assessment of students, and the broader aims of learning via activities of institutional learning communities.

The central foci of QD are on transformation and educational development also in their broadest sense. QD also attempts to integrate the processes of quality assurance with quality enhancement within institutions by identifying changes to the educational process that can bring about improvement in it. The QD model encourages greater reflective practice throughout the entire educational process that in turn addresses many of the expectations of both internal and external quality assurance systems. In common with other quality activities, QD is a dynamic process. Its key dimensions are that:

- the emphasis is on key elements of the pedagogical process: curriculum development, learning and teaching activities and SoTL;
- effective action and appropriate change are at teaching–learning interface and central to the quality process;
- the process is non-burdensome to faculty/staff and the institution.

(see Horsburgh 1999; Lauvås 2000)

The work of QD involves applying new measures of quality that are developmentally focused and centre on the managing and integrating of three major areas of work in universities: academic development, learning development and quality development. The linkages between these three are illustrated in Figure 8.1.

In our earlier work on quality development (Gosling and D'Andrea 2001), we placed this relationship within the larger conceptual frame of educational development, where educational development encompasses the entire range of learning-related work within the university, from policy to practice.

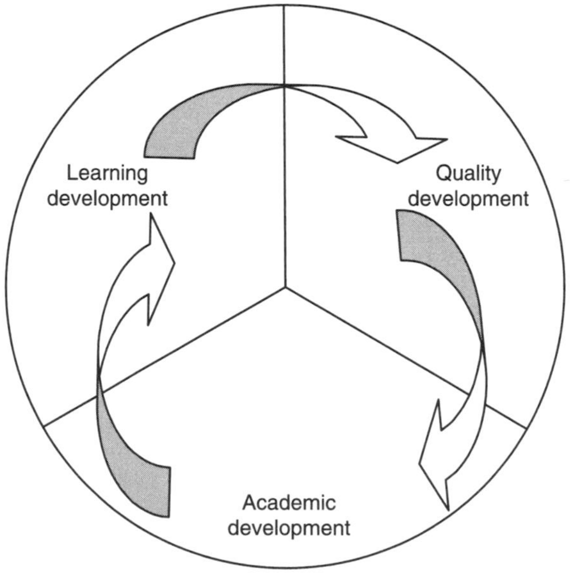

Figure 8.1 Holistic educational development

As Gosling (1996, 2001b) has reported, many educational development centres in the UK have had a remit to support educational change at all of these levels. Where they exist in universities they are especially well placed to carry out the task of linking them for the purpose of quality development.

Academic development in this model includes a wide range of activities and goes beyond the usual emphasis on developing staff per se. It emphasizes the connection between the three key dimensions of QD that we noted above: curriculum development, learning and teaching activities, and SoTL. In this model, the focus is on the academic role, instead of the academic per se, and the way that these three areas are integral to this role.

The model of learning development that we described in Chapter 4 includes a comprehensive support system for student learning directly linked to subject discipline and curricular expectations. It encourages the creation of learning enhancement activities for all students and is not just for those needing remedial support. It allows any student to increase their learning skills and to develop a repertoire of competences that can be applied to any learning situation in or outside the university. Improving reading, writing, speaking and computing skills, for example, are among a wide range of proficiencies that students of all abilities and educational backgrounds and at any stage in their learning career would find useful.

The QD model involves the holistic development, implementation and evaluation of the educational provision. It informs the process of curriculum development with knowledge of current pedagogical theory, practice and scholarly reflections on teaching and learning. It also provides professional development for faculty/staff on teaching–learning approaches that is constructively aligned to meet the educational aims of the curriculum and their role as teaching scholars. It engages all students in activities that are aimed at helping them to achieve the best results in their current studies and prepares them for lifelong learning. And, it provides guidance on appropriate mechanisms to evaluate the outcomes of learning. In combination, these provide the basis for a link between all three major areas of the higher education experience: academic development, learning development and quality development.

Additionally, the emphasis of QD is not on documentation produced only for quality assurance purposes but rather on the collection of useful evaluative data and scholarly papers, so that these can be used as a means to improve the educational experience of students. The outcomes are not measurable scores but development of skills and processes that have been determined by academics to be of value to the students' learning experience. The measurements are based on systematic reflection on each area of development with decisions taken based on these reflections that are appropriate for achieving the goals set. Quality development replaces trust in academics to investigate and evaluate their work and to find ways of improving quality through a developmental process (Elton 1996). Potentially there is a route to achieve fundamental changes as well, although this does depend on building a consensus among the various learning communities within the institution.

Table 8.2 Comparison of quality assessment with quality development approaches in higher education

	Quality assessment	*Quality development*
Focuses on intrinsic values		✓
Focuses on extrinsic values	✓	✓
Linked to external authority	✓	
Linked to internal authority		✓
Provides a measure of accountability	✓	✓
Based on peer review		✓
Process provides support to departments to improve teaching and learning		✓
Streamlines quality activities		✓
Holistic approach to quality assurance		✓
Helps disseminate institutional policies		✓
Potential for greater consistency of standards		✓
Increases student support		✓
Emphasis on documentation	✓	
Emphasis on educational experience		✓
Focuses on learning outcomes		✓
Focuses on measurable data and scores	✓	
Driven by scholarly reflection		✓
Driven by quantitative methodology	✓	
Trusts academic judgements		✓
Potential to achieve fundamental changes in higher education		✓

Table 8.2 compares the key features of a quality development approach to quality assurance with a quality assessment approach.

Quality development – some examples

Probably the best way to understand how QD works in practice, and how it is different from quality assessment, is for us to provide some examples. We begin with two areas that as Mathias (2003: 14) has noted 'should be primarily developmental activities, such as . . . observation of teaching and student feedback [which] are increasingly used as crude performance measures of individual teachers in the quest to assure quality and standards by managers'.

Teaching observation

There has been a history of hostility to the observation of teaching among academics because it has often been used by heads of departments to aid decisions about promotion and performance-related pay (Allen n.d.). In this context the observations are conducted to achieve a summative judgement of the teaching observed, they involve little or no formative feedback by the observer, nor do they require any reflection on the part of the teacher observed. The focus of the observation is mostly on the stated outcomes for the session and whether the observer judges that the students have achieved them. Observations of this kind provide snapshot data that look at teaching at a single moment in time, allowing for no other comparisons of the learning experience of the students. When all this is added to the distortion created by the stress of a managerial colleague judging the teacher's work, there is little redeeming educational value to the process.

In order to reconceptualize the role and function of peer observation of teaching within a QD model, it is necessary to frame the exercise within the broader aims of assisting departments to provide a high-quality educational experience for its students and to encourage all staff to reflect on the effectiveness of their own teaching and identify their development needs. This can only be achieved if there is an ethos of collegial discussion about teaching and the exchange of views about what is suited to the learning goals of the department. An important principle governing the process within a developmental observation model is that feedback to individual staff/faculty must be confidential. For observations to be developmental they must also be separated from other university assessment processes, such as those for probationary staff, for underperformance or promotion, or as part of the ongoing performance review process. It is also important that all staff with teaching responsibilities, whatever their grade or status, participate in the observation scheme. In order to ensure that the process is carried out constructively and sensitively it is essential that all observers learn appropriate methods of observation and giving constructive feedback.

Research undertaken at the University of East London shows that, when guidelines such as these are used, objections to having teaching observed become much weaker and largely disappear. Although there is also some evidence that the willingness of faculty/staff to be observed was related to, at the time of the study, the threat of external assessment, the way in which the observation has been built into a departmentally based development process creates a different view of the process (Gosling 2005).

Student evaluations

Student evaluations have been increasingly used within quality assurance systems as a means to judge the work of individual teachers with students. In the USA, where student evaluation has had a chequered history, the student movement of the 1960s demanded that the student 'voice' be heard to improve the learning experience, redress the power balance between teacher and student, and bring about changes to make the curriculum more relevant to the times and student needs. Students believed that student evaluations would be a vehicle for bringing about these changes. However, over time, student evaluations in the USA have come to be used primarily to evaluate the performance of faculty/staff and have become focused almost entirely on an attempt to identify teachers whose work with students was labelled as problematical. This emphasis on the summary judgement of teachers and not on the relevance of the curriculum has decreased the power of the student voice to bring about improvements in the total learning experience.

The QD model argues for a need to return to the original aims of student evaluations and to take the process away from managerial purposes. The research evidence (Braskamp and Ory 1994; Cashin 1995) indicates analysis of student feedback on teaching has had little or no effect on identifying areas of change for individual staff. Student views about the personal performance of staff are therefore of little use for this purpose but can be used as part of a dialogue between teachers and students for review of the curriculum. It is essential that the analysis of student responses is as much about the student's engagement with the course and the success of their learning as it is about the teacher's role in teaching and supporting learning. Ramsden's (1991) Course Experience Questionnaire (CEQ) is a good example of a way in which student responses can be used to evaluate the outcomes of a programme rather than the performance of the teacher. The data from student evaluation tools such as the CEQ can be used for a wide range of developmental goals, such as identifying areas for improvement for teachers as well as strengths and weaknesses of the course in promoting approaches to learning. Instruments like the CEQ can provide data to enhance the teaching and learning process overall whereas faculty/staff-focused student evaluations are limited to assessment functions. However, in Australia the CEQ has been used by central government to publish league tables of university performance, which has coloured faculty/staff perceptions of its value as a developmental tool. It appears likely that a similar development will be initiated in the UK (DfES 2003a). In this increasingly political context, it becomes all the more important not to lose sight of the potential educational and developmental value of student evaluations.

Two other examples that help us to illustrate the QD approach centre on learning as the central developmental device, these are: student learning development (study skills) and committees as learning communities

Student learning development

If one of the major reasons for engaging with QA activities is to bring about improvement in the learning experience of students then it is important that its direct impact on student learning is taken into account. As we have noted earlier, QA processes tend to examine inputs, that is, what systems are in place to support students' learning and outputs, as measured by so-called performance indicators, such as pass rates, retention and progression data, postgraduate employment and further study. Both are less successful in enabling an analysis of the factors that have been instrumental in influencing these data. Where institutions have different student profiles and different missions, the significance attached to the indicators will vary considerably. Although some efforts have been made to take this into account in recent revisions to performance indicators in the UK (HEFCE 2000c), the main purpose of these changes appears to be the option to create university league tables of student performance, rather than to support a developmental process of meeting student needs.

A QD approach focuses on each subject or department undertaking a self-analysis of the impact of the interaction between students and staff, the effectiveness of the learning materials available, the use students make of those materials. More difficult for departments to identify are the ways in which their programmes may be responsible for disadvantaging certain categories of students. There is evidence (Seymour and Hewitt 1997; Yorke 1999) that the traditions within subjects have a powerful influence on the styles of teaching adopted and these may be responsible for student failure and withdrawal. There are also qualitative considerations which are much harder to capture in any description which relate to issues such as the ways in which the curriculum and teaching methods have embedded assumptions relating to student demographic characteristics such as race, ethnicity, gender and class, as discussed in Chapter 4.

Learning communities, networks and committees

Universities that create an environment that is conducive to the support of a learning community and the structural platforms for them to thrive will, as we have suggested in Chapter 2, ensure the conditions for the success of learning committees and learning networks which are well placed to contribute to a quality development approach to improving the learning experience of students. They are well placed in the sense that the goals and purposes of learning communities, and their constituent parts, have similar goals to the QD approach to quality assurance. Thus, there could easily be a learning network that focuses on specific QD activities across the university or within a school or department, for example a student evaluation network. Equally, university quality committees could be reinvented as learning committees and commit themselves to learning about how to lever change and improve student learning through the systematic analysis, consideration and reflection on QD data.

It is only when students and faculty/staff are facilitated to enquire into their practices through self-investigation and discussion, in an ethos that is not potentially punitive, that issues such as these can be fully acknowledged and effectively dealt with. Both QD processes and the systematic creation of acknowledged learning communities within the university can contribute to a conscious improvement of the learning experience. Quality assurance, with its emphasis on measurement, external accountability and regulatory control, can identify issues and possibly shame departments into taking some actions to comply with the regulatory framework, but it cannot in and of itself bring about improvements and does not necessarily engender an attitude among staff which is focused on improvement. In various chapters in this book we have discussed ways of using peer review of teaching, student evaluations, curriculum development and analysis of learning support that will ultimately bring greater benefits to students and achieve improvements in the learning experience of students. Quality development processes take account of the need to focus on developmental indicators such as the ones we have used as examples in this section. Instead of using the traditionally overvalued quantitative performance indicators (see Vught 1994; Stoddard 1995), we suggest that these equally useful qualitative indicators can be directly applied to the transformative process of improving student learning.

Conclusion

As Stefani and Matthew (2002: 48) have suggested:

> It is rare for staff to value something which has been imposed. Developmental approaches while taking more time and energy (and consequently cost[ing] more, even if only in human resource terms) are more likely to lead to real change which those who implement it believe in and will strive to make work.

Additionally, a developmental model also deals with what Newton's respondents called the 'so what' factor. It helps to create a meaning structure for academic work on quality issues. As one of Newton's respondents stated:

> What differences, if any, are these systems, which are claiming time and energy from staff, making to our performance in terms of the quality of the courses . . .? If you believe as staff operating these systems that they'll not make any difference, they're wasting your time, they're meaningless rituals . . . Because if they're not working and not making any difference, and you don't believe in them, let's forget it.
>
> (Newton 2000: 156)

Other staff in Newton's study suggested that improvements were not always tied to quality systems and that developments would occur with or without them. This stands to logic in as much as improvements in teaching and learning had been occurring for centuries, long before quality systems were in place. However, what we are suggesting is that they are more likely and more predicable if there is a systematic approach that is agreed and acknowledged by all parties involved, takes account of the expectations and values of both faculty/staff and students, and is developmentally focused. 'This is particularly so if it is assumed that sustained quality improvement in teaching and learning is premised upon the energies and initiatives of staff at ground level' (Newton 2000: 160).

From our perspective, this is a win–win model for the entire higher education sector. If used properly it can satisfy the need for public accountability while affirming trust in academics by allowing them to do what they do best: develop, ensure, enhance and deliver educational programmes of study, while giving students the opportunity to achieve their educational goals in a supportive learning community. To paraphrase Harvey (2001) for those universities where the quality development process has barely started, the trick is, it seems, to ensure that the outcome is better learning rather than bigger and better bureaucracies. What is now required is 'guarded trust' (Yorke cited in Elton 1996) which is not only about 'doing the right thing but doing it right' (D'Andrea 1994).

Notes

1. Newton (2001: 6) has added quality as 'customer satisfaction' and quality as 'peer review' to this list as well.
2. Throughout this chapter we draw on our previous work on quality development: see Gosling and D'Andrea (2001).
3. Each country in Britain has its own funding council for higher education; however, each is within the remit of the Quality Assurance Agency for Higher Education.
4. It should be noted that prior to HEQC there was the Council for National Academic Awards (CNAA) which provided the quality assurance function for the former polytechnics. See R.B. Brown (2004a) for a discussion of the comparative histories of the CNAA and HEQC/QAA.
5. This process has become known as appreciative enquiry.

Part 3

Developing Institutional Strategies to Improve the Quality of the Student Experience

9

Strategies to Enhance Teaching and Learning

> Over the long haul, we are not likely to see extravagantly more effort on the part of our students. Neither are we, their teachers, likely to be able to devote a lot more effort to our teaching than we already are.
>
> Rocklin 2001: 2

In this final chapter we summarize the main elements for developing a whole institution strategic approach to improving learning and teaching. We also present the case for the need to evaluate the impact of the strategies being adopted. In the closing section, we reflect on the role of educational development centres within the framework for improving teaching and learning. We suggest that educational development should be understood as a function of the whole institution rather than of a single organizational office, and that this function should be central to strategic change within institutions.

The realities that constrain any institutional attempt to bring about improvements in teaching and learning are that there is a fixed amount of time and effort available for these activities and that teaching in higher education continues to be perceived as the poor relation to research. Throughout this book we have been proposing an approach to improving student learning that is based on the principle that there are core values that are distinct to the academic culture which need to be sustained. We believe that the trend towards increased managerial control is in danger of damaging these core values and that higher education needs to restore trust in its relations with professional staff and enable conversations about teaching to occur in a constructive framework.

We have also suggested that the changes occurring in higher education are presenting teachers with new challenges that require all academic staff to think critically about their teaching. Teaching needs to adapt and respond to widening access and greater student diversity by focusing on the academic development needs of students, rather than operating with a deficit model of student capabilities. We have advocated that this should occur through the systematic academic orientation of students, within disciplines, in ways that recognize the distinctive features of 'pedagogical communities' and discipline cultures.

In this complex and shifting environment, institutions need to promote the learning of academic staff as well as of students. Learning implies that academic staff become more 'learned'. Yet in the competitive world of modern higher education, 'learnedness' is not always valued, and where it is, it relates exclusively to subject knowledge and subject-based research. We have also suggested teaching is a scholarly activity and 'learnedness' needs to be valued in the work that teachers undertake to support students as well as in their research.

The intellectual challenge of teaching can be recognized by consciously working towards the ideal of scholarly teaching, with the inherent implications that this has for reflexivity and evaluation. However, teaching is not only intellectually challenging, and potentially as scholarly as conducting research, it is also, to use some old-fashioned words, a noble and worthwhile activity. Aspiring to teach well entails an ethically, and emotionally, charged commitment to improving the lives of students through their education. Nevertheless, the ultimate responsibility for learning lies with the individual learner, whether a student or a teacher.

Whole institution approach for improving teaching and learning: a summary

We have attempted to steer a course between the competing institutional cultures of managerialism and collegiality by suggesting ways for institutions to create more of what Bergquist (1992) has called a 'developmental culture'. In each of the key areas of higher education that we have discussed, managerial solutions have been rejected in favour of strategies that are more in accord with academic values. While we agree that teaching has been undervalued compared with research in the traditional collegial culture, we do not think that the solution lies in 'human resource management' alone, for example through new career paths, recognition and rewards. While these structural changes are necessary conditions for change, they are not sufficient. Attention must be focused on the culture of the departments, through both discipline-specific and cross-disciplinary professional development that encourages teachers to debate teaching and educational values utilizing various kinds of collaborative peer review.

The major concepts relating to each of our chapters are summarized in Table 9.1. This summary provides a quick reference point to the key domains where we think most strategies for improvements in teaching and learning are currently being promoted. The table also links these domains to the major debates surrounding the shifting value structures related to these changes.

All too often, improvement strategies in teaching and learning are based on an oversimplified approach of setting goals and targets, and then identifying 'development' activities that are designed to enable the targets to be

Table 9.1 Summary of whole institution approach for improving teaching and learning

Changes/tensions in higher education	*Managerial values*	*Academic values*
Goals of higher education	Corporate identity, financially driven	Transformational
Change model	Rational planning model	Learning university, holistic
Academic Identity	Human resources	Collegial culture, discipline-based
Diversity	Student as customer/client	Student identity, inclusivity, social justice
Curriculum content	Commodification of knowledge (McDonalization), marketization	Academic freedom, learning-centred, epistemological basis
Learning technologies	Technical innovation focus	Pedagogical innovation focus
Research–teaching nexus	Separation of functions	Scholarly approach to teaching and learning
Accountability	Quality assurance	Quality development
Organizational goals	Efficiency	Educational development

met for academics and all those who support learning. We agree with others that it is important to caution those adopting such approaches not to be seduced by a 'false certainty' of so-called action plans and change strategies (Fullan and Hargreaves 1998). Complexity theory provides a counterview to this approach by pointing out that, in complex organizations, progress is rarely linear, outcomes are often 'fuzzy' and contradictions are inherent in the system (Stacey 1996).

Additionally, setting targets is too often a substitute for dialogue or can even be intended as a means to shut down dialogue by treating some matters as 'non-negotiable'. Although engaging in dialogue about change can sometimes increase the time needed for it to occur, it is critical to the successful implementation of change (Eckel *et al.* 1999; Clegg 2003). It is only through a dialogue that alternative interpretations of policy can be aired and debated (Berg and Ostergren 1979). This step cannot be missed out because 'any significant innovation, if it is to result in change, requires individual implementers to work out their own meaning' (Fullan 2001: 108). As we noted in Chapter 2, involving academics in this way is to give them an opportunity to shape and 'take ownership' of the direction in which the policy is moving.

> One cannot design the practices that will emerge in response to institutional systems. One can design roles, but one cannot design the identities that that will be constructed through these roles. One can design visions, but one cannot design the allegiance necessary to align energies behind those visions.
>
> (Wenger 1998: 229)

To work with academic allegiances it is essential to respect academic identities, as we have discussed in Chapter 3; but this does not mean treating them as unchanging reifications. Improving teaching and learning means challenging what has been taken for granted while also recognizing that 'existing patterns of teaching are tailored to [academics'] priorities of purpose and [are] highly adapted to the circumstances in which they find themselves' (S. Brown 2000: 2). If some innovation in teaching and learning is to become adopted it must be accepted as a potentially more adequate response to a perceived need than existing practice by the very academic teachers being asked to implement the innovation. This is one way in which the specificity of local circumstances influences the nature of the improvement, since the perceived need will vary in specific organizational contexts.

In Chapter 2 we outlined the processes needed for creating a culture of improvement within a 'learning university'. Others have described this approach as creating a 'supportive culture for change' (Dempster & Deepwell 2002). The principles underlying this process include collaboration across all levels of the hierarchy of the institution, promotion of informed and scholarly dialogue, and organizational structures to facilitate different forms of communication and enquiry. By way of summary, we provide a checklist of the activities discussed throughout the book that are designed to create a developmental culture aimed at improvement in teaching and learning.

Activities proposed to support improvement in teaching and learning

Collaboration across all levels of the hierarchy of the institution

- Institutional ethos makes clear commitment to teaching and sees itself as a learning community fostering critical debate to improve teaching and learning.
- Leadership statements and behaviour clearly support learning and teaching.
- Committees are used as learning communities as well as to make decisions.
- Student networks are supported to facilitate input into debate about teaching.
- A programme of events and courses is run by an educational development centre in association with teaching departments.

Promotion of informed and scholarly dialogue

- Learning sets and reading groups on teaching and learning are initiated.
- Course approval, review and accreditation processes are used to increase professional knowledge of teaching.
- High-profile events are held to recognize innovation and development in teaching and learning.
- Publicity is given to teaching and curriculum developments through a variety of media.
- Publications of scholarship on teaching and learning are funded and distributed.
- Involvement in national teaching projects is encouraged and fully supported by the institution.
- Visiting teaching scholars are invited to support scholarship of teaching.
- Evaluations of aspects of teaching and learning strategy are funded and used to review the strategy.

Organizational structures to facilitate change

- Learning communities are encouraged and supported.
- Responsibilities for development of teaching is devolved to school or departments through teaching and learning 'co-ordinators'.
- Support is given for the work of the teaching co-ordinators by facilitating networking between them and a central educational development centre.
- Induction/orientation of faculty/staff provides an introduction to teaching quality and sets out the expectations of the university.
- Professional development courses enable development of scholarly approach to teaching.
- Continuing professional development (CPD) requirements have a clear reference to development of teaching.
- Peer review of teaching is encouraged and supported.
- Promotion and reward panels use peer review of teaching.
- Funding is made available for teaching, curriculum, learning and assessment to encourage development projects in these areas.
- Resources on teaching and learning are available on the university intranet with links to external resources.
- Strategy for development of teaching and learning is a high priority and leads subsidiary strategies for human resources, ICT, estates, finances.
- Quality audit is used to promote quality development in teaching and learning.
- Examining is valued as an opportunity for professional development.
- National/international networking is encouraged and funded.

Although not a comprehensive list of possible strategies, this list is indicative of the many ways that institutions can act to bring about improvements in teaching and learning while at the same time addressing their needs to manage effectively both their day-to-day functioning and the many and varied changes they are facing. Again, as we have set out in Table 9.2, we would emphasize that these actions can also support the traditional core values of higher education.

Table 9.2 Institutional cultures and improving teaching and learning

Managerialist culture methods	*Collegial culture methods*
Teaching has been undervalued compared with research in the traditional collegial culture. It should be given greater prominence, recognition and reward. Professional development is an important means to achieving this end.	Both discipline-specific and cross-disciplinary professional development are advocated. This encourages teachers to debate teaching and educational values utilizing peer review and promotes a scholarship of teaching.
Teaching needs to change to respond to widening access and greater student diversity focusing on the development needs of students, rather than operating with a deficit model of student capabilities.	Academic orientation of students should happen within disciplines in ways that recognize the distinctive features of pedagogical communities and discipline cultures.
Course design should take account of outcome-based and student-focused approaches to teaching.	Critiques rationalistic basis of 'constructive alignment' and recognizes that changes to course design occurs in response to multiple personal, subject-based and institutional influences and choices.
It is important to recognize the contribution that learning technologies can make to teaching in higher education.	Uses learning technologies that are pedagogically, not technologically, driven and controls their use by keeping them in the hands of teachers, not technologists.
Accepts that some form of quality assurance and public accountability is a political expectation within higher education today.	Quality development rather than assurance is a cost-effective way to achieve a lasting impact and create a culture of improvement.

Source: adapted from Bergquist (1992).

Evaluation of changes to improve teaching and learning

Improving teaching and learning also involves careful evaluation of the approaches and strategies that have been chosen to effect change. However, evaluating the success of strategies to improve teaching and learning is a complex process. This is because: (a) definitions of improving teaching and learning are varied, local and contingent upon the nature of the teaching situation, and the desires of the teachers, and (b) teaching and learning involve numerous actors; teachers, students, university management, employers, professional bodies, funding agencies, who themselves may define improvement in different ways. Furthermore, participants' views of improvements in higher education are not static but evolve in response to their experience of engaging with the process of change itself.

In any case, if the change is to be successful it is important that the impact of the processes being undertaken should be investigated as events unfold rather than waiting until the end phase of a change strategy. Evaluation data, when collected and interpreted appropriately, provide evidence to answer the key questions about a change strategy. What impact is the strategy having? Where is change occurring? Are there barriers to be overcome? And, is there evidence that the improvements the strategy was designed to promote are occurring?

Despite the potential value that evaluation has for understanding the impact of the change strategy, it has been suggested that UK higher education does not take evaluation seriously enough.

> Academic decisions are on the whole made by academic men . . . yet all over the country these groups of scholars, who would not make a decision about the shape of a leaf, or the derivation of a work, or the author of a manuscript without painstakingly assembling the evidence, make decisions about admissions policy, size of universities, staff–student ratios, content of courses and similar issues based on dubious assumptions, scrappy data and mere hunch.
>
> (Ashby cited in Elton 1987: 163)

Institutions undoubtedly have far more data available to them now to make strategic decisions than Ashby did in 1963, but 40 years on, the lesson of evaluating initiatives had not been fully learned by UK universities: 'Strategic decisions are too often made on hunch or prejudice, or even for sectional advantage, rather than after a clear-sighted review or on the basis of thorough investigation' (Shattock 2003: 65).

One example of the limited use of evaluation, in the UK, was cited in the review of institutional learning and teaching strategies submitted to the Higher Education Funding Council for England (HEFCE). It was found that

> almost half of HEIs [higher education institutions] content themselves with monitoring or review procedures rather than with evaluation as such. We discovered only a few examples of institutions which were in the process of creating an actual evaluation strategy.
>
> (Badley and Wicks 2002: para 78)

The experience of the USA has been somewhat different. In the 1970s, faculty development centres began investigating institutional climates and culture, student learning styles, and stages of development and institutional goals and priorities (Bergquist 1992). Strongly influenced by the behavioural sciences, institutional research tools were developed using inventories and batteries of tests that enabled comparative analysis to be undertaken. These 'effectively demonstrated that knowledge about an institution's life and culture that has been systematically acquired can enhance the quality and success of institutional change efforts' (Bergquist 1992: 100 citing Chickering and Linquist).

It has been suggested that one reason that evaluation has not taken place more often as a part of the process of change is that universities are unwilling to specify their goals in such a way that they can be evaluated. Again, an example of this was evident in the review of the first round of learning and teaching strategies submitted to the HEFCE in 1999.

> Many strategies specify goals in ways which would preclude attempts to evaluate their achievement. Only half the strategies specify targets and these are usually specified in terms of inputs (what actions will take place) rather than in terms of outcomes. Specification of outcomes for students is very rare. Plans for evaluation are usually missing or are intended to be developed at some later date.
>
> (Gibbs 2001a: para 5)

Evaluations of change strategies need to focus on outcomes as well as on inputs if they are to be useful as a planning tool or a part of the change agency itself. For example, reporting that 80 development events have been held and 300 faculty/staff have attended them does not reveal whether there has been any change, let alone improvement, in those areas addressed by the events.

But evaluation is not simply about making judgements about whether the concrete goals in an institutional change strategy have been achieved. It is also about ways of capturing transitional shifts in the institutional culture, which may not be possible to measure quantitatively, but which are important to understanding the outcomes of improvements made. Achieving an adequate insight into these transitions requires a different approach to evaluation from one that simply attempts to measure observable outputs. As well as collecting data on whether targets have been met, evaluation is also about understanding what is happening and giving a vivid account of the 'state of play'. Cousin (2003) talks of 'the evaluator giving rich descriptive passages, vignettes, anecdotes, photographs, drawings, metaphoric usage to offer the readers a vicarious experience of being there'. Descriptions of a scene observed in the library, impressions of the mood of a meeting, absorbing a feel for the attitudes and values of a group of faculty/staff or students, observing the body language of a faculty/staff at a professional development event, these are all data sources that can be valuable in assessing the culture and the underlying feelings of faculty/staff and students towards an improvement.

Furthermore, evaluation is more likely to have impact if it is collaborative, involving others in the process of change through dialogue and feedback. As we noted in Chapter 2, learning communities are a useful institutional structure for creating these conditions to carry out evaluations. The guidelines offered by Deepwell and Cousin (2002) (see Figure 9.1) also make the assumption that beneficiaries should be involved in a collaborative way with the development and implementation of evaluation, rather than having it visited upon them. The development of a scholarship of teaching and learning is an indication that there are growing numbers of teachers in higher education who are also involved in evaluating the impact of attempted improvements in their own work.

Change requires faculty/staff and students to reconceptualize their roles and ways of working. The extent to which people are willing to make changes depends on a variety of contextual factors, as we have discussed throughout this book, some of which will be drivers for change and some of which will be inhibitors. It is only through an iterative process of action, reflection and evaluation that the agents of change can understand the context in which they are working and those they are hoping to influence and actively engage in development activities. This also suggests that those leading change must take account of the findings of evaluation, be flexible and responsive to the concerns identified, and revise strategies and targets in the light of the data collected.

Evaluation activity adds value to the change process when it is built into the design of the teaching and learning improvements themselves. In this

- Offer a draft evaluation strategy for comment and refinement with stakeholders
- Set up a shared resource base, e.g. intranet or website – allow a range of stakeholders/evaluators to contribute
- Encourage devolved ownership of the evaluation
- Invite feedback and discussion (online and face-to-face) regularly
- Include differing perspectives and voices
- Propose dates for the different phases of the evaluation and convene feedback and discussion meetings
- State the expected results of each phase of the intervention and the data needed to support them. Provide all stakeholders with access to ongoing evaluation research
- Allow for a mix of quantitative and qualitative data
- Develop a structure for the collection, management and analysis of data
- Look beyond goal fulfilment for unexpected outcomes and their implications

Figure 9.1 Guidelines for evaluating teaching and learning.
Source: Deepwell and Cousin (2002: 25).

way it can provide information on the change process, engage faculty/staff and students in feedback on activities being undertaken, inform ongoing decisions that need to be made and acquire evidence of the effectiveness of the change strategy over any given period of time. Evaluation is not an activity that only occurs at the end of a phase or towards the final stages of the implementation of the strategy, but is an integral part of the change strategy itself. By building evaluation into the improvement activities the opportunity is created to reveal understandings about the process of innovation, its outcomes and impacts.

It is always important to build some flexibility into the evaluation of teaching and learning initiatives. Life in higher education institutions is often far from rational and reality rarely fits into what the improvement planning envisaged would happen. Evaluation in this context therefore needs to consider not only whether planned changes have taken place but also what unintended consequences may have occurred. Some questions that can help to determine this include:

- How far were the planned outcomes achieved?
- What unintended outcomes occurred?
- How much did unintended outcomes affect the original planning?
- Did the initial plans need to be modified in the light of experience?
- How were unexpected outcomes incorporated into revised planning?

There are a number of ways to find the answers to these kinds of questions. Figure 9.2 summarises the ones most commonly used in higher education.[1]

Evaluation should be considered an integral part of any change process. Despite the difficulties in defining improvement, there will always be some change of structure, process or attitude that is being aimed for and which is

- **Benchmarking:** internal and external benchmarking
- **Observation:** in person or recorded
- **Archival materials:** content analysis, discourse analysis
- **Interviews:** individual and focus groups
- **External audit:** QAA reviews, professional body accreditations
- **Narratives:** personal, key informants, group
- **Journals:** diaries, records, reports
- **Questionnaires:** surveys – paper, electronic, telephone
- **Checklists:** feedback on teaching methods or learning materials
- **Critical incident analysis:** narratives, observation
- **Visual representations:** drawings, concept maps

Figure 9.2 Examples of common forms of evaluation in higher education

intended to be better, in some sense, than what existed before. The purpose of evaluation is to attempt to capture whether that change has occurred and whether it has delivered the improvements hoped for. We have argued for a collaborative form of evaluation that can contribute to the change process and not simply measure its outcomes.

Educational development to support change in teaching and learning

Effective teaching involves making a personal commitment to students, being excited by their achievements and caring about their failures and confusions. It is for this reason that the central philosophy of this book is the idea that educational development most usefully occurs within teaching departments. Within this context the principal responsibility of educational managers is to provide an institutional environment that encourages individual teachers to be motivated to be creative and, where necessary, take risks to improve their teaching, course design and assessment. Improving teaching and learning happens when teachers and students explore the creation of knowledge, engage in critical debate and develop new ways of thinking about problems. It is about finding effective ways of understanding students' learning and the difficulties they face, whatever their background or prior experience, whether PhD students or on first degrees. It is about allowing students freedom to learn within a structure that helps them to succeed.

If the principal responsibility for improving teaching lies with teachers themselves, what is the role of a central office dedicated to supporting teaching and learning? To answer this question we would like to make some comments in this concluding section regarding the central educational development function. We have referred on a number of occasions throughout the book to the important role that educational development staff can play, in particular within the 'quality development' model (Chapter 8). We have also acknowledged the difficulties that sometimes exist with respect to the perception of those charged with this role by mainstream academics. How can educational development departments/centres contribute to the improvement of teaching and learning?

Educational development centres (EDCs) in the UK go under a variety of names, are located in different places within institutional structures and have a variety of remits. They vary in size from a one- or two-person section within a larger organizational unit, such as the registry, human resources or academic services, to whole free-standing departments reporting directly to a pro-vice-chancellor for teaching and learning (Gosling 2001b). Some have a strong learning technology or distance learning focus, whereas others have a broader academic staff development role. Sometimes the activity of such centres is conceptualized in terms of aligning quality enhancement with quality assurance. In some cases there is a clear remit to both undertake and promote pedagogical research. In many institutions, EDCs have responsibility for teaching and assessing participants on courses relating to teaching and learning in higher education. In those institutions where the EDC is conceptualized as a university 'service' there may be little or no role in undertaking or supporting academic work.

Educational development has been defined as the 'systematic and scholarly support for improving both educational processes and the practices and capabilities of educators' (Stefani 2003: 10). In this book we have suggested that the key concept which runs through a great array of different activities aimed at improving teaching and learning is learning: the learning of organizations, the learning of academics and the learning of students. Using this approach, educational development may be characterized as the following types of activity.

- *Organizations' learning.* Assisting organizational and policy development; facilitating institutional and departmental learning about teaching; and developing, through consultation guidelines, policies and strategies on matters relating to teaching and learning.
- *Academics' learning.* Providing support to improve teaching and assessment practices, curriculum design, learning support and creating formal and informal opportunities for the professional development of academic staff and all those involved in supporting student learning.
- *Students' learning.* Supporting the learning development of students by the provision of services and advice to students and to teaching departments.

We have also noted that central to the work of educational development is the 'scholarship of teaching'. This is important enough to suggest that it constitutes a fourth type of activity which relates to each and all of the three key areas of learning mentioned above. This fourth area includes the activities discussed in Chapter 7. In Badley's words these are:

> Supporting the scholarship of teaching through classroom inquiry and action research; providing opportunities for critical dialogue and conversation about teaching and learning in departmental and institutional settings, and promoting learning as the critical link between teaching, research, scholarship, inquiry and dialogue.
>
> (Badley 1998: 71)

Across the developed world, more staff are being appointed to undertake these educational development activities than ever before. As we saw in Chapter 3, there has been a considerable increase in the number of career tracks for individuals involved in educational development as broadly understood. In addition to the growing number of posts within educational development centres, there are increasing numbers of school/faculty learning and teaching co-ordinators, teaching fellows with development responsibilities, and project leaders, on either internal or externally funded initiatives. Within the UK over the past decade there has also been more educational development activity being undertaken at a national level, for example, in the Higher Education Academy and its constituent subject centres. The Centres for Excellence in Teaching and Learning are creating further growth, both in new appointments to establish and carry out the work of the centres, and in the numbers of academics within those centres who will take on a developmental role.

We have suggested that in undertaking these roles there must be recognition that teaching is a disciplinary, interdisciplinary or professionally based activity and that the nature of 'development' must be contextualized within the specific values, purposes and contexts of the disciplinary teaching being undertaken. This means working in partnership with teachers to both stimulate and facilitate improvement by providing specialist expertise on broader higher education issues and knowledge. We have also suggested that there is a role for cross-institutional development, working with managers and strategy makers to help inform decisions and to bring teachers together into various kinds of learning communities (see Chapters 2 and 3). This cross-institutional role can be to provide advice and facilitation for strategies that are agreed to be implemented institution-wide. Additionally, as we have also emphasized, it is about facilitating dialogue about teaching and student learning.

To be effective, educational developers, whatever their role, must have expertise and knowledge that is recognized and valued by teaching staff and their managers. This knowledge base should include an understanding of the management of change as well as of the empirical and theoretical literature on a wide range of teaching and learning areas. In order to foster informed discussion through the types of learning committees, networks and activities we have described in this book and to promote the scholarship of teaching, educational developers need to be well grounded in theoretical frameworks for this work as well. Currently, people working in educational development come from a variety of academic and non-academic backgrounds and their preferred theoretical frameworks can vary quite significantly. It is our view that educational development is in essence an academic role and those undertaking those roles must earn respect from other academics by engagement with scholarship and undertaking higher education research.

Higher education pedagogy is an increasingly complex field with a fast-growing literature. While a minority of subject-based academics develop an interest in this literature, the majority of subject specialists have neither the time nor the inclination to become experts in it themselves. The growth of knowledge in the disciplines is such that all researchers and teachers have difficulty in keeping up to date with the flood of relevant publications appearing every year relating to their specialism. It is unreasonable to expect the majority of academics to acquire the same level of expertise in higher education research. However, those with educational development roles need to have the level of knowledge of their field that subject specialists are expected to have of theirs. This is what provides them with the authority to undertake a 'developmental' role.

We have also emphasized that the knowledge that educational developers draw on is as much based on values and viewpoint as that in any other field of study. Value assumptions underpinning proposals for teaching methods, course design and assessment need to be made explicit, if they are to be opened up to critical debate by all those who might want to use them or have a reasoned basis for rejecting them. Malcolm and Zukas (2001) and Lindsay (2004) have criticized 'educational developers' for having a single hegemonic view that has been insufficiently interrogated before becoming taken for granted and used in their work. Examples addressed in this critique have been the concepts of 'deep' and 'surface' learning, 'learning styles' and the use of learning outcomes in course design. However, focusing on these examples does not recognize the diversity of views, based on a rich pedagogical literature, that exists among those responsible for developing teaching and learning within higher education institutions. Land (2001) has shown that educational development, far from being restricted to a single methodology, has been characterized by a wide variety of different 'approaches'.

In the first part of this chapter we noted that the position being adopted in this book, which we have called a 'developmental approach', represents a way forward that is neither managerialist nor a traditional collegial approach to higher education. What, then, are the implications of a developmental approach for educational development?

Some have argued that the recent growth of educational development is an extension of managerialism into the area of academic life, namely teaching, which had previously been the preserve of the autonomous professional. The growth in the UK of institutional learning and teaching strategies, recognition and reward for teaching performance, and funding in support of 'excellence in teaching and learning' might all be cited, following Foucault, as examples of 'micro-technologies of power' that support the implementation of neo-liberal managerialism.

Olssen *et al.* (2004) argue that the characteristics of the neo-liberal approach are the emphasis on individual 'flexibility' in the working lives of teachers in order to achieve greater 'efficiency' and 'effectiveness', and the shifting of responsibility for adapting to this need for 'flexibility' on to the individual teacher. 'Professional development' becomes the means of achieving this end, managed through use of devices such as record keeping (for example, teaching portfolios), performance targets, quality control, and monitoring of outputs or learning outcomes. The increasing use of competitive processes, for example for teaching awards, bidding for teaching enhancement funds and claiming 'excellence', might also be seen as characteristic of an environment that values individual performance over collaborative endeavour and sharing of expertise. The result is, according to Olssen *et al.* (see also Nixon *et al.* 2001), a reduction in professional autonomy and loss of trust. Although the educational development movement has presented itself as non-ideological, pragmatic and eclectic, taking this view it could be seen as potentially managerialist and neo-liberal.

We do not accept that educational development is necessarily implicated in advancing the goals of neo-liberalism. However, like all members of higher education communities, those working in educational development often find themselves being required to engage in activities while personally disagreeing with the ideological basis that underpins the very things they are required to do. Competitive bidding for teaching improvement funds is a case in point. Working with departments that are subject to external quality assurance processes might be another example. The assumptions of neo-liberalism are pervasive throughout western societies at present and therefore hard to resist or avoid. Faced with the world of higher education as it is currently constructed, what can be done? Olssen *et al.* (2004: 196) suggest that:

> First, academics and teachers should strive to change their own individual practices, refusing where possible to enact neo-liberal accountability rituals. Second, they should endeavour to promote democratic models of management based upon co-operation and collegial relationships.

We agree that democratic models of management are desirable. We have also suggested ways in which the character of managerial changes can be shifted to achieve a developmental rather than a managerial purpose. It may be, for example that learning technologies are becoming ubiquitous, but, as we argued in Chapter 6, we must hold on to the principle that they are used to advance pedagogical, not purely technological, purposes. Or, to take another example, widening access to higher education certainly does challenge some assumptions about teaching in higher education, but adopting the learning development approach discussed in Chapter 4 does not by any means treat students as simply 'products' of the system. Enhancing quality is not just a matter of meeting the arcane requirements of external agencies, but can be a process in which everyday teaching practices are subjected to critical scrutiny and improvements evaluated in scholarly ways.

We, therefore, hold on to the hope that improving teaching and learning can be taken seriously as an institutional priority and in ways that mean that educational development is not simply the servant of managerialist goals. We have discussed how teaching is as intellectually challenging, and as important, as undertaking research and should have an equal place in institutional planning. The precise ways in which teaching and learning can be improved are, as we have said, contested territory and, in this book, we have not attempted to suggest the details of what are 'improvements'. What those improvements are will be contextually specific and will only emerge from critical self-scrutiny within teaching and learning departments. Rather, we have focused on ways in which higher education institutions can orientate themselves to give due importance to the scholarly engagement and dialogue about teaching and student learning by focusing on the learning that is a prerequisite of change.

Note

1. A similar list with some additional methods and further detail on each is located at: http://www.icbl.hw.ac.uk/ltdi/cookbook/recipes.html#endhead

Appendix A

Possible SoTL Journals

The following examples are from Carfax (Taylor & Francis Group).

Accounting Education: An International Journal
Editor: Richard M. S. Wilson, Loughborough University Business School, UK
Editorial information
Publication details: 4 issues per year

Action Learning: Research and Practice
Editor: Mike Pedler, The Revans Institute for Action Learning and Research, University of Salford, UK
Editorial information
Publication details: 2 issues per year

ALT-J: Research in Learning Technology
Editors: Professor Grainne Conole, Research and Graduate School of Education, University of Southampton, UK
Dr Martin Oliver, Education and Professional Development, University College London, UK
Dr Jane K. Seale, Research and Graduate School of Education, University of Southampton, UK
Editorial information
Publication details: 3 issues per year

Assessment and Evaluation in Higher Education
Editor: Professor William Scott, Department of Education, University of Bath, UK
Editorial information
Publication details: 6 issues per year

British Educational Research Journal
Editor: David Hustler, Institute of Education, Manchester Metropolitan University, 799 Wilmslow Road, Manchester M20 2RR, UK

Editorial information
Publication details: 6 issues per year

British Journal of Religious Education
Editor: Professor Robert Jackson, Institute of Education, University of Warwick, UK
Editorial information
Publication details: 3 issues per year

Cambridge Journal of Education
Editors: Dr Paul Andrews, University of Cambridge, UK
Dr Nalini Boodhoo, University of East Anglia, UK
Peter Cunningham, University of Cambridge, Faculty of Education, UK
Lani Florian, University of Cambridge, Faculty of Education, UK
Professor Donald McIntyre, University of Cambridge, UK
Professor Nigel Norris, University of East Anglia, UK
Professor Jean Rudduck, University of Cambridge, UK
Professor Les Tickle, University of East Anglia, UK
Executive Editor: Paula Peachy, University of Cambridge, UK
Editorial information
Publication details: 3 issues per year

Curriculum Journal
Editors: Bob McCormick, The Open University, UK
Bob Moon, The Open University, UK
Editorial Information
Publication details: 3 issues per year

Communication Education
Editor: Don Rubin, University of Georgia, USA
Editorial information
Publication details: 4 issues per year

Communication Teacher
Editor: Scott A. Myers, West Virginia University, USA
Publication details: 4 issues per year

Community College Journal of Research and Practice
Editor-in-Chief: D. Barry Lumsden, Professor of Higher Education, University of North Texas, PO Box 311337, Denton, TX 76203-1337, USA
Publication details: 10 issues per year

Education and the Law
Co-Editors: Professor Geoffrey Bennett, University of Notre Dame, UK
David Palfreyman, New College, Oxford, UK
Editorial information
Publication details: 4 issues per year

Educational Media International
Editor: Professor John Hedberg, National Institute of Education, Nanyang Technological University, Singapore
Editorial information
Publication details: 4 issues per year

Gender and Education
Becky Francis, London Metropolitan University, UK and **Christine Skelton**, University of Newcastle upon Tyne, UK
Editorial information
Publication details: 4 issues per year

Globalisation, Societies and Education
Editors: Professor Roger Dale, University of Auckland, New Zealand/ University of Bristol, UK
Dr Susan Robertson, School of Education, University of Bristol, UK
Editorial information
Publication details: 3 issues per year

Higher Education in Europe
Senior Editor: Leland C. Barrows, CEPES c/o UNESCO, Romania
Editorial information
Publication details: 4 issues per year

Higher Education Research and Development
Editors: Margot Pearson, Centre for Educational Development and Academic Methods, Australia National University, Canberra, Australia
Linda Hort, Centre for Educational Development and Academic Methods, Australia National University, Canberra, Australia
Editorial information
Publication details: 3 issues per year

Innovations in Education and Teaching International
formerly Innovations in Education and Training International
Editors: Philip Barker, University of Teesside, UK
Gina Wisker, Anglia Polytechnic University, UK
Editorial information
Publication details: 4 issues per year

Intercultural Education
Formerly European Journal of Intercultural Studies
Editors: Pieter Batelaan, IAIE, Hilversum, The Netherlands
Barry Van Driel, Anne Frank Stichting, The Netherlands
Editorial information
Publication details: 4 issues per year

International Journal for Academic Development
Editors: Dr Angela Brew, University of Sydney, Australia
Lynn McAlpine, McGill University, Canada
Rhonda Sharpe, Oxford Brookes University, UK
Reviews Editor:
Ray Land, University of Edinburgh, UK
Publication details: 2 issues per year

International Journal of Inclusive Education
Editor: Roger Slee, Education Queensland, Australia
Editorial information
Publication details: 4 issues per year

International Journal of Lifelong Education
Editors: Peter Jarvis, School of Educational Studies, University of Surrey, Guildford, GU2 5XH, UK
Stella Parker, School of Continuing Education, University of Nottingham, Jubilee Campus, Wollaton Road, Nottingham, UK
Editorial information
Publication details: 6 issues per year

International Journal of Mathematical Education in Science and Technology
Editor: Dr Martin Harrison, Department of Mathematical Sciences, Loughborough University, Loughborough, LE11 3TU, UK
Editorial information
Publication details: 6 issues per year

International Journal of Qualitative Studies in Education
Editors: James Scheurich and **Angela Valenzuela**, University of Texas at Austin, Texas, USA
Editorial information
Publication details: 6 issues per year

Journal of Curriculum Studies
Editor: Ian Westbury, University of Illinois at Urbana-Champaign, USA
Editorial information
Publication details: 6 issues per year

Journal of Education for Teaching: International Research and Pedagogy
Editors: Edgar Stones, University of Birmingham, UK
Peter Gilroy, Manchester Metropolitan University, UK
Editorial information
Publication details: 3 issues per year

Journal of Further and Higher Education
Editor: Jennifer Rowley, University of Wales, UK

Editorial information
Publication details: 4 issues per year

Journal of Geography in Higher Education
Editors: Martin Haigh, Oxford Brookes University, UK and **David Higgitt**, University of Durham, UK
Editorial information
Publication details: 3 issues per year

Journal of Moral Education
Editor: Monica J. Taylor, UK
Editorial information
Publication details: 4 issues per year

Journal of Peace Education
Editor: John Synott, Queensland University of Technology, Australia
Editorial information
Publication details: 2 issues per year

London Review of Education
Editor: Professor David Halpin, Institute of Education, University of London, UK
Editorial information
Publication details: 3 issues per year

Music Education Research
Editor: Sarah Hennessy, School of Education, University of Exeter, UK
Editorial information
Publication details: 3 issues per year

Open Learning: The Journal of Open and Distance Learning
Editor: Graham Gibbs, The Open University, Walton Hall, Milton Keynes, MK7 6AA, UK
Editorial information
Publication details: 3 issues per year

Oxford Review of Education
Editors: David Phillips, Fellow of St Edmund Hall and Reader in Comparative Education, University of Oxford, UK
Editorial information
Publication details: 4 issues per year

Pharmacy Education: An International Journal for Pharmaceutical Education
Editor: Ian Bates, Head of Educational Development, Department of Practice and Policy School of Pharmacy, University of London, 29/39 Brunswick Square, London, WC1N 1AX, UK

Editorial information
Publication details: Quarterly

Quality in Higher Education
Editor: Professor Lee Harvey, Surrey Building, Sheffield Hallam University, City Campus, Howard Street, Sheffield, S1 1WB, UK
Editorial information
Publication details: 3 issues per year

Race, Ethnicity and Education
Editor: David Gillborn, University of London, Institute of Education, UK
Editorial information
Publication details: 4 issues per year

Religious Education
Editor-in-Chief: Theodore Brelsford, Emory University, Bishops Hall, Box 39, Atlanta, GA, 30322, USA
Editorial information
Publication details: 4 issues per year

Research in Dance Education
Editor: Linda Rolfe, School of Education, University of Exeter, UK
Editorial information
Publication details: 2 issues per year

Research in Drama Education
Editors: John Somers, University of Exeter, UK
E-mail: **j.w.somers@exeter.ac.uk**
Editorial information
Publication details: 2 issues per year

Research in Science and Technological Education
Editor: Chris Botton, Science Education Centre, University of Hull, UK
Editorial information
Publication details: 2 issues per year

Review of Education, Pedagogy and Cultural Studies
Editors: Henry A. Giroux, Susan Searls Giroux, Patrick Shannon, Department of Curriculum and Instruction, Pennsylvania State University, Chambers Building, University Park, PA 16802, USA
Editorial information
Publication details: Quarterly

Social Work Education: The International Journal for Social Work and Social Care Education, Training and Staff Development
Editor: Michael Preston-Shoot, Department of Applied Social Studies, University of Luton, UK

Editorial information
Publication details: 6 issues per year

Studies in Continuing Education
Editors: Professor David Boud, Associate Professor Clive Chappell, Associate Professor Nicky Solomon, all at the Faculty of Education, University of Technology Sydney, Australia
Editorial information
Publication details: 2 issues per year

Studies in Higher Education
Editor: Professor Malcolm Tight, Department of Continuing Education, University of Warwick, UK
Editorial information
Publication details: 4 issues per year

Teaching in Higher Education
Founding Editor: Len Barton, Institute of Education, University of London, UK
Editor: Jon Nixon, School of Education, University of Sheffield, UK
Editorial information
Publication details: 4 issues per year

Westminster Studies in Education
Editor: Dr David Palacio, Westminster Institute of Education, Oxford Brookes University, Oxford OX2 9AT, UK
Editorial information
International Advisory Board Membership
Publication details: 2 issues per year

Appendix B
SoTL Conferences

Annual International SoTL Conference held in London currently organized by City University (http://www.city.ac.uk/edc/SoTLConference.htm). One more annual event is planned after which this conference will be joined with the International Society for SoTL (see below).

Improving Student Learning Symposium (ISL) has been a major forum in the UK for reporting on SoTL work for over a decade. http://www.brookes.ac.uk/services/ocsd/1_ocsld/isl2004/callforpapers.html

International Society for SoTL (IS-SOTL). The Society's first conference was held in October 2004 in Bloomington, Indiana, USA. The plan is to alternate international sites.

Society for Research in Higher Education (SRHE) (www.srhe.ac.uk). The SRHE annual conference held in December has begun to address SoTL areas of work.

References

Adia, E. (1996) *Higher Education: The Ethnic Minority Experience.* Leeds: HEIST.

Ainley, P. (1994) *Degrees of Difference: Higher Education in the 1990s.* London: Lawrence & Wishart.

Allen, L. (n.d.) *Consenting Adults in Private: Union and Management Perspectives on Peer Observation of Teaching.* Higher Education Academy, CPD011[1] at http://www.heacademy.ac.uk/resources (accessed February 2005).

Allen, R. and Layer, G. (1995) *Credit-based Systems as Vehicles for Change in Universities and Colleges,* London: Kogan Page.

Alley, L.R. (1996) An instructional epiphany, *Change,* 28 (2): 49–54.

Andresen, L.W. (1995) Accredited courses in teaching and learning in A. Brew (ed.), *Directions in Staff Development,* pp. 36–50. Buckingham, SRHE/Open University Press.

Andresen, L.W. (2000) A useable, trans-disciplinary conception of scholarship, *Higher Education Research and Development,* 19 (2): 137–53.

Andrews, B. and Wilding, J.M. (2004) The relation of depression and anxiety to life stress and achievement in students, *British Journal of Psychology,* 95 (4): 509–21.

Angelo, T.A. (1995) Teaching Goals Inventory. Presentation to Improving Student Learning Conference, Exeter, UK, September.

Angelo, T.A. and Cross, P.J. (1993) *Classroom Assessment Techniques: A Handbook for College Teachers.* San Francisco: Jossey-Bass.

Archer, L. and Leathwood, C. (2003) Identities, inequalities and higher education, in L. Archer, M. Hutchings and A. Ross (eds) *Higher Education and Social Class,* pp. 175–92. London: Routledge Falmer.

Archer, L., Hutchings, M. and Ross, A. (2003) *Higher Education and Social Class.* London: Routledge Falmer.

Arora, R. (1995) *Experiences of Ethnic Minority Students in Higher Education for a Multicultural University,* working paper no. 3. London: New Ethnicities Unit, University of East London.

Ash, J. (2001) Student induction into studying at university, in P. Frame (ed.) *Student Induction in Practice,* pp. 75–82. Birmingham: SEDA.

Astin, A.W. (1993) *What Matters in College: Four Critical Years Revisited.* San Francisco: Jossey-Bass.

Badley, G. (1998) Making the case for educational development in times of drift and shift, *Quality Assurance in Education,* 6 (2): 64–73.

Badley, G. and Wicks, K. (2002) *Learning and Teaching Strategies: A Preliminary Analysis.* Milton Keynes: National Co-ordination Team, Open University.

Baker, P. (1999) Creating learning communities: the unfinished agenda, in B.A. Pescosolido and R. Aminzade (eds) *The Social Worlds of Higher Education,* pp. 95–109. Thousand Oaks, CA: Pine Forge Press.

Bamber, V. (2002) To what extent has the Dearing policy recommendation on training new lecturers met acceptance? Where Dearing went that Robbins didn't dare, *Teacher Development,* 6 (3): 433–59.

Bamber, V. (2003) Is there an ideal method for evaluating new lecturer development? *Educational Developments,* 4 (3): 16–21.

Bandura, A. (1986) *Social Foundations of Thought and Action: A Social Cognition Theory.* Englewood Cliffs, NJ: Prentice Hall.

Barker, P., van Schaik, P., Hudson, S. and Tan, C.M. (1997) Mental models and their role in the teaching and learning of human–computer interaction. Paper presented at the SEDA Conference, Winter.

Barnes, J. (1999) Funding and university autonomy, in M. Henkel and B. Little (eds) *Changing Relationships between Higher Education and the State,* pp. 162–90. London: Jessica Kingsley.

Barnett, R. (1990) *The Idea of Higher Education.* Buckingham: SRHE/Open University Press.

Barnett, R. (1997) *Higher Education: A Critical Business.* Buckingham: SRHE/Open University Press.

Barnett, R. (2000) *Realizing the University in an Age of Supercomplexity.* Buckingham: SRHE/Open University Press.

Barnett, R. and Griffin, A. (eds) (1997) *The End of Knowledge in Higher Education.* London: Cassell.

Barr, R. and Tagg, J. (1995) From teaching to learning: a new paradigm for undergraduate education, *Change,* 27 (6): 13–25.

Bateson, T. and Bass, R. (1996) Teaching and learning in the computer age, *Change,* 28 (2): 42–7.

Baume, D. (1994) *Developing Learner Autonomy,* SEDA paper 84. Birmingham: SEDA.

Baume, C., Martin, P. and Yorke, M. (2002) *Managing Educational Development Projects.* London: SEDA/Kogan Page.

Beaty, L. and McGill, I. (1995) *Developing Reflective Practice: Observing Teaching as a Component of Professional Development.* Brighton: University of Brighton.

Beaty, L., Gibbs, G. and Morgan, A. (1997) Learning orientations and study contracts, in F. Marton, D. Hounsell and N. Entwistle (eds) *The Experience of Learning,* pp. 72–88. Edinburgh: Scottish Academic Press.

Becher, T. (1989) *Academic Tribes and Territories: Intellectual Enquiry and the Cultures of Disciplines.* Milton Keynes: SRHE/Open University Press.

Becher, T. (1994) The significance of disciplinary differences, *Studies in Higher Education,* 19 (2): 151–61.

Becher, T. and Kogan, M. (1992) *Process and Structure in Higher Education.* London: Routledge.

Becher, T. and Trowler, P.R. (2001). *Academic Tribes and Territories.* Buckingham: SRHE/Open University Press.

Beck, U. (1992) *Risk Society: Towards a New Modernity.* London: Sage.

Beetham, H. and Bailey, P. (2001) *Career Development of Learning Technology Staff Scoping Study: EFFECTS Project.* Plymouth: Plymouth University. Also at http://sh.plym.ac.uk/eds/effects/jcalt-project/ (accessed November 2004).

Bell, M. (2001) Supported reflective practice: a programme of peer observation and feedback for academic development, *International Journal for Academic Development*, 6 (1): 29–39.

Bennett, S. and Marsh, D. (2002) Are we expecting online tutors to run before they can walk?, *Innovations in Education and Teaching International*, 39 (1): 14–20.

Berg, B. and Ostergren, B. (1977) *Innovations and Innovation Processes in Higher Education.* Stockholm: National Board of Universities and Colleges.

Berg, B. and Ostergren, B. (1979) Innovative processes in higher education, *Studies in Higher Education*, 4 (2): 261–7.

Berger, P. and Luckman, T. (1967) *The Social Construction of Reality.* London: Allen Lane.

Bergquist, W. (1992) *Four Cultures of the Academy.* San Francisco: Jossey-Bass.

Bernstein, B. (2000) *Pedagogy, Symbolic Control and Identity: Theory, Research, Critique.* Oxford: Rowman & Littlefield.

Biggs, J. (1999) *Teaching for Quality Learning at University: What the Student Does.* Buckingham: SRHE/Open University Press.

Blackburn, R.T. and Lawrence, J.H. (1995) *Faculty at Work: Motivation, Expectation, Satisfaction.* Baltimore, MD: The Johns Hopkins University Press.

Blackwell, R. (2003) The future of quality enhancement, *Educational Developments*, 4 (3): 10–12.

Blackwell, R. and McLean, M. (1996) Mentoring new university teachers, *International Journal for Academic Development*, 1 (2): 80–5.

Blackwell, R. and Preece, D. (2001) Changing higher education, *International Journal of Management Education*, 3: 4–14.

Boud, D. (1995) Meeting the challenges, in A. Brew (ed.) *Directions in Staff Development*, pp. 203–13. Buckingham: SRHE/Open University Press.

Boud, D. and Miller, N. (1996) *Working with Experience: Animating Learning.* London: Routledge.

Boud, D. and Walker, D. (1993) *Using Experience for Learning.* Buckingham: SRHE/Open University Press.

Boughey, C. (2002) Naming students' problems: an analysis of language related discourses at a South African university, *Teaching in Higher Education*, 7 (3): 295–308.

Bourdieu, P. (1988) *Homo Academicus.* Cambridge: Polity Press.

Bourdieu, P. (1998) *Acts of Resistence: Against the New Myths of our Times.* Cambridge: Polity Press.

Bourner, T., Cooper, A. and France, L. (2000) Action learning across a university community, *Innovations in Education and Training International*, 37 (1): 2–9.

Bourner, T., France, L. and Blake, M. (2003) The learning outcomes of courses that accredit university teachers, in D. Gosling and V. D'Andrea (eds) *International Conference on the Scholarship of Teaching: Proceedings 2001 and 2002*, pp. 65–78. London: Educational Development Centre, City University.

Bowden, J. and Marton, F. (1998) *The University of Learning: Beyond Quality and Competence in Higher Education.* London: Kogan Page.

Boyer, E. (1990) *Scholarship Reconsidered: Priorities of the Professoriate.* Princeton, NJ: Carnegie Foundation for the Advancement of Teaching.

Boyer, E. (1994) Scholarship reconsidered: priorities for a new century, *Universities in the Twenty-First Century*, pp. 110–31. Washington, DC: National Commission on Education.

Braskamp, L.A. and Ory, J.C. (1994) *Assessing Faculty Work: Enhancing Individual and Institutional Performance.* San Francisco: Jossey-Bass.

Breen, R. (2002) Different disciplines require different motivations for student success, *Oxford Brookes Teaching Forum*, 50: 39–40. Also at http://www.brookes.ac.uk/virtual/NewTF/index.html (accessed August 2004).

Brennan, J.L., Brighton, R., Moon, N., Richardson, J., Rindl, J. and Williams, R. (2003) *Collecting and Using Student Feedback on Quality and Standards of Learning in HE: A Report to HEFCE*, RD08.03, Centre for Higher Education Research and Information (Open University), NOP Research Group and SQW Ltd. Bristol: Higher Education Funding Council for England.

Brew, A. (1999) Research and teaching: changing relationships in a changing context, *Studies in Higher Education*, 24 (3): 291–391.

Brew, A. (2004) Closing the gap between teaching and research at an institutional level: a case study. Paper presented to Research and Teaching: Closing the Divide? An International Colloquium, Winchester, UK, 18–19 March.

Brew, A. and Boud, D. (1995a) Research and learning in higher education, in Smith, B. and Brown, S. (eds) *Research, Teaching and Learning in Higher Education*, pp. 30–9. London: Kogan Page.

Brew, A. and Boud, D. (1995b) Teaching and research: establishing the vital link with learning, *Higher Education*, 29 (3): 261–73.

Brew, A. and Boud, D. (1996) Preparing new academic roles: an holistic approach to development, *International Journal for Academic Development*, 1 (2): 17–25.

Brien, A. (1998) Professional ethics and the culture of trust, *Journal of Business Ethics*, 17 (4): 391–409.

Brookfield. S. (1985) *Understanding and Facilitating Adult Learning*. San Francisco: Jossey-Bass.

Brookfield, S.D. (1995) Changing the culture of scholarship to the culture of teaching: an American perspective, in T. Schuller (ed.) *The Changing University?* pp. 128–38. Buckingham: SRHE/Open University Press.

Brown, H. (2001) Reflections on the development of a collaborative learning community for continuing professional development (CPD): the creative network. Paper presented to the Higher Education Close Up Conference 2, Lancaster University, 16–18 July.

Brown, J.S. (2000) Growing up digital: how the web changes work, education and the way people learn, *Change*, 32 (2): 11–20.

Brown, J.S. and Duguid, P. (2000) *The Social Life of Information*. Boston, MA: Harvard Business School Press.

Brown, R.B. (1998a) Teaching and research: friends or foes? Inaugural Professorial Lecture, Roehampton Institute London, 26 October.

Brown, R.B. (1998b) Co-operation or compliance? The National Committee of Inquiry proposals on quality and standards, *Quality in Higher Education*, 2 (1) 85–96.

Brown, R.B. (2000a) Accountability in higher education: have we reached the end of the road? The case for a Higher Education Audit Commission. Professorial Lecture, University of Surrey Roehampton, 24 October.

Brown, R.B. (2000b) Funding and policy drivers, in *The Relationship between Research and Teaching in Higher Education: Present Realities, Future Possibilities*, pp. 65–69. Southampton: Southampton Institute/Higher Education Funding Council for England.

Brown, R.B. (2000c) The new UK quality framework, *Higher Education Quarterly*, 54 (4): 323–42.

Brown, R.B. (2000d) Teaching is the main event, not a sideshow to research, *Research Fortnightly*, 12 January, p. 17.

Brown, R.B. (2001) Evidence-based policy making or policy-based evidence? The case of quality assurance in higher education. Professorial Lecture, City University, 11 December.

Brown, R.B. (2002a) One half of double act, *Times Higher Education Supplement*, 15 February, p. 14.

Brown, R.B. (2002b) *Scholarship, On Learning, Teaching and Higher Education*, Academic Development Service Working Papers, Vol. 1, paper 16 (July).

Brown, R.B. (2002c) Linking research and teaching – repairing the damage, *Exchange*, 3 (Autumn): 29–30.

Brown, R.B. (2003) *The Current Position on Quality Assurance.* SCOP Quality Management Group, 6 March.

Brown, R.B. (2004a) *Quality Assurance in Higher Education: The UK Experience since 1992.* London: Routledge Falmer.

Brown, R.B. (2004b) Keynote Speech, Why link your personal research and your teaching? Research and Teaching: Closing the Divide? An International Colloquium, Winchester, UK, 18–19 March.

Brown, S. (1999) *Assessment Matters in Higher Education: Choosing and Using Diverse Approaches.* Buckingham: SRHE/Open University Press.

Brown, S. (2000) Influences on the effectiveness of teaching and learning innovations in higher education, *SRHE News*, 44: 1–3.

Brown, S. (2003) Recognising and rewarding excellence, *Exchange*, 5: 4–6.

Cambridge, B. (1999) The scholarship of teaching and learning: questions and answers from the field, *AAHE Bulletin*, 52 (4): 7–10.

Cambridge, B. (2001) Fostering the scholarship of teaching and learning: communities of practice, in D. Lieberman and C. Wehlberg (eds) *To Improve the Academy*, pp. 3–16 Bolton, MA: Anker.

Cambridge, B. (2002) Fostering the scholarship of teaching and learning: communities of practice. Plenary Panel IV, Annual International SoTL Conference, London 23–24 May.

Cambridge, B. (2004) *Campus Progress: Supporting the Scholarship of Teaching.* Washington DC: American Association for Higher Education.

Capstick, S. and Fleming, H. (2003) Peer assisted learning in an undergraduate hospitality course, *Journal of Hospitality, Leisure, Sport and Tourism Education*, 1 (1): 69–75.

Carnegie Foundation for the Advancement of Teaching (2000) Informational Program Booklet. Menlo Park: CA: Carnegie Academy for the Scholarship of Teaching and Learning.

Carter, J., Fenton, S. and Modood, T. (1999) *Ethnicity and Employment in HE.* London: Policy Studies Institute.

Cashin, W.E. (1995) *Student Ratings of Teaching: The Research Revisited*, IDEA paper no. 32. Manhattan, KS: Center for Faculty Evaluation and Development in Higher Education.

Castells, M. (2001). The new global economy in A. Muller, N. Cloete and S. Badat (eds) *Challenges of Globalisation*, pp. 2–21. Cape Town: Makew Miller Longman.

Chang, C-C. (2003) Towards a distributed web-based learning community, *Innovations, In Education and Teaching International*, 40 (1): 27–42.

Chen, T-M. and Barnett, G.A. (2000) Research on international student flows from a macro perspective: a network analysis of 1985, 1989 and 1995, *Higher Education*, 39: 433–53.

Chickering, A.W. and Ehrmann, S.C. (1996) Implementing the seven principles: technology as lever, *AAHE Bulletin*, October. Also at www.aahe.org/bulletin/SevenPrinciples.htm

Chism, N.V. (2002) Valuing student differences, in W.J. McKeachie (ed.) *Teaching Tips: Strategies, Research, and Theory for College and University Teachers*, pp. 128–47. Boston, MA: Houghton Mifflin.

CIHE (2004) *Higher Education and the Public Good*. London: Council for Industry and Higher Education.

Clark, B.R. (1997) The modern integration of research activities with teaching and learning. *Journal of Higher Education*, 68: 241–56.

Clark, B.R. (1998) *Creating Entrepreneurial Universities: Organizational Pathways of Transformation Issues in Higher Education*. Oxford: IAU/Pergamon.

Clegg, S. (2003) Learning and teaching policies in higher education: mediations and contradictions of practice, *British Educational Research Journal*, 29(6): 803–19.

CNAA (1992) *Case Studies in Student-centred Learning*. London: Council for National Academic Awards.

Cohen, P. (1995) *For a Multicultural University: The Crisis of the Western University*. London: University of East London.

Colbeck, C.L. (1998) Merging in a seamless blend: how faculty integrate teaching and research, *Journal of Higher Education*, 69 (6): 647–71.

Connor, H., Dewson, S., Tyers, C., Eccles, J., Regan, J. and Aston, J. (2001) *Social Class and Higher Education: Issues Affecting Decisions on Particpation by Lower Social Class Groups*, DfES Research Report 267. London: Institute for Employment Studies.

Connor, H., Tyers, C., Modood, T. and Hillage, J. (2004) *Why the Difference? A Closer Look at Higher Education Minority Ethnic Students and Graduates*, DfES Research Report 552. Sheffield: Department for Education and Skills.

Conole, G. (2001) Drivers and barriers to utilising information and communication technologies. Keynote Address and Paper, *IEE International Symposium on Engineering Education: Innovations in Teaching, Learning and Assessment*, 2: 22/1–22/10.

Cooke, R. (2002) *Information on Quality and Standards in Higher Education: Final Report of the Task Group*, Report 02/15. Bristol: Higher Education Funding Council for England.

Cooper, A. (2000) The state of mind we're in, *Soundings*, 15 (summer): 118–38.

Cooper, A. (2003) Exploring the social context of learning to teach in HE, *Educational Developments*, 4 (3): 1–7.

Cooper, A. (2004) Leading programmes in learning and teaching, in D. Baume and P. Kahn (eds) *Enhancing Staff and Educational Development*, pp. 56–80. London: Routledge Falmer.

Corbett, A. (2003) 'Europe': a threat or an opportunity for national systems of higher education? *SRHE News*, 23 (1): 4.

Cosh, J. (1998) Peer observation in higher education: a reflective approach, *Innovations in Education and Teaching International*, 35 (2): 171–6.

Cottrell, S. (2001) *Teaching Study Skills and Supporting Learning*. London: Palgrave.

Cousin, G. (2003) Less is more: evaluations research for educational development. Keynote Address, SEDA Conference, Bristol, 9–11 April.

Cox, M.D. (1998) Long-term patterns in a successful mentoring program for junior faculty: recommendations for building a teaching and learning culture on your campus. Paper presented at the Lilly Conference on College Teaching, Towson University, Baltimore, MD, 3–5 April.

Cox, M.D. (2004) Introduction to faculty learning communities, in Cox, M. and Richlin, L. (eds) *Building Faculty Learning Communities*, pp. 5–23. San Francisco: Jossey-Bass.

Cox, M.D. and Richlin, L. (2004) *Building Faculty Learning Communities*. San Francisco: Jossey-Bass.

Curzon-Hobson, A. (2002) Higher education in a world of radical unknowability: an extension of the challenge of Ronald Barnett, *Teaching in Higher Education*, 7 (2): 179–92.

D'Andrea, V. (1994) Higher education quality assurance systems in Europe and the United States: doing the right thing and/or doing it right. Paper presented to the American Sociological Association Annual Meeting, Los Angeles, CA.

D'Andrea, V. (1996) *Recent Developments in Teaching and Learning: Roehampton Institute London 1993–1995* (with S. Dhaliwal). London: Roehampton Institute London.

D'Andrea, V. (1997) IT and Dearing: the implications for HE – response to the report, in H. Beetham (ed.) *IT and Dearing: The Implications for HE – Colloquium Proceedings*, pp. 28–9. London: CTISS Publications.

D'Andrea, V. (1999) Organising teaching and learning: outcomes-based planning, in H. Fry, S. Ketteridge and S. Marshall (eds) *A Handbook on Teaching and Learning in Higher Education*, pp. 41–57. London: Kogan Page.

D'Andrea, V. (2001) Peer review in the USA. *Learning and Teaching Support* Network (LTSN) website at www.heacademy.ac.uk.

D'Andrea, V. (2003) Organising teaching and learning: outcomes-based planning, in H. Fry, S. Ketteridge and S. Marshall (eds) *A Handbook on Teaching and Learning in Higher Education*, pp. 26–41. London: Kogan Page.

D'Andrea, V. and Allan, C. (eds) (2002) Linking research and teaching, *Exchange*, 3 (Autumn).

D'Andrea, V. and Ewens, B. (1990) *Discussion in the College Classroom*. Washington, DC: American Sociological Association.

D'Andrea, V. and Gosling, D. (2000a) Creating meta-learning communities to model inclusive learning. Paper presented to the Towards the Global University II; Redefining Excellence in the Third Millennium, Cape Town, South Africa, 16–20 April.

D'Andrea, V. and Gosling, D. (2000b) Promoting research in teaching and learning in higher education: two case studies of multi-disciplinary pedagogic research. Paper presented to the ESRC-TLRP Conference, Leicester, UK, November.

D'Andrea, V. and D. Gosling. (2001) Joining the dots: reconceptualising educational development, *Active Learning*, 2 (1): 65–81.

D'Andrea, V., Davies, A., Gosling, D. and Jackson, B. (2001) Linking educational development and information technology (EDIT): integrating learning and teaching strategies with information technology strategies in UK universities. Paper presented to the 9th International Symposium on Improving Student Learning: Improving Student Learning using Learning Technology, September.

Davis, J.R. (1976) *Teaching Strategies for the College Classroom*. Boulder, CO: Westview.

Day, D. (1999) *New Technology in Teaching and Learning – A RIL Perspective*. London: University of Surrey Roehampton.

Dearing, R. (1997) *Higher Education in the Learning Society* (Dearing Report). National Commission of Inquiry into Higher Education. London: HMSO.

Deepwell, F. and Cousin, G. (2002). A developmental framework for evaluating institutional change, *Educational Developments*, 3 (1): 24–6.

Delanty, G. (2001) *Challenging Knowledge: The University in the Knowledge Society*. Buckingham: SRHE/Open University Press.

Deming, W.E. (1988) *Out of Crisis*. Cambridge: MA: MIT, Center for Advanced Engineering Study/Cambridge University Press.

Dempster, J. and Deepwell, F. (2002). *A Review of Successful Project Approaches to Embedding Educational Technology Innovation into Institutional Teaching and Learning Practices in Higher Education*. York: Generic Centre.

Department of Education (1997) *A Programme for the Transformation of Higher Education*, Education White Paper, no. 3, *Government Gazette* no. 18207 (15 August). Pretoria, Republic of South Africa: Government Printers.

Department of Educational Research (2002) *Evaluating the Learning and Teaching Support Network: Third Biannual Report to the LTSN Executive*. Lancaster, UK: University of Lancaster.

De Vries, P. (1997) Self-assessment within the quality assessment process: a critical perspective, in J. Radford, K. Raaheim, P. de Vries and R. Williams (eds) *Quantity and Quality in Higher Education*, Higher Education Policy Series 40. London: Jessica Kingsley.

DfES (2003a) *The Future of Higher Education*. London: HMSO.

DfES (2003b). *Towards a Unified e-Learning Strategy Consultation 2003*. London: HMSO. Also at http://www.dfes.gov.uk/elearningstrategy/strategy.stm

DfES (2003c) *Widening Participation in Higher Education*. Sheffield: Department for Education and Skills.

Diamond, R.M. and Adam, B.E. (2004) Balancing institutional, disciplinary and faculty priorities with public and social needs: defining scholarship for the 21st century, *Arts and Humanities in Higher Education*, 3 (1): 29–40.

Dumaine, B. (1989) What the leaders of tomorrow see, *Fortune*, 120 (1): 48–62.

Dweck, C.S. (1999) *Self-Theories: Their Role in Motivation, Personality and Development*. Philadelphia, PA: Psychology Press.

Eckel, P., Hill, B. and Green, M. (1998) *On Change: En Route to Transformation*. Washington, DC: American Council on Education.

Eckel, P., Green, M., Hill, B. and Mallon, W. (1999) *Taking Charge of Change: A Primer for Colleges and Universities*. Washington, DC: American Council on Education.

Ehrmann, S.C. (2000) Computer-intensive academic programs: how to evaluate, plan, support and implement (in that order) your campus technology investments, *AAHE Bullentin*, 53 (3): 7–11.

Ehrmann, S.C. (2002a) *Evaluating (and Improving) Benefits of Educational Uses of Technology*, December. Also at http://www.tltgroup.org/resources/Flashlight/Benefits.html

Ehrmann, S.C. (2002b) Using technology to improve the outcomes of higher education: learning from past mistakes, in C. Rust (ed.) *Proceedings of the 9th International Symposium Improving Student Learning: Improving Student Learning Using Learning Technology*, pp. 11–26. Oxford: Oxford Centre for Staff and Learning Development, Oxford Brookes University.

Ellis, R. (ed.) (1993) *Quality Assurance for University Teaching*. Buckingham: SRHE/Open University Press.

Elmore, R. (1995) Getting to scale with good educational practice, *Harvard Educational Review*, 66 (1): 1–26.

Elton, L. (1986) Research and teaching: symbiosis or conflict, *Higher Education*, 15: 299–304.

Elton, L (1987). *Teaching in Higher Education: Appraisal and Training*. London: Kogan Page.

Elton, L. (1995a) Is university teaching researchable? Professorial Inaugural Lecture, University College London, 9 March.

Elton, L. (1995b) An institutional framework, in *Directions in Staff Development*, pp.177–88. Buckingham: SRHE/Open University Press

Elton, L. (1996) Partnership, quality and standards in higher education, *Quality in Higher Education*, 2 (2): 95–104.

Elton, L. (2000) Research and teaching: possible future contexts and considerations, in *The Relationship between Research and Teaching in Higher Education: Present Realities, Future Possibilities*, pp. 37–43. Southampton: Southampton Institute/Higher Education Funding Council for England.

Elton, L. (2003), Some Thoughts on Scholarship, Educational Developments, 4 (4): 7–8.

Elton, L. (2004) Response to 'Mohammad Qamar uz Zaman, review of the academic evidence on the relationship between teaching and reseach in higher education' [Dfes Research Report RR506]. Paper presented to Research and Teaching: Closing the Divide? An International Colloquium, Winchester, UK, 18–19 March.

Elton, L. and Partington, P. (1993) *Teaching Standards and Excellence in Higher Education*, Occasional Green Paper no. 1. London: Committee of Vice Chancellors and Principals.

Engestrom, Y. and Miettinen, R. (1999) *Perspectives on Activity Theory*. Cambridge: Cambridge University Press.

Entwistle, N. (2000) Promoting deep learning through teaching and assessment: conceptual frameworks and educational contexts. Paper presented to ESRC Teaching and Learning Programme Conference, Leicester, November.

Entwistle, N., Thompson, S. and Tait, H. (1992). *Guidelines for Promoting Effective Learning in Higher Education*. Edinburgh: Centre for Research on Learning and Instruction.

Eraut, M. (2000) Non-formal learning and tacit knowledge in professional work, *British Educational Journal of Educational Psychology*, 70: 113–36.

Evans, C. (1988) *Language People*. Milton Keynes: Open University Press.

Evans, C. (1993) *The English People*. Buckingham. SRHE/Open University Press.

Evans, G. (1999) *Calling Academia to Account: Rights and Responsibilities*. Buckingham: SRHE/Open University Press.

Evans, G. (2002) *Academics and the Real World*. Buckingham: SRHE/Open University Press.

Fanghanel, J. (2004) Capturing dissonance in university teacher education environments, *Studies in Higher Education*, 29 (5): 575–90.

Feito, J. (2003) Exploring intellectual community: reflections on the evolution of a seminar, in D. Gosling and V. D'Andrea (eds) *International Conference on the Scholarship of Teaching and Learning: Proceedings 2001–2002*, pp. 141–9. London: Educational Development Centre, City University.

Foucault, M. (1970) *The Order of Things: An Archaeology of the Human Sciences*. New York: Vintage Books.

Fox, D. (1983) Personal theories of teaching, *Studies in Higher Education*, 8 (2): 151–63.

Frame, P. (2001) *Student Induction in Practice*, paper 113. Birmingham: Staff and Educational Development Association.

Frame, P., Johnson, M. and Rosie A. (2003) How does it feel to be top of the class? Reflections on being a National Teaching Fellow. Paper presented at the 3rd International Conference on the Scholarship of Teaching and Learning, London, 5–6 June.
Friedlander, L. (2000) *New Spaces for New Times.* Stanford Learning Laboratory, Palo Alto, CA: Stanford University.
Fullan, M. (2001) *The New Meaning of Educational Change.* London: Routledge Falmer.
Fullan, M. (2003) Planning, doing, and coping with change, in M. Preedy, R. Glatter and C. Wise (eds) *Strategic Leadership and Educational Improvement,* pp. 185–97. London: Paul Chapman.
Fullan, M. and Hargreaves, A. (1998) *What's Worth Fighting For in Education?* Buckingham: SRHE/Open University Press.
Fullerton, H. (1999) Observation of teaching, in Fry, H. Marshall, S. Ketteridge, S. Marshall (eds) *A Handbook for Teaching and Learning in Higher Education: Enhancing Academic Practice,* pp. 226–41. London: Kogan Page.
Gaff, J.G., Pruitt-Logan, A.S. and Webl, R.A. (2000) *Building the Faculty We Need.* Washington, DC: Association of American Colleges and Universities/Council of Graduate Schools.
Gardner, H. (1991). *The Unschooled Mind: How Children Think and How Schools Should Teach.* New York: Basic Books.
Garvin, D.A. (1993) Building a learning organisation, *Harvard Business Review,* 7 (4): 78–91.
Geras, N. (1998) *The Contract of Mutual Indifference: Political Philosophy After the Holocaust.* London: Verso.
Gibbons, M., Limoges, C., Nowotny, H., Schwartzman, S., Scott, P. and Trow, M. (1994) *The New Production of Knowledge: The Dynamics of Science and Research in Contemporary Societies.* London: Sage.
Gibbs, G. (1992) *Independent Learning with More Students.* Oxford: Oxford Centre for Staff Development.
Gibbs, G. (2001a). *Analysis of Strategies for Learning and Teaching,* Research Report 01/37A. Bristol: Higher Education Funding Council for England.
Gibbs, G. (2001b) HEFCE Project Brief: Maximising the Benefits to Teaching of Research, ciculated to R & T Group, October.
Gibbs, G. and Coffey, M. (2004) The impact of training on university teachers on their teaching skills, their approach to teaching and their approach to learning of their students, *Active Learning,* 5 (1): 87–100.
Gibbs, G., Holmes, A. and Segal, R. (2002). *Funding Innovation and Disseminating New Teaching Practices: A Guide to Good Practice.* Milton Keynes: National Co-ordination Team, Open University.
Giddens, A. (1973) *The Class Structure of Advanced Societies.* London: Hutchinson.
Giddens, A. (1991) *Modernity and Self Identity.* Oxford: Blackwell.
Gilbert, S. (1997) Re: AAHESGIT 154: 3rd vision – face-to-face/telecommunications. aahesgit@list.cren.net, 27 June.
Gilbert, S. (1999) AAHESGIT118: Gilbert Q & A from SUDU – audio-narrated slideshow. aahesgit@list.cren.net, 26 September.
Gilbert, S. (2000) *A New Vision Worth Working Toward – Connected Education and Collaborative Change.* http://www.tltgroup.org/gilbert/NewVwwt2000–2–14–00.htm (accessed August 2004).
Gilbert, S. (2001) *Why Bother?,* 4 October, TLT Group, http://www.tltgroup.org/gilbert/WhyBother.htm (accessed August 2004).

Gilchrist, R., Phillips, D. and Ross, A. (2003) Participation and potential participation in UK higher education, in L. Archer, M. Hutchings and A. Ross (eds) *Higher Education and Social Class: Issues of exclusion and inclusion*, pp. 75–96. London, Routledge Falmer.

Giroux, H. (1996) *Counternarratives. Cultural Studies and Critical Pedagogies in Post-modern Spaces.* London: Routledge.

Gordon, G. (2001) *The Roles of Leadership and Ownership in Building an Effective Quality Culture.* Strathclyde: Centre for Academic Practice, University of Strathclyde.

Gordon, G. (2004) Locating educational development: identifying and working with national contexts, policies and strategies, in D. Baume and P. Kahn (eds) *Enhancing Staff and Educational Development*, pp. 9–17. London: Kogan Page.

Gordon, G., D'Andrea, V, Gosling, D. and Stefani, L. (2003) *Building Capacity for Change: Research on the Scholarship of Teaching, Review Report for the HEFCE.* Bristol: Higher Education Funding Council for England.

Gosling, D. (1996) What do UK educational development units do?, *International Journal for Academic Development*, 1 (1): 75–83.

Gosling, D. (1997) Recruiting good teachers, *The New Academic* 6 (1): 11–15.

Gosling, D. (2000) Using Habermas to evaluate two approaches to negotiated assessment, *Assessment and Evaluation in Higher Education*, 25 (3): 293–304.

Gosling, D. (2001a) Lost opportunity: what a credit framework would have added to the National Qualification Frameworks, *Higher Education Quarterly* 55 (3): 270–84.

Gosling, D. (2001b) What educational development units do – five years on, *International Journal for Academic Development*, 6 (1): 74–92.

Gosling, D. (2003) *Personal Development Planning.* Birmingham: Staff and Educational Development Association.

Gosling, D. (2004) Talking about teaching: overcoming some difficulties in peer review. Paper presented to the Annual International Conference on the Scholarship of Teaching and Learning, London, May.

Gosling, D. (2005) *Peer Observation of Teaching.* Birmingham: SEDA (forthcoming).

Gosling, D. and D'Andrea, V. (2000) Research and teaching: revaluing pedagogic research in higher education. Paper presented to the SRHE Conference, Leicester.

Gosling, D. and D'Andrea, V. (2001) Quality development: a new concept for higher education, *Quality in Higher Education*, 7 (1): 7–17.

Gosling, D. and Jiwani, A. (1997) Curriculum design for multi-ethnic higher education, *Curriculum Design for Improving Student Learning*, pp. 314–380. Oxford: Oxford Brookes University.

Gosling, D. and Moon, J. (2003) *How to Use Learning Outcomes and Assessment Criteria.* London: SEEC.

Gosling, D. and Ritchie, S. (2003) *Research Project on Peer Observation of Teaching, ESCALATE* http://www.escalate.ac.uk/initiatives/DavidGosling.php (accessed 1 June 2004).

Graff, G. (2002) The problem problem and other academic oddities, *Arts and Humanities in Higher Education*, 1 (1): 27–42.

Graham, D.N. (2001) Unplugged classrooms: are chalk-talks still in play?, *On the Horizon*, November/December: 10–12.

Graves, N. (ed.) (1993) *Learner Managed Learning: Practice, Theory and Policy.* London: Higher Education for Capability/World Education Fellowship.

Greatrix, P. (2001) Quality assurance in the 21st century: command and control or enlightened accountability?, *Perspective*, 5 (1): 12–16.

Griffin, A. (1997) Knowledge under Attack: Consumption, Diversity and the Need for Values, in R. Barnett (ed.) *The End of Knowledge in Higher Education*, pp. 2–12. London: Cassell.

Griffiths, R. (2004) Knowledge production and the research-teaching nexus: the case of the built environment disciplines, *Studies in Higher Education*, 29 (6): 709–26.

Griffiths, S. (1996) *The Professional Development of Academic Staff in their Role as Teachers*. Ulster: UCOSDA, University of Ulster.

Habermas, J. (1984) *The Theory of Communicative Action*. London: Heinemann.

Halsey, A.H. and Trow, M.A. (1971) *The British Academics*. London: Faber & Faber.

Hanks, W.F. (1991) Foreword, *Situated Learning: Legitimate Peripheral Particpation*, pp. 13–24. Cambridge: Cambridge University Press.

Hannan, A. (2002) Innovating in UK universities since the late 1990s. Paper presented to British Educational Research Association Annual Conference, University of Exeter, September.

Hannan, A. and Silver, H. (2000) *Innovating in Higher Education: Teaching, Learning and Institutional Cultures*. Buckingham: SRHE/Open University Press.

Harvey, L. (1995) The key issues: the quality agenda, *Quality in Higher Education*, 1 (1): 5–12.

Harvey, L. (2001) The end of quality? Keynote address to the Sixth Quality in Higher Education Seminar 'The End of Quality', Birmingham, UK, May.

Harvey, L. (2002) Evaluation for what? *Teaching in Higher Education*, 7 (3): 245–64.

Harvey, L. and Green, D. (1993) Defining quality, *Assessment and Evaluation in Higher Education*, 18 (1): 9–34.

Hativa, N. and M. Marincovich (1995) *Disciplinary Differences in Teaching and Learning: Implications for Practice*. San Francisco, Jossey-Bass.

Hattie, J. and Marsh, H.W. (2004) On journey to unravel the relationship between research and teaching. Paper presented to Research and Teaching: Closing the Divide? An International Colloquium, Winchester, UK, 18–19 March.

Hayes, D. and Wynyard, R. (2002) *The McDonaldization of Higher Education*. Westport, CT: Bergin & Garvey.

Healey, M. and Jenkins, A. (2003) Discipline-based educational development, in H. Eggins and R. Macdonald (eds) *The Scholarship of Academic Development*, pp. 47–57. Buckingham: SRHE/Open University Press.

Hegarty, S. (2000) Teaching as a knowledge-based activity, *Oxford Review of Education*, 26 (3–4): 451–65.

Helm, P. (1997) Teaching and learning with the new technologies: for richer, for poorer; for better, for worse, in J. Field (ed.) *Electronic Pathways*, pp. 41–52. Leicester: National Institute of Adult Continuing Education.

Hendricks, M., and Quinn, L. (2000) Teaching referencing as an introduction to epistemological empowerment, *Teaching in Higher Education*, 5 (4): 447–57.

Henkel, M. (2000) *Academic Identities and Policy Change in Higher Education*. London: Jessica Kingsley.

Henkel, M. (2001) Policy change and academic identities, UCL/EPD Seminar, November.

HEFCE (2000a) *Better Accountability for Higher Education: A Review for the HEFCE by PAQ Consultaing*. Bristol: Higher Education Funding Council for England.

HEFCE (2000b) Council Briefing, December. Bristol: Higher Education Funding Council for England.

HEFCE (2000c) *Performance Indicators in Higher Education in the UK, 1997–1998, 1998–1999, 00–04*. Bristol: Higher Education Funding Council for England.

HEFCE (2001) *Supply and Demand in Higher Education*, 01:62. Bristol: Higher Education Funding Council for England.

HEFCE (2002) *Teaching Quality Enhancement Fund: Funding Arrangements 2002–03 to 2004–05*. Bristol: Higher Education Funding Council for England.

Higher Education Academy (2004) Supporting New Academic Staff (SNAS). York: LTSN Generic Centre. Also at http://www.heacademy.ac.uk/SNAS.htm (accessed 29 November 2004).

Horsburgh, M. (1999) Quality monitoring in two institutions, *Quality in Higher Education*, 5 (1): 9–25.

Hounsell, D. (2003) Student feedback, learning and development, in M. Slowey and D. Watson (eds) *Higher Education and the Lifecourse*, pp. 67–78. Buckingham: SRHE/Open University Press.

Huber, M.T. (1999) Developing discourse communities around the scholarship of teaching, *Carengie Chronicle – Supplemental Material*, 8 (6): 1–10.

Huber, M.T. (2002) Evaluating Outreach: scholarship assessed's approach, *Outreach*, http://www.outreach.psu.edu/News/Pubs/Monographs/eval.html (accessed 22 May 2002).

Huber, M.T. (2003) Disciplines and the development of a scholarship of teaching and learning in the United States of America, in D. Gosling and V. D'Andrea (eds) *International Conference on the Scholarship of Teaching and Learning: Proceedings 2001 and 2002*, pp. 88–97. London: Educational Development Centre, City University.

Huber, M.T. (2004) *Balancing Acts: The Scholarship of Teaching and Learning in Academic Careers*. Washington, DC: American Association for Higher Education.

Hutchings, M. (2002) Enhancing learning with computer mediated communication: teacher intentions and student conceptions of online learning, in C. Rust (ed.) *Proceedings of the 9th International Symposium Improving Student Learning: Improving Student Learning Using Learning Technology*, pp. 99–111. Oxford: The Oxford Centre for Staff and Learning Development, Oxford Brookes University.

Hutchings, M. (2003) *Financial Barriers to Participation: Higher Education and Social Class*. London: Routledge Falmer.

Hutchings, P. (1995) *From Idea to Prototype: The Peer Review of Teaching – A Project Workbook*. Washington DC: American Association for Higher Education.

Hutchings, P. (ed.) (2000) *Opening Lines: Approaches to the Scholarship of Teaching and Learning*. Palo Alto, CA: Carnegie Foundation for the Advancement of Teaching.

Hutchings, P. and Shulman, L. (1999) The scholarship of teaching: new elaborations, new development, *Change*, 31 (5): 11–15.

Huxley, L. (n.d.) Institute for Learning and Research Technology: Feasibility Report on E-learning – A summary. Sheffield: Higher Education Staff Development Agency.

Hyland, P. (2000). Learning from feedback on assessment, in A. Booth and P. Hyland (eds) *The Practice of University History Teaching*, pp. 233–249. Manchester: Manchester University Press.

Illingworth, S. (2004) *Approaches to Ethics in Higher Education: Learning and Teaching in Ethics across the Curriculum*. Leeds: Philosophy and Religious Studies Learning and Teaching Support Network.

Jackson, N. and Ward, R. (eds) (2001) *Personal Development Planning: Institutional Case Studies*. York: Learning and Teaching Support Network.

Jarvis, P. (2001) *Universities and Corporate Universities*. London: Kogan.

Jenkins, A. (1995) The Research Assessment Exercise, funding and teaching quality, *Quality Assurance in Education*, 3 (2): 4–12.

Jenkins, A. (2000) Summary/review of the research and scholarly evidence on teaching/research relationships in higher education, *The Relationship between Research and Teaching in Higher Education: Present Realities, Future Possibilities,* pp. 23–33. Southampton: Southampton Institute and the Higher Education Funding Council for England.

Jenkins, A., Blackman, T., Lindsay, R. and Paton-Saltzberg, R. (1998) Teaching and research: student perceptions and policy implication, *Studies in Higher Education,* 23 (2): 127–42.

Jenkins, A., Breen, R. and Lindsay, R. (2003) *Reshaping Teaching in Higher Education: Linking Teaching with Research.* London: Kogan Page.

Jiwani, A. and Gosling, D. (1997) Course design for multi-ethnic student groups, in C. Rust and G. Gibbs (eds) *Curriculum Design for Improving Student Learning,* pp. 314–30. Oxford: Oxford Brookes University.

Johnston, V. (2003) Mission Impossible? Promoting transformation and change through a student retention project, in H. Edwards, D. Baume and G. Webb (eds) *Staff and Educational Development: Case Studies, Experiences and Practice from Higher Education,* pp. 114–24. London: Kogan Page.

Jonassen, D., Peck, K. and Wilson, B. (1999) *Learning with Technology: A Constructivist Approach.* Upper Saddle River, NJ: Prentice Hall.

Jones, S. and Little, B. (1999) Higher Education in the UK: the Pushme–Pullyou effects, in M. Henkel and B. Little (eds) *The Changing Relationships between Higher Education and the State,* pp. 125–41. London: Jessica Kingsley.

Kahn, P. (2004) Careers within staff and educational development, in D. Baume and P. Kahn (eds) *Enhancing Staff and Educational Development,* pp. 154–69. London: Routledge Falmer.

Kember, D. and Gow, L. (1994). Orientations to teaching and their effect on the quality of student learning, *Journal of Higher Education,* 65: 59–74.

Kiechel, W. (1990) The organisation that learns, *Fortune,* 121 (6): 133–6.

King, C. (2003) 'Fair Access' means different things to different gifted and talented people, *Guardian,* 15 April, p. 12.

Knight, P.T. (2002) *Being a Teacher in Higher Education.* Buckingham: SRHE/Open University Press.

Knight, P. and Trowler, P. (2001) *Departmental Leadership in Higher Education.* Buckingham: SRHE/Open University Press.

Knight, P. and Yorke, M. (2003) *Assessment, Learning and Employability.* Buckingham: SRHE/Open University Press.

Kogan, M. (2000) Higher education communities and academic identity, *Higher Education Quarterly,* 54 (3): 207–16.

Kolb, D. A. (1984). *Experiential Learning: Experience as the Source of Learning and Development.* Englewood Cliffs, NJ: Prentice Hall.

Kreber, C. (2000a) How university teaching award winners conceptualise academic work: some further thoughts on the meaning of scholarship, *Teaching in Higher Education,* 5 (1): 61–78.

Kreber, C. (2000b) Integrating teaching with other aspects of professorial work: a comparison of experienced and inexperienced faculty's role conceptualizations, *Canadian Journal of Higher Education,* 30(3): 79–113.

Kreber, C. and Cranton, P.A. (2000) Exploring the scholarship of teaching, *Journal of Higher Education,* 71 (4): 466–95.

Land, R. (2001) Agency, context and change in academic development, *International Journal for Academic Development,* 6 (1): 4–20.

Lauvås, P. (2000) Quality enhancement systems to improve teaching and learning. Paper presented to the 3rd Conference of the International Consortium for Educational Development, Bielefeld, Germany, July.

Lave, J. (1993) The practice of learning, in S. Chaiklin, and J. Lave (eds) *Understanding Practice. Perspectives on Activity and Context*, pp. 3–34. Cambridge: Press Syndicate of the University of Cambridge.

Lave, J. and Wenger, E. (1991) *Situated Learning: Legitimate Peripheral Participation.* New York: Cambridge University Press.

Law I. (2003) University teaching in ethnicity and racism studies: context, content and commitment, *Ethnic and Racial Studies*, 26 (3): 517–22.

Law, I., Turney, L. and Phillips, D. (2002) *Institutional Racism in Higher Education.* Leeds: Centre for Ethnicity and Racism Studies, University of Leeds.

Law, I., Phillips, D. and Turney, L. (2004) *Institutional Racism in Higher Education.* Stoke-on-Trent: Trentham Books.

Lawler, P. and King, K. (2000) *Planning for Effective Faculty Development using Adult Learning Strategies.* Malabar, FL: Krieger.

Lawler, S. (2000). Escape and escapism: representing working class women, in *Cultural Studies and the Working Class: Subject to Change.* London: Cassell.

Laycock, M. (1997) QILT: a whole-institution approach to quality improvement in learning and teaching, in P. Armstrong (ed.) *Facing up to Radical Changes in Universities and Colleges*, pp. 75–83. London: Kogan Page.

Layer, G. (1995) Changing the approach, in M. Slowey (ed.) *Implementing Change from Within*, pp. 113–24. London: Kogan Page.

Lea, M.R. and Street, B. (1998) Student writing in higher education: an academic literacies approach, *Studies in Higher Education*, 23 (2): 157–72.

Leach, J. (2002) Emotional Health and University Learning. Oxford Brookes Teaching Forum, 50: 31–2.

Lessem, R. (1991) *Total Quality Learning: Building a Learning Organisation.* Oxford: Basil Blackwell.

Lieberman, A. (1999) Community means more than team work, *Journal of Staff Development*, Spring: 47–8.

Light, G. and Cox, R. (2001) *Learning and Teaching in Higher Education: The Reflective Professional.* London: Paul Chapman.

Lindsay, R. (2004) Review of Biggs' *Teaching for Quality Learning* and Ramsden's *Learning to Teach in Higher Education, Studies in Higher Education,* 29 (2): 279–86.

London Metropolitan University, Centre for Academic and Professional Development, *Innovations.* London: London Metropolitan University.

Longden, B. (2004) Interpreting students early departure from higher education through the lens of cultural capital, *Tertiary Education and Management*, 10 (2): 121–38.

Lotus Institute (1996) *Distributed Learning; Approaches, Technologies and Solutions*, White Paper. Cambridge, MA: Lotus Development Corporation.

Lueddeke, G. (1997). Educational development units in higher education: much ado about nothing?, *Quality in Higher Education*, 3 (2): 155–70.

Lyotard, J-F. (1984) *The Postmodern Condition: A Report on Knowledge.* Manchester: Manchester University Press.

Macfarlane, B. (2003) *Teaching with Integrity.* London: Routledge Falmer.

Malcolm, J. and Zukas, M. (2001) Bridging pedagogic gaps: conceptual discontinuities in higher education, *Teaching in Higher Education*, 6 (1): 33–42.

Mann, S. (2003) Alternative perspectives on professional practice in academic development, in H. Eggins and R. Macdonald (eds) *The Scholarship of Academic Development*, pp. 80–90. Buckingham: SRHE/Open University Press.

Marginson, S. and Rhoades, G. (2002) Beyond national states, markets, and systems of higher education, *Higher Education*, 43 (3): 281–310.

Martin, E. (1999) *Changing Academic Work: Developing the Learning University*. Buckingham: SRHE/Open University Press.

Martin, E. and Ramsden, P. (1993) An expanding awareness: how lecturers change their understanding of teaching, *Research and Development in Higher Education* 15: 148–55.

Martin, E. and Ramsden, P. (2000) Introduction, *Higher Education Research and Development*, 19: 133–5.

Marton, F. and Saljo, R. (1976) On qualitative differences in learning: outcome and process, *British Journal of Educational Psychology*, 46: 4–11.

Marton, F., Hounsell, D.J. and Entwistle, N.J. (1997) *The Experience of Learning*. Edinburgh: Scottish Academic Press.

Massy, W.F., Wilger, K. and Colbeck, C. (1994) Departmental cultures and teaching quality, overcoming 'hollowed' collegiality, *Change*, 26 (4): 11–20.

Mathias, H. (2003) Putting the 'E' into 'QA', *Educational Developments*, 4 (2): 13–16.

Mathieu, R.D. (2004) Teaching-as-research: a concept for change at research universities. Paper presented to Research and Teaching: Closing the Divide? An International Colloquium, Winchester, UK, 18–19 March.

Mayes, T. (2001) Learning technology and learning relationships, in J. Stephenson (ed.) *Teaching and Learning Online*, pp. 16–25. London: Kogan Page.

McCarthy, T. (1984) *The Critical Theory of Jurgen Habermas*. London: Polity Press.

McGettrick, A., Dunnett, A. and Harvey, B. (1997) Continuous quality improvement in higher education, *Quality in Higher Education*, 3 (3): 235–47.

McGill, I. and Beaty, L. (1995) *Action Learning: A Guide for Professional, Management and Educational Development*. London: Kogan Page.

McLennan, G. (2001). Problematic multiculturalism, *Sociology*, 35(4): 985–89.

McNay, I. (1995) From collegial academy to corporate enterprise: the changing cultures of universities, in T. Schuller (ed.) *The Changing University?*, pp. 105–15. Buckingham: SRHE/Open University Press.

McNay, I. (1999) The paradoxes of research assessment and funding, in *Changing Relationships between Higher Education and the State*, pp. 191–203. London: Jessica Kingsley.

McWilliam, E. (2002) Against professional development, *Educational Philosophy and Theory*, 34 (3): 289–99.

Meade, P. (1995) Utilising the university as a learning organisation to facilitate quality improvement, *Quality in Higher Education*, 1 (2): 111–21.

Megginson, D. and Clutterbuck, D. (1995) *Mentoring in Action: Practical Guide for Managers*. London: Kogan Page.

Metcalf, H. (2003) Increasing inequality in higher education: the role of term time working, *Oxford Review of Education*, 29: 315–28.

Meyer, J.H.F. and Land, R. (2003) Threshold concepts and troublesome knowledge. Paper presented to Research, Scholarship and Teaching Conference, Society for Research into Higher Education, Royal Holloway, University of London, London, December.

Middlehurst, R. (2000) *The Business of Borderless Education: UK Perspectives*. London: Committee of Vice Chancellors and Principals.

Mill, J.S. (1962) On Liberty, in M. Warnock, *Utilitarianism*, pp.126–250. London: Collins (first published 1859).

Mitchell, S. and Riddle, M. (2000) *Improving the Quality of Argument in Higher Education.* London: School of Lifelong Learning, Middlesex University.

Moore, R. (2003) Curriculum restructuring in South African higher education, *Studies in Higher Education*, 28 (3): 303–19.

Morey, A.I. (2003) Major trends impacting faculty roles and rewards: an international perspective, *SRHE International News*, 52: 2–5.

Morley, L. (2003a) *Quality and Power in Higher Education.* Buckingham: SRHE/Open University Press.

Morley, L. (2003b) Reconstructing students as customers: power and assimilation?, in M. Slowey and D. Watson (eds) *Higher Education and the Lifecourse.* Buckingham: SRHE/Open University Press.

Moses, I. (1990) Teaching, research and scholarship in different disciplines, *Higher Education*, 19 (1): 351–75.

Murray, K. and Macdonald, R. (1997) The disjunction between lecturers' conceptions of teaching and their claimed educational practice, *Higher Education* 33 (3): 331–49.

Nehusi, K. and Gosling, D. (2001) Travellers' tales from the University of East London: the experience of 'Black' adult learners, in L. West, N. Miller, D. O'Reilly and R. Allen (eds) *Travellers' Tales: From Adult Education to Lifelong Learning and Beyond, Proceedings of the 31st Annual Conference of SCUTREA*, pp. 293–7. London: University of East London, Standing Conference on University Teaching and Research in the Education of Adults (SCUTREA).

Newman, J.H. (1976) *The Idea of a University.* Oxford: Oxford University Press (first published 1853).

Newton, J. (2000) Feeding the beast or improving quality? Academic staff perceptions of quality assurance and quality monitoring, *Quality in Higher Education*, 6 (2): 153–63.

Newton, J. (2001) Views from below: academics coping with quality. Keynote Address, 6th QHE Seminar, Birmingham, UK, 26 May.

Nixon, J., Marks, A., Rowland, S. and Walker, M. (2001) Towards a new academic professionalism: a manifesto of hope, *British Educational Journal of Sociology of Education*, 22 (2): 227–44.

NSSE (2002) *National Survey of Student Engagement*, annual report, http://www.indiana.edu/~nsse/2002_annual_report/html/

Ofori-Dankwa, J. and Lane, R.W. (2000) Four approaches to cultural diversity: implications for teaching at institutions of higher education, *Teaching in Higher Education*, 5 (4): 493–500.

O'Hagan, C. (2001) The campus university and *e*-learning: *e*volution and r*e*volution. Professorial Inaugural Lecture, University of Derby, 7 February.

Oliver, M. and Plewes, L. (2002) Academics' curriculum development practices at UCL: a preliminary study for the Imaginative Curriculum project. York: LTSN Generic Centre. Also at http://www.imaginativecurriculum.net/

Olssen, M. (2001) *The Neo-liberal Appropriation of Tertiary Education Policy: Accountability, Research and Academic Freedom.* New Zealand Association for Research in Education, State of the Art Monograph No. 8., October.

Olssen, M., Codd, J. and. O'Neill, A-M. (2004) *Education Policy: Globalization, Citizenship and Democracy.* London: Sage.

O'Reilly, D. (1996) Becoming a master in learning and teaching in higher education:

some issues raised by problematizing 'mastery' on a learner-led MA programme, *International Journal for Academic Development*, 1 (2): 80–5.
O'Reilly, D., Cunningham, L. and Lester, S. (1999) *Developing the Capable Practitioner.* London: Kogan Page.
O'Reilly, D., Weaver, N. and Caddick, M. (2000) Disciplining interdisciplinarity: pedagogic tensions within architectural education, in C. Rust (ed.) *Improving Student Learning: Improving Student Learning through the Disciplines*, pp. 294–303. Oxford: Oxford Centre for Staff and Learning Development.
O'Toole, J. (1995) *Leading Change: Overcoming the Ideology of Comfort and the Tyranny of Custom.* San Francisco: Jossey-Bass.
Ottewill, R. (2001) Tutors as professional role models with particular reference to undergraduate business education, *Higher Education Quarterly*, 55 (4): 436–51.
Outram, S. (2004) 53 interesting ways in which colleagues resist change, *Educational Developments*, 5 (2): 1–4.
Ozga, J. and Sukhnandan, L. (1998). Undergraduate non-completion: developing an explanatory model, *Higher Education Quarterly*, 52: 316–33.
Palmer, P.J. (1998) *The Courage to Teach.* San Francisco: Jossey-Bass.
Parker, V. (1998) UK initiatives to promote inclusion in HE for students with disabilities, *European Journal of Special Needs Education*, 13 (2): 189–200.
Percy, A. (2001) Student induction: the psychology of transition, in P. Frame (ed.) *Student Induction in Practice*, pp. 95–104. Birmingham: Staff and Educational Development Association.
Perlman, B., Gueths, J. and Weber, D.A. (1988) *The Academic Intrapreneur: Strategy, Innovation and Management in Higher Education.* New York: Praeger.
Perry, W. (1999) *Forms of Intellectual and Ethical Development in the College Years.* San Francisco: Jossey-Bass (first published 1968).
Pirsig, R.M. (1974) *Zen and the Art of Motorcycle Maintenance.* New York: Bantam Books.
Popper, K. (1966) *The Open Society and Its Enemies: The High Tide of Prophecy: Hegel, Marx and the Aftermath.* London: Routledge & Kegan Paul.
Pratt, J. (1997) *The Polytechnic Experiment 1965–1992.* Buckingham: SRHE/Open University Press.
Prensky, M. (2002) Not only the lonely: implication of 'social' online activities for higher education, *On the Horizon*, 10 (4): 28–32.
Prosser, M. and Trigwell, K. (1999) *Understanding Learning and Teaching: The Experience in Higher Education.* Buckingham: SRHE/Open University Press.
QAAHE (1998) *Graduate Standards Programme: Report on Subject Association Pilot Projects.* London: Quality Assurance Agency for Higher Education.
Radford, J., Kjell, R., De Vries, P. and Williams, R. (1997) *Quantity and Quality in Higher Education*, Higher Education Policy Series 40. London: Jessica Kingsley.
Ramsden, P. (1991) A performance indicator of teaching quality in higher education: the course experience questionnaire, *Studies in Higher Education*, 16 (2): 129–50.
Ramsden, P. (1992) *Learning to Teach in Higher Education.* London: Routledge.
Ramsden, P. and Martin, E. (1996) Recognition of good university teaching: policies from an Australian study, *Studies in Higher Education*, 21 (3): 299–315.
Reay, D. (1998) 'Always knowing' and 'never being sure': institutional and familial habituses and higher education choice, *Journal of Education Policy*, 13 (4): 519–29.
Rice, R.E. (1992) Toward a broader conception of scholarship: the American context, in T.G. Whiston and R.L. Geiger (eds) *Research and Higher Education: The United Kingdom and the United States*, pp. 117–29. Buckingham: SRHE/Open University Press.

Richlin, L. (2001) Scholarly teaching and the scholarship of teaching, in C. Kreber (ed.) *New Directions in Teaching and Learning*, Perspectives on the Scholarship of Teaching and Learning no. 86, pp. 57–68. San Francisco: Jossey-Bass.

Rickinson, B. and Rutherford, D. (1996) Systematic monitoring of the adjustment to university of undergraduates: a strategy for reducing withdrawal rates, *British Journal of Guidance and Counselling*, 24: 213–25.

Riddell, S., Tinklin, T. and Wilson, A. (2003) Disabled students in higher education: legislation, teaching, learning and assessment, in M. Slowey and D. Watson, *Higher Education and the Lifecourse*, pp. 36–50. Buckingham: SRHE/Open University Press.

Ritzer, G. (1993) *The McDonaldization of Society: An Investigation into the Changing Character of Contemporary Social Life*. London: Sage/Pine Forge Press.

Robbins, D. (1988). *The Rise of Independent Study: the Politics and Philosophy of an Educational Innovation, 1970–87*. Buckingham: SRHE and Open University Press. Committee on Higher Education ('The Robbins Report') 1963, Higher Education: Report of the Committee appointed by the Prime Minister under the Chairmanship of Lord Robbins, London, HMSO.

Roberts, D. and Allen, A. (1997). *Young Applicants' Perceptions of Higher Education*. Leeds: Heist.

Robertson, D. (1994) *Choosing to Change*. London: Higher Education Quality Council.

Rocklin, T. (2001) Do I dare? Is it prudent?, *The National Teaching and Learning Forum*, 10 (3): 1–4.

Rorty, R. (1989) *Contingency, Irony and Solidarity*. Cambridge: Cambridge University Press.

Rowland, S. (1996) Relationships between teaching and research, *Teaching and Learning in Higher Education*, 1 (1): 7–20.

Rowland, S. (2000) *The Enquiring University Teacher*. Buckingham: SRHE/Open University Press.

Rowland, S. (2003). Academic development: a practical or theoretical business?, in H. Eggins and R. Macdonald (eds) *The Scholarship of Academic Development*, pp. 13–22. Buckingham: SRHE/Open University Press.

Rowland, S. (2004) *MA in Academic Practice: Ethos and Learning Process*. London: University College London. Also at http://www.ucl.ac.uk/epd/masters/maap.html (accessed November 2004).

Rowley, R. (1996) *Student Support Services*. Buckingham: SRHE/Open University Press.

Rushing, W. (2001). Inequality and education reform: formulating a macro-historical sociology perspective, *Race Ethnicity and Education*, 4 (1): 29–43.

Rust, C. (2000) Do initial training courses have an impact on university teaching? The evidence from two evaluative studies, *Innovations in Education and Teaching International*, 37 (3): 254–62.

Rustin, M. (2001) *Quality Improvement in Learning and Teaching (QILT) Research Project on Student Retention*, Interim Report, Social Sciences. Barking: University of East London.

Rutherford, J. (2004). Editorial, *Soundings*, 26: 11–17.

Ryan, A. (2004) *Times Higher Education Supplement*, 6, August p. 13.

Salter, B. and Tapper, T. (1994) *The State and Higher Education*. London: Woburn Press.

Schein, E.H. (1992) *Organizational Culture and Leadership*. San Francisco: Jossey-Bass.

Schon, D. (1987) *Educating the Reflective Practitioner: How Professionals Think in Action.* London: Temple Smith.

Schuller, T. (1995) *The Changing University?* Buckingham: SRHE/Open University Press.

Schuller, T. (2002) Thinking about social capital, in R. Edwards, J. Clarke and N. Miller (eds) *Supporting Lifelong Learning: Working Papers.* Milton Keynes: Open University/University of East London.

Scott, P. (1995) *The Meanings of Mass Higher Education.* Buckingham: SRHE/Open University Press.

Scott, P. (1997) Changes in knowledge production and dissemination in the context of globalisation knowledge, *Identity and Curriculum Transformation in Africa,* pp. 17–42. Cape Town: Maskew Miller Longman.

Scott, P. (2002) Let's stop trying to separate the inseparable, *Exchange,* 3: 27–8.

SEEC (2003) *Credit Level Descriptors for Further and Higher Education.* London: Southern England Consortium for Credit Accumulation and Transfer.

Segal, R. (2003) Working on educational development projects, in P. Kahn and D. Baume (eds) *A Guide to Staff and Educational Development,* pp. 128–42. London: Kogan Page.

Sekers, A. (2000) The context of this discussion. Paper presented to the EDIT Seminar, London Institute, 12 July.

Senge, P.M. (1990a) *The Fifth Discipline: The Art and Practice of the Learning Organization.* London: Century Business.

Senge, P.M. (1990b) The leader's new work: building learning organizations, *Sloan Management Review,* Fall: 7–23.

Senge, P.M. (1996) Leading learning organizations: the bold, the powerful and the invisible, in F. Hasselbein, M. Goldsmith and R. Beckhard (eds) *The Leader of the Future,* pp. 42–57. San Francisco: Jossey-Bass.

Seymour, E. and Hewitt, N.M. (1997) *Talking About Leaving: Why Undergraduates Leave the Sciences.* Oxford: Westview Press.

Sharpe, R. (2004). How do professionals learn and develop, in D. Baume and P. Kahn (eds) *Enhancing Staff and Educational Development,* pp. 132–53. London: Routledge Falmer.

Shattock, M. (2003) Research, administration and university management: what can research contribute to policy?, in R. Begg (ed.) *The Dialogue between Higher Education Research and Practice,* pp. 55–66. London: Kluwer Academic.

Shay, S.B. (2004) The assessment of complex performance: a socially situated interpretive act, *Harvard Educational Review,* 74 (3): 307–29.

SHEFC (2000) *Consultation on Quality Enhancement Strategy,* HEC07/00. Edinburgh: Scottish Higher Education Funding Council.

SHEFC (2004). *Higher Education: A Baseline Report.* Edinburgh: Scottish Higher Education Funding Council.

Shore, C. and Wright, S. (1999) Audit culture and anthropology: neo-liberalism in British higher education, *Journal of the Royal Anthropological Institute,* 5 (4): 557–75.

Shore, C. and Wright, S. (2000) Coercive accountability: the rise of audit culture in higher education, in M. Strathem (ed.) *Audit Cultures,* pp. 57–89. London: Routledge.

Shrives, L. and Bond, C. (2003) Consultancy in educational development, in P. Kahn and D. Baume (eds) *A Guide to Staff and Educational Development,* pp. 61–75. London: Kogan Page.

Shuell, T.J. (1986) Cognitive conceptions of learning, *Review of Educational Research*, 56: 411–36.

Shulman, L.S. (1993) Teaching as community property: putting an end to pedagogical solitude, *Change*, 26 (6): 6–7.

Simpson, R. (1996). Learning development in HE: deficit or different?, in S. Wolfendale (ed.) *Opening Doors*, pp. 17–30. London: Cassell.

Sipress, M. (1997) Re: AAHESGIT 158: support service crisis. aahesgit@list.cren.net, 3 July.

Skelton, A. (2002) Towards inclusive learning environments in higher education: reflections on a professional development course for university lecturers, *Teaching in Higher Education*, 7 (2): 194–214.

Skelton, A. (2004) Understanding 'teaching excellence' in higher education: a critical evaluation of the National Teaching Fellowships Scheme, *Studies in Higher Education*, 29 (4): 451–68.

Smith, R.S. (1992) The university – some differences from other organizations, *Canadian Society for the Study of Higher Education*, 12 (Winter): 1–11.

Spangehl, S.D. (2001) Quality Improvement alive and vital in US accreditation, paper presented at the *Quality in Higher Education Conference*, Birmingham, May.

Stacey, R. (1996) *Strategic Management and Organizational Dynamics*. London: Pitman.

Stefani, L. (2003) What is staff and educational development?, in P. Kahn and D. Baume (eds) *A Guide to Staff and Educational Development*, pp. 9–23. London: Kogan Page.

Stefani, L. and Matthew, B. (2002) The difficulties of defining development, *International Journal for Academic Development*, 7 (1): 41–50.

Stephenson, J. and Laycock, M. (1993) *Using Learning Contracts in Higher Education*. London: Kogan Page.

Stiles, M. (2000) Overview of the use of virtual learning environments and web-based learning support at Staffordshire University, *Learning Matters*, 1: 8–16.

Stoddard, J. (1995) Collective key to standards, *Times Higher Education Supplement*, 12 May, p. 11.

Stuart, M. (2001) Standards, standards, standards: the unintended consequences of widening participation, *Journal of Access and Credit Studies*, 3 (2): 180–90.

Taylor, C. (1995) *The Politics of Recognition Multiculturalism*. Princeton, NJ: Princeton University Press.

Talbot, C. (1996) Re: revolutionizing strategy. Message posted to the Staff-development@mailbase.ac.uk, 1 August.

Taylor, L. (2004) Farewell to cuddly ethos of yesteryear, *Times Higher Education Supplement*, 19 March, pp. 20–1.

Taylor, P.G. (1999) *Making Sense of Academic Life: Academics, Universities and Change*. Buckingham: SRHE/Open University Press.

Taylor, R., Barr, J. and Steele, T. (2002) *For a Radical Higher Education: After Postmodernism*. Buckingham: SRHE/Open University Press.

Thomas, E. (2001) *Widening Participation in Post-compulsory Education*. London: Continuum.

Thompson, S. (2004) Leading an educational development unit, in D. Baume and P. Kahn (eds) *Enhancing Staff and Educational Development*, pp. 36–55. London: Kogan Page.

Thune, C. (2002) Future relationships and dilemmas of quality assurance and accreditation. Plenary Address, 24th EAIR Forum, Prague, 8–11 September.

Timmis, S. (2003) Embedding learning technology institutionally new roles, structures and alliances, *JISC Senior Management Briefing Paper*, April. Also at http://www.jisc.ac.uk/projects/

Tinto, V. (1993) *Leaving College: Rethinking the Causes and Cures of Student Attrition.* Chicago: University of Chicago Press.

Tomusk, V. (1999). East-European university on the crossroad: its glorious past and unclear future, *Universities in Modern Society.* Oslo: University of Oslo. Also at http://www.tf.uio.no/etikk/artikler/tomusk.htm (accessed November 2004).

Tooey, S. (1999) *Designing Courses for Higher Education.* Buckingham: SRHE/Open University Press.

Trigwell, K. and Prosser, M. (1996) Changing approaches to teaching: a relational perspective, *Studies in Higher Education*, 21 (3): 275–84.

Trigwell, K., Martin, E., Benjamin, J. and Prosser, M. (2000) Scholarship of teaching: a model, *Higher Education Research and Development*, 19 (2): 155–68.

Trow, M. (1973) *Problems in the Transition from Elite to Mass Higher Education.* Berkeley, CA: Carnegie Commission on Higher Education.

Trow, M. (1994) *Managerialism and the Academic Profession: Quality and Control*, Higher Education Report no. 2, Quality Support Centre. London: The Open University.

Trow, M. (1996) *Trust, Markets and Accountability in Higher Education: A Comparative Perspective*, paper CSHE1-96, Center for Studies in Higher Education, http://repositories.cdlib.org/cshe/CSHE1–96

Trowler, P.R. (1998) *Academics Responding to Change.* Buckingham: SRHE/Open University Press.

Turner-Bisset, R. (1999) Knowledge bases for teaching, *British Educational Research Journal*, 25 (1): 39–55.

University of Glamorgan, Centre for Lifelong Learning, *Occasional Papers Educational Development Series.* Pontypridd, Wales: University of Glamorgan.

Usher, R., Bryant, I. and Johnston, R. (1997) *Adult Education and the Postmodern Challenge.* London: Routledge.

UUK/SCOP (2004). *Towards a Framework of Professional Teaching Standards: National Consultation.* London: Universities UK/Standing Conference of Principals.

Vught, F.A. van (1994) Intrinsic and extrinsic aspects of quality assessment in higher education, in D.F. Westerheijden, J. Brennan and P.A.M. Maassen (eds) *Changing Context of Quality Assessment: Recent Trends in West European Higher Education*, pp. 31–50. Utrecht: CHEPS.

Wagenaar, T.C. (1978) *Curriculum Workshop Materials.* Oberlin, OH: ASA Projects on Teaching Undergraduate Sociology.

Walker, M. (1998) Response III: identities and contexts, in J. Nixon, M. Beattie, M. Challis and M. Walker (eds) What Does It Mean to be an Academic? A Colloquium, *Teaching in Higher Education*, 3 (3): 277–98.

Walker, M. (2001a) Collaboration within a critical community of practice, in M. Walker (ed.) *Reconstructing Professionalism in University Teaching*, pp. 39–56. Buckingham: SRHE/Open University Press.

Walker, M. (2001b) *Reconstructing Professionalism in University Teaching.* Buckingham: SRHE/Open University Press.

Walker, M. (2002). Pedagogy and politics and purposes of higher education, *Arts and Humanities in Higher Education*, 1 (1): 43–58.

Ward, R. (2001) Developing and implementing institutional policy on personal development planning, in N. Jackson and R. Ward (eds) *Personal Development Planning: Institutional Case Studies*, pp. 2–6. York: Learning and Teaching Support Network.

Wareham, T. (2002). Failing teachers, failing students: learning about failure from a teaching development programme, in M. Peelo and T. Wareham (eds) *Failing Students in Higher Education*, pp. 85–97. Buckingham: SRHE/Open University Press.

Warren, D. (2003). Developing academic literacy: a discipline-based approach, *Investigations*, 1 (1): 46–51.

Watkins, K.E. and Marsick, V.J. (1993) *Sculpting the Learning Organization*. San Francisco: Jossey-Bass.

Watson, D. (2000) Assuring standards: bench-marking and beyond. Presentation to the Student Assessment and Classification Working Group 6th National Workshop: Defining Subject Standards: Benchmarks and Classifications, 23 November, Wolverhampton, UK.

Webb, G. (1996) *Understanding Staff Development*. Buckingham: SRHE/Open University Press.

Webber, T., Bourner, T. and O'Hara, S. (2003) Practioner-centred research on academic development in higher education, in H. Eggins and R. Macdonald (eds) *The Scholarship of Academic Development*, pp. 117–28. Buckingham: SRHE/Open University Press.

Webster, J. (2002). My troubles with Perry: developmental scheme or humanities curriculum, in D. Gosling and V. D'Andrea (eds) *International Conference on the Scholarship of Teaching and Learning: proceedings 2001 and* 2002, pp. 118–21. London: Educational Development Centre, City University.

Weimer, M. (1993) The disciplinary journals on pedagogy, *Change*, 25 (6): 44–51.

Welton, M.R. (1995) *In Defense of the Lifeworld*. Albany, NY: State University of New York.

Wenger, E. (1998) *Communities of Practice, Learning, Meaning and Identity*. Cambridge: Cambridge University Press.

Wenger, E. (2004) *Communities of Practice: A Brief introduction*. http://www.ewenger.com/theory/index.htm (accessed July 2004).

Wilkinson, J. (2001). Designing a new course, in M. Walker (ed.) *Reconstructing Professionalism in University Teaching*, pp. 149–69. Buckingham: SRHE/Open University Press.

Williams, J. (1997) The discourse of access: the legitimation of selectivity, in J. Williams (ed.) *Negotiating Access to Higher Education*, pp. 24–46. Buckingham: SRHE/Open University Press.

Williams, P. (2002) Anyone for enhancement?, *Higher Quality*, 11: 1–2.

Wolf, A. (2002) *Does Education Matter? Myths about Education and Economic Growth*. London: Penguin.

Woodhouse, D. (2001) *The Research/Teaching Nexus in New Zealand Universities, 1999–2001*, The Nexus Project. The Vice-Chancellor's Symposium on the Teaching–Research Nexus: Enhancing the Links. http://cedir.uow.edu.au.nexus/dwoodhse. html

World Bank (2001) *Constructing Knowledge Societies: New Challenges for Tertiary Education – A World Bank Strategy*, Vol. II. Washington, DC: World Bank.

Wright, A. (2001) *Of Promise and Challenge: First Report of the External Project Evaluator SkillsPlus Project 2004*. http://www.open.ac.uk/vqportal/Skills-Plus/documents/ProjPaper6.pdf

Yorke, M. (1999) *Leaving Early: Undergraduate Non-completion in Higher Education.* London: Falmer.

Yorke, M. (2000) A cloistered virtue? Pedagogical research and policy in UK higher education, *Higher Education Quarterly*, 54 (2): 106–26.

Yorke, M. and Knight, P. (2004) Self-theories: some implications for teaching and learning in higher education, *Studies in Higher Education*, 29 (1): 25–38.

Index

Page numbers in *italics* refer to tables and figures.

The Society for Research into Higher Education

The Society for Research into Higher Education (SRHE), an international body, exists to stimulate and coordinate research into all aspects of higher education. It aims to improve the quality of higher education through the encouragement of debate and publication on issues of policy, on the organization and management of higher education institutions, and on the curriculum, teaching and learning methods.

The Society is entirely independent and receives no subsidies, although individual events often receive sponsorship from business or industry. The Society is financed through corporate and individual subscriptions and has members from many parts of the world. It is an NGO of UNESCO.

Under the imprint *SRHE & Open University Press*, the Society is a specialist publisher of research, having over 80 titles in print. In addition to *SRHE News*, the Society's newsletter, the Society publishes three journals: *Studies in Higher Education* (three issues a year), *Higher Education Quarterly* and *Research into Higher Education Abstracts* (three issues a year).

The Society runs frequent conferences, consultations, seminars and other events. The annual conference in December is organized at and with a higher education institution. There are a growing number of networks which focus on particular areas of interest, including:

Access
Assessment
Consultants
Curriculum Development
Eastern European
Educational Development Research
FE/HE
Graduate Employment
New Technology for Learning
Postgraduate Issues
Quantitative Studies
Student Development

Benefits to members

Individual

- The opportunity to participate in the Society's networks
- Reduced rates for the annual conferences
- Free copies of *Research into Higher Education Abstracts*
- Reduced rates for *Studies in Higher Education*

- Reduced rates for *Higher Education Quarterly*
- Free online access to *Register of Members' Research Interests* – includes valuable reference material on research being pursued by the Society's members
- Free copy of occasional in-house publications, e.g. *The Thirtieth Anniversary Seminars Presented by the Vice Presidents*
- Free copies of *SRHE News* and *International News* which inform members of the Society's activities and provides a calendar of events, with additional material provided in regular mailings
- A 35 per cent discount on all SRHE/Open University Press books
- The opportunity for you to apply for the annual research grants
- Inclusion of your research in the *Register of Members' Research Interests*

Corporate

- Reduced rates for the annual conference
- The opportunity for members of the Institution to attend SRHE's network events at reduced rates
- Free copies of *Research into Higher Education Abstracts*
- Free copies of *Studies in Higher Education*
- Free online access to *Register of Members' Research Interests* – includes valuable reference material on research being pursued by the Society's members
- Free copy of occasional in-house publications
- Free copies of *SRHE News* and *International News*
- A 35 per cent discount on all SRHE/Open University Press books
- The opportunity for members of the Institution to submit applications for the Society's research grants
- The opportunity to work with the Society and co-host conferences
- The opportunity to include in the *Register of Members' Research Interests* your Institution's research into aspects of higher education

SRHE

Membership details: SRHE, 76 Portland Place, London W1B 1NT, UK Tel: 020 7637 2766. Fax: 020 7637 2781. email: srheoffice@srhe.ac.uk
world wide web: http://www.srhe.ac.uk./srhe/
Catalogue: SRHE & Open University Press, McGraw-Hill Education, McGraw-Hill House, Shoppenhangers Road, Maidenhead, Berkshire SL6 2QL. Tel: 01628 502500. Fax: 01628 770224. email: enquiries@openup.co.uk – web: www.openup.co.uk

Open up your options
Education
Health & Social Welfare
Management
Media, Film & Culture
Psychology & Counselling
Sociology
Study Skills
for more information on our publications visit www.openup.co.uk
OPEN UNIVERSITY PRESS
McGraw - Hill Education